Starring Women

WOMEN, GENDER, AND SEXUALITY
IN AMERICAN HISTORY

Editorial Advisors:
Susan K. Cahn
Wanda A. Hendricks
Deborah Gray White
Anne Firor Scott,
Founding Editor Emerita

*A list of books in the series appears
at the end of this book.*

STARRING WOMEN

CELEBRITY, PATRIARCHY,
AND
AMERICAN THEATER,
1790–1850

SARA E. LAMPERT

**UNIVERSITY OF
ILLINOIS PRESS**
Urbana, Chicago, and Springfield

Publication of this book was supported by funding
from University of South Dakota College of Arts and Sciences.

⊚ This book is printed on acid-free paper.

Library of Congress Cataloging-in-Publication Data
Names: Lampert, Sara E., 1982– author.
Title: Starring women: celebrity, patriarchy, and American theater,
    1790–1850 / Sara E. Lampert.
Description: Urbana: University of Illinois Press, 2020. | Series:
    Women, gender, and sexuality in American history | Includes
    bibliographical references and index.
Identifiers: LCCN 2020017015 (print) | LCCN 2020017016 (ebook) | ISBN
    9780252043352 (cloth) | ISBN 9780252085260 (paperback) | ISBN
    9780252052231 (ebook)
Subjects: LCSH: Women in the theater—United States—History—19th
    century. | Actresses—United States—Biography. | Theater—United
    States—History—19th century. | Theater and society—United
    States—History—19th century.
Classification: LCC PN1590.W64 L355 2020 (print) | LCC PN1590.W64
    (ebook) | DDC 792.082/0973—dc23
LC record available at https://lccn.loc.gov/2020017015
LC ebook record available at https://lccn.loc.gov/2020017016

For Eva and Esther

Contents

Acknowledgments

As an avid consumer of popular media, I have long been fascinated by the capacity of women entertainers to both transgress and reify gender norms. When I showed interest in dance and theater as a girl, I learned that my grandmother Eva Doerstling Schimert had pursued an acting career in interwar Berlin, but the devastation of war and prospect of marriage led her to reorient her life. She immigrated to America and raised five daughters, but she never performed again. My other grandmother, Esther Kopelman Lampert, also grew up in Berlin, escaped the Nazi genocide, and made her way to London. As a teenage refugee, she watched opera under the roof of Covent Garden. Decades later, she instilled in her granddaughter a love of opera and musical theater. For hundreds of years, women entertainers have offered subversive fantasies for their publics while navigating contradictory gendered expectations. These tensions are at the center of this book.

To truly trace this project's origins and honor my debts, I must begin at Rutgers University, where Paul Clemens, Ann Fabian, and Jennifer Morgan nurtured my undergraduate research and helped me imagine new possibilities. At the University of Michigan, my advisor, Jay Cook, pushed me intellectually and provided key support through the dissertation process, along with Susan Juster and the members of my committee, Mary Kelley, June Howard, and Ann Fabian. In graduate school, I discovered a rich intellectual community of scholars and friends, especially Allison Abra, Diana Mankowski, Susanna Linsley, Sarah McDermott, Sara Babcox First, Clayton Howard, Amanda Hendrix-Komoto, Elspeth Martini, and Cookie Woolner.

In the years since, my scholarship has benefited from new intellectual relationships and the interdisciplinary feminist community I have found at the University of South Dakota. My USD History colleague Molly Rozum read every word of this book, some chapters multiple times, and provided meaningful feedback and support through this process. This book is a testament to her mentorship and friendship. Two of my colleagues in USD English, Heather Love and Lisa Ann Robertson, also read sizable portions of this book as part of our interdisciplinary reading group. Many more people provided support at key stages, serving as sounding boards for ideas and reading and commenting on drafts. Thank you to Allison Abra, Amanda Hendrix-Komoto, Clayton Howard, Cookie Woolner, Sarah Ehlers, Andrew Ross, Aston Gonzalez, Elyssa Ford, Elena Solodow, and Dave Moskowitz. I am likewise so grateful for the wonderful friends and colleagues with whom I've enjoyed drinks, food, and moral support these past six years. Shout-out to The Bean!

As this project took shape, I was able to draw on a rich body of research from my dissertation and explore new research avenues. I am grateful for research support from the Department of History and Rackham Graduate School at the University of Michigan, the Massachusetts Historical Society for a Ruth R. and Alyson R. Miller Fellowship, the Andrew W. Mellon Foundation for a fellowship to conduct research at the Library Company of Philadelphia and the Historical Society of Pennsylvania, the Harry Ransom Center at the University of Texas at Austin for a dissertation fellowship, the American Antiquarian Society for a Kate B. and Hall J. Peterson Fellowship, and the College of Arts & Sciences and the James & Ruth Ann Weaver History Department Enrichment Fund at the University of South Dakota.

Thank you to the librarians, archivists, and staff who made this research possible, tracking down obscure materials and suggesting still others. These institutions include the American Antiquarian Society, Boston Athenæum, Boston City Archives, Boston Public Library Special Collections, Rare Book and Manuscript Library at Columbia University, Folger Shakespeare Library, Harry Ransom Center at the University of Texas at Austin, Historical Society of Pennsylvania, Houghton Library at Harvard University, Library Company of Philadelphia, Manuscript Division at the Library of Congress, Massachusetts Historical Society, Missouri History Museum Library and Research Center, New-York Historical Society, New York Public Library Performing Arts Library, and Schlesinger Library. I am also grateful for the friends and family who opened their homes to me on many of these trips, particularly my aunt Cornelia Schimert and uncle Bill Solodow. Thank you as well to those who located and emailed scans of key documents to a scholar living miles away in South Dakota.

Digitization makes historical research possible, democratizing access to the archive. Almost a decade ago at the University of Michigan, I read Anna Mowatt's 1854 memoir on a microfilm reader, transcribing carefully while rationing twenty-five-cent printouts. This text has since been digitized by Google Books, along with so many of my sources. The digital platforms I used to conduct this research include Google Books, Internet Archive, Hathi Trust Digital Library, Readex Early American Newspapers, Gale 19th-Century U.S. Newspapers, Accessible Archives, American Periodical Series, Ancestry.com, Genealogy Bank, and Newspapers.com.

My editor at the University of Illinois Press, Dawn Durante, showed steady interest in and support for this project, shepherding it along with a light but deft hand. Thank you to the external reviewers for their thoughtful, constructive feedback and questions. This book is better for them. Some material from chapter 4 first appeared in "'Thy *First* Temple in the Far, Far West!': Re/Shaping Theater in St. Louis, MO 1837–1839," *Ohio Valley History*, Summer 2018, but has since undergone substantial revision. I developed additional content on Josephine Clifton (chapter 6) in "'Instruction Which She Should Avoid': Reflections on 1830s Theater Manager Thomas Hamblin in the #MeToo Era," *Nursing Clio*, February 8, 2018, https://nursingclio.org/2018/02/08/reflections-on-1830s-theater-and-metoo/.

This book explores the many ways family can shape a woman's career. I am grateful for a large, loving, and supportive family. Thank you to my aunts, uncles, and cousins; grandfather Sam Lampert; father, Jordan Lampert; brothers, Marcus Lampert and Julian Lampert; and mother, Catharina Schimert, whose identity as a feminist artist shaped my early relationship with feminism, influencing my development as a scholar. I reserve my most profound sentiments for Dave Moskowitz and Jack, who transformed my life in the years I wrote this book and whose love, support, and faith in me kept me going. You all mean so much to me.

Starring Women

Introduction

In her 1854 *Autobiography of an Actress*, retired actress, playwright, and author Anna Cora Ogden Mowatt recalled her first visit to the theater twenty years earlier. She had gone to see English actress Fanny Kemble "take her farewell of the stage" at New York's Park Theatre. Mowatt was then fifteen, and, as she explained to readers, her minister had furnished her with a grim view of the moral perils of the theater. But Anna's vow never to "enter such a dreadful place" could not withstand the teenager's desire to see a woman "whose name was on everybody's lips." She had read "critiques upon [Kemble's] acting in the papers, and heard her talked of as a most devoted daughter and truly excellent woman."[1] When Anna's father announced he had bought tickets, she decided to go. She would see Fanny Kemble in her most celebrated and closely identified role, as Julia in James Sheridan Knowles's play *The Hunchback*. The experience transformed Anna.

Kemble was "bewitching," Mowatt recalled. "The tones of her voice were richest music, and her dark, flashing eyes seemed to penetrate my very soul." These were qualities Kemble apparently shared with her great-aunt Sarah Siddons, regarded as the finest tragic actress of the Georgian stage. During her brief career, Kemble was celebrated as the heir and conduit of the great Siddons and welcomed in America as an avatar of uplift for the drama. Mowatt's account captured what many theatergoers experienced during Kemble's two years on northeastern stages. Anna saw "a reality from beginning to end," and she "laughed and wept immoderately."[2]

This compelling story might have been true. This may have been Mowatt's first visit to the theater. Veracity notwithstanding, connecting Mowatt's first visit to a commercial playhouse to the tour of English celebrity Fanny Kemble performed important work in Mowatt's narrative, establishing a frame of reference for readers that linked Mowatt to dramatic uplift. When she came to the United States in 1832, Fanny Kemble had been only two years on the stage but was celebrated as the pinnacle of English dramatic acting of her generation, recognized as a woman of letters and thus a literary actress. She was also praised for being a virtuous and dutiful daughter who went on the stage to help her actor-manager father get out of debt. Kemble's American celebrity provided an accessible point from which Mowatt could begin to explore the power, meaning, and legitimacy of the theater, in turn establishing a framework in which her own career could be evaluated.

Mowatt embarked on a dramatic career in 1845 following the success of her comedy *Fashion*. She came from New York Knickerbocker elite, eloped as a teenager, and attempted to salvage her husband's financial losses by entering first into publishing and then testing her draw as an elocutionist in 1840. Published in 1854 shortly before Mowatt retired, the *Autobiography of an Actress* challenged lingering Protestant condemnation of the morality of the theater while asserting the legitimacy of the stage as a sphere of labor and artistic endeavor for genteel white women. It drew on discourses of domesticity and "redemptive womanhood" to challenge persistent prejudices about theater and its effect on women as both performers and spectators.[3] As Mowatt explained, when she saw Kemble perform, her girlhood "prejudices against the theatre melted" away, and she realized it was not an "evil" amusement; rather, any "harm" came from "abuses which had nothing to do with the drama itself." Mowatt reframed "evil" as a function of environment, not intrinsic to drama itself. Theater was as good or bad as the character of those constituting it, both performers and audience. "Evil minds" could "draw . . . poison . . . from the rose whence the bee sucks but honey," Mowatt ruminated. She pointed, by way of example, to the "chastely-graceful girls" who performed a *"pas de deux"* or dance duet that evening. In the intervening decades, they had become "refined and accomplished ladies, exemplary wives . . . gracing the high sphere in which they move."[4] When the truly virtuous were the drama's votaries, a respectable audience would only draw honey from this flower. Mowatt and her champions in the press had mobilized this idea to promote her own dramatic career, positioning her as an agent of uplift within the theater. In the *Autobiography*, she argued against lingering suspicion of actresses as lacking in womanly virtues by asserting that women in this line of work continued to successfully conform to standards of domestic femininity embraced by their publics. Thus Mowatt participated in the respectability politics around stage performers that supported the recent gentrification (and corresponding market segmentation) of theater. This involved some historical revisionism, however.

Mowatt constructed the theater in which Fanny Kemble had performed two decades earlier as a respectable, morally elevating, and female-centered world. By the time Mowatt was crafting her memoir, reforms to the interior organization and marketing of theater had gone far to transform it from its origins as a male-dominated place of social mixture that was potent with threats of riots and disorder and home to the vice trades. Theater at midcentury was becoming a space of genteel feminized family amusement, while theater in the early 1830s was a socially contested and morally suspect place and by no means economically secure. Theater in the early decades of the century brought together a volatile social mixture, with white men of different social classes occupying pit benches, white women and middling to elite men in the boxes of the lower tiers, the third tier reserved for prostitutes and their patrons, and "colored people" restricted to either the third tier or a gallery. Many theaters contained barrooms. Theatergoers, especially in the pit and galleries, interacted with the performers, demanding encores, occasionally hurling projectiles, and sometimes starting theater riots, which occurred frequently in this era.

But though early theater culture was dominated by men, women were prominent as both stars and theatergoers. English actresses like Kemble were commercially viable and culturally significant, especially with genteel white women, whom managers were anxious to court. Fanny Kemble's 1832–34 tour occurred in the context of efforts by managers and performers to establish English theater in the United States as stable and profitable while appealing to the broadest possible public. Through her tidy account of Fanny Kemble's 1832 American debut, Mowatt glossed decades of struggle over the gender and class composition of theater audiences and debates about the legitimate gender performance and national identity of stage performers. These struggles played out around starring women. Foreign actresses like Kemble were at the center of efforts to establish theater as a viable institution in America. As some of the most visible and celebrated women in America, they were likewise drawn into contests over the acceptable parameters of female entertainment and celebrity.

Starring Women examines the careers and celebrity of the white women and girls who toured theaters in the expanding United States in the decades spanning Kemble's tour, from 1790 through midcentury. Starring women were, next to writers, the most publicly visible, celebrated, and often polarizing female public figures in the young republic.[5] While Fanny Kemble's tour remains an important watershed in the history of transatlantic female stage celebrity, she was part of a much larger cohort of women and girls who developed careers and renown in the context of the "starring system," which grew American theater by drawing upon the talents, labor, and ambition of predominantly foreign performers from England and continental Europe. Starring women drove the expansion of English theater in America from the eastern seaboard into the trans-Appalachian West both through their itinerancy and the circulation of their celebrity. They connected American theatergoers to a transatlantic entertainment culture and western regions into the expanding nation. In so doing, starring women were drawn into contemporary battles involving tastemakers, theater managers, and American publics over the definition of American culture and its relationship with Europe and over the social ownership of American entertainment. Finally, as women with lucrative public careers who operated on the margins of intensifying white middle-class politics of respectability, stars offered a series of contradictory lessons about the terms of women's labor and publicity.

During the half century that saw the institutionalization of urban theater in the United States, men both controlled the theater industry and dominated debates about its changing structure, content, and audiences. Yet women and girls remained active participants and agents of these transformations, however much their voices recede from the published archive and are fragmentary in surviving manuscript sources. In fact, women occupied every level of the theater industry, including management, though women's tenures were usually embattled and short-lived. Theater was also one of the few industries in which women were able to earn equal pay with men, though it is difficult to determine the degree to which women controlled their earnings or the terms of their careers. Patriarchal family structures that governed women's lives and careers in turn conditioned their participation in the entertainment industry. As with other economic opportunities for women in America's expanding market society, women's pursuit of new opportunities in theater involved negotiation of their place within patriarchal structures. Over the first half of the nineteenth century, the family-based artisan system declined, and theater began to look more like a modern business contracting wage-earning employees, yet men remained the major architects and power brokers of the industry. Starring became one of the few avenues for women to achieve professional and personal autonomy—to a point.

And starring women in turn became vital to the success of American theater.

Beginning in the 1810s, managers in the United States and their agents increased recruiting of performers from England and continental Europe to tour as headliners. The rise of itinerant starring created new professional opportunities. While managers increasingly bemoaned their diminished creative control and struggles for economic solvency, for performers, starring was a bid for economic solvency and creative control that held particular significance for women. But unlike men, early starring women like Agnes Holman and Clara Fisher were rarely able to operate as if they were independent agents; decisions about the allocation of their labor were made in the context of the patriarchal family. Professional success did not necessarily release them from the control and legal authority exercised by parents or husbands, from marriage, or from bearing and raising children. In the case of Mary Ann Duff and Frances Denny Drake, family responsibilities came at the expense of a starring career. Women also navigated patriarchal business structures that demanded conformity to gendered scripts and standards of respectability, which reinforced larger promarital pressures. But as the new financial and artistic possibilities of starring caused families to renegotiate allocation of their labor, some women, like Lydia Kelly, were able to pursue greater professional and personal autonomy, introducing new entertainments or, in Elizabeth Blanchard Hamblin's case, leaving bad marriages. Over the 1820s and 1830s, the number of foreign stars increased, with figures like Kelly and Celeste Elliott introducing new genres of performance and forms of female celebrity. In the 1830s, American entertainers like Josephine Clifton deployed surging nationalism to compete with foreign celebrities. These women became flash points in intensifying struggles over entertainment content, social ownership, and foreign influence.

The starring system built upon and accelerated a transatlantic traffic in entertainers and reinforced the foreign, mainly English, character of American culture. English acting companies and English and continental European stars dominated early US theater. At key moments, such as occurred around the tours of Fanny Kemble in 1832–34 and Fanny Elssler in 1840–42, the foreign character of American entertainment catalyzed debates about the economic and cultural independence of the new nation. As foreign women popularized new types of entertainment, they became flash points in debates about the intellectual and moral implications of foreign imports and their effect on American culture and society. Given the socially diverse composition of theater audiences in this period, struggles over the content of theatrical amusements often pitted elite male tastemakers against the theatergoing habits of both plebeian and elite publics. Foreign starring women, including Kelly and Fisher in the 1820s, Elliott and Ellen Tree in the 1830s, and Elssler in 1840, consistently disrupted the categories tastemakers used to shape American entertainment, especially by popularizing breeches performance, protean melodramas (in which girls and women performed multiple roles, including boy roles), and dance pantomime and ballet. These women catalyzed debates about what American culture and entertainment *should* look like and whether theater as an institution aligned with or jeopardized national identity, taste, and morality. As tastemakers debated whether foreign stars represented a gendered foreign threat, their arguments often involved assessment of the class and gender of the majority white theatergoing public.

As highly visible and celebrated public figures, starring women also became touchstones for changing and contested gender roles in American society. The height of women's participation in the starring system coincided with the mobilization of frameworks of true womanhood and domestic femininity, part of an expanding middle-class culture of sentimentality. The theater and stage celebrity were among the purveyors of sentimental domestic ideals, as the popularity of domestic melodrama underscores. How we interpret the controversial popularity of starring women in this moment depends in part upon readings of the theater audience, which, though dominated by men, included women. Female spectators become much more visible in historical sources around the celebrity of starring women, even across very different genres of entertainment, and were often problematized by the same critics who noted their presence. This suggests that starring women's celebrity, which encompassed their onstage performances, could and did offer possibilities that ran against narrowing definitions of womanhood and constructions of woman's public role. But in their efforts to appeal to new publics, particularly the expanding middle classes, architects of stage celebrity consistently deployed narratives about starring women that aligned with values of white middle-class domestic womanhood.

The culture of celebrity that developed alongside the starring system looked to stage performers to model standards of domesticity and respectability in their private lives, evaluating their success in terms of both their onstage performances and their private lives and character offstage. Starring women such as Kemble and Elssler neither represented a subversive challenge to emerging nineteenth-century gender ideology, which pressured women to link their identities and labors to the private family and orient their labors around values of Christian domesticity, nor entirely conformed to or epitomized these ideals. Rather, they discovered that sustaining a broader purchase as public figures in American society required a careful negotiation of gendered respectability politics in the public deployment of their private lives. Particularly with the rise of the literary weekly, the penny press, and other forms of cheap print sensationalism from the 1830s on, starring women like Clifton, Elssler, and later Charlotte Cushman and Matilda Heron found themselves navigating the strategic deployment of "public intimacy" to sustain their purchase as celebrated public figures.[6]

However, the strategic deployment of the lives of starring women existed in tension with the structural realities of their lives, even and especially as female stage celebrity came to be legitimized through white middle-class constructions of womanhood. On the one hand, starring women seemed to defy emerging strictures governing women's lives in the early nineteenth century. These were high-earning, mobile, and visible public figures, most of whom supported families, while some remained unmarried and childless. Yet with few exceptions, they all faced similar pressures to serve the interests of their families as children, siblings, spouses, and parents. The stories told about starring women's lives, stories that were legible to their publics, often involved alienating them from their own ambition (or ambivalence about a stage career) and deploying explanatory frameworks of genius, triumph over adversity, and orientation toward domestic ideals and respectability. The celebrity of starring women thus spoke to questions about the acceptable parameters of female ambition and the degree to which women could live in public life while preserving their womanhood. To the central question of the nineteenth century, whether true womanhood could *only* be nurtured in a domestic-oriented life at a remove from market society, female stage celebrity offered a highly qualified no. In their visible defiance of narrowing gendered frameworks, starring women were exceptional figures who mapped these boundaries. Their celebrity produced a contradictory message: women could stretch the gendered boundaries of their lives so long as they performed conformity to the domestic and moral standards of a white middle-class ideal.

Structure and Content of Early US Theater

Starring Women draws together and engages literature on the changing structure and content of antebellum American theater, women's changing relationship with public life, and the rise of modern celebrity culture. Women drove the growth and expansion of American theater through their labors and celebrity, catalyzing debates about the terms of women's publicity and, increasingly from the 1830s on, deploying sentimental domesticity in a bid for expanding publics and wider cultural legitimacy. *Starring Women* thus brings the history of dramatic performance into dialogue with the themes and patterns of women's history by exploring the connection between the height of women's participation in the starring system and the mobilization of frameworks of domestic femininity and "redemptive womanhood."[7]

The prevailing image of early nineteenth-century theater as a rowdy, boisterous, and fundamentally masculine urban space connects with one of the familiar watersheds in the history of American commercial entertainment, the 1849 New York Astor Place Riot. Historians argue that the Astor Place Riot was a crucial tipping point that led theater managers to more purposefully reshape the culture of amusements over the 1850s. They exerted more control over the behavior of audiences, pushed out the working-class publics who had rioted in the context of their exclusion from new venues like the Astor Place Opera House, and redesigned theater to appeal to the feminized middle class. However, the centrality of this event to narratives about the shifting structure, content, and market for American theater has rendered women marginal if not invisible as historical actors prior to midcentury.[8]

Scholars point to the 1850 tour of Swedish opera singer Jenny Lind as further demonstrating the viability of new promotional strategies, a watershed in the development of modern celebrity. Manager P. T. Barnum marketed Lind as simultaneously popular and elite—but emphatically respectable. The tour created a sensation across demographics, including groups who remained suspicious of the theater. Much of this was possible because unlike previous touring singers, who sang in theaters, Lind sang in hybrid venues that had more democratic seating arrangements. Women and children were also prominent in her audiences. The Lind tour demonstrated the economic potential of marketing entertainment as genteel feminized family fare.[9]

While the broad public enthusiasm around Lind's tour and the terms of her celebrity may have been unprecedented both in New York and in her extensive touring, "Lindomania" was merely a new phase in a longer history of public enthusiasm for foreign stars that inspired debates about the nature of American society and culture. The use of "mania" to describe the public response to foreign celebrities first appeared in the 1820s around Edmund Kean and Clara Fisher. In 1840 "Elsslermania" became a way of describing public responses to Viennese dancer Fanny Elssler's 1840–42 tour. English stars of the dramatic theater (Fanny

Kemble in 1832–34, Edmund Kean in 1820 and 1825, and George Frederick Cooke in 1811) generated a popular excitement while sparking discussion about American taste and the acceptable parameters of public enthusiasm. However, the period spanning the Kemble and Elssler tours has been underserved by existing scholarship. The women and girls who preceded Kemble revealed the viability of the American market, catalyzing debates about American entertainment, and those who followed her continued to grow and transform theater in America into midcentury.

With key exceptions, scholarship on women and the growth of entertainment capitalism in the United States focuses on the second half of the nineteenth century. This literature examines the expansion and consolidation of a consumer-oriented leisure culture in which female performance explored the new possibilities of a self-reflexive and consumption-oriented sense of self. Much of this occurred outside of formal theater, in the dynamic and more ethnically diverse worlds of variety, which originated as a working-class-oriented entertainment culture in reaction to the gentrification of the theater.[10] Renewed scholarly interest in early national and antebellum entertainment, however, has not involved sustained examination of women and gender.[11]

The most important scholarly works on women and early national and antebellum entertainment remain Faye Dudden's *Women in the American Theatre: Actress and Audiences, 1790–1870*, which concentrates on theater in the Northeast, especially New York, reflecting the bias of much nineteenth-century entertainment history; and Elizabeth Reitz Mullenix's *Wearing the Breeches: Gender on the Antebellum Stage*.[12] Dudden maps a shift from a culture of aurality to visuality in American theater, which Dudden argues narrowed expressive possibilities for women and ensured their exclusion from control of the industry. While sharing Dudden's attention to shifting realms of opportunity for women in theater, *Starring Women* analyzes overlapping systems of patriarchal control across the transformation of American theater, demonstrating that mobility through starring offered the greatest realm of possibility for women's personal and professional autonomy. Reitz Mullenix periodizes the rise in the 1830s and 1840s of women's breeches performance and its waning popularity after midcentury, which she connects with the politicization of women's rights and the shifting gender and class politics of public amusement. *Starring Women* incorporates the periodization suggested by Reitz Mullenix while considering how female stage celebrity engaged with questions of woman's place throughout the early nineteenth century. While theater remained a male-dominated space to midcentury, women were central to its growth and expansion as performers and as publics. By the 1820s, starring had emerged as the form of entertainment entrepreneurship most available to women, yet with the exception of Kemble, women rarely appear prominently in discussions of starring. This has constituted a missed opportunity to situate women and girls within histories of theater and market capitalism, thereby highlighting the relationship between capitalist innovation in theater and the family.

Starring Women highlights starring women as active participants in a larger culture of experimental market capitalism, as much "proto-capitalists" as the managers who hired them, though their participation in these innovations was largely shaped by gendered divisions of labor and hierarchies.[13] While nineteenth-century theater resembled the artisan workshop far more than the factory floor, starring made it possible for workers trained in this artisan system to break out of long-standing professional hierarchies, enhance their earning potential, and assert new levels of creative control. As independent contractors, touring stars were uniquely able to intervene in the management decisions of a particular theater by defining their own repertoire. This was particularly significant for women, given the gender imbalance of the repertoire, which meant fewer stock positions for women and limited control over casting.[14] However, while starring women's attempts to "elevat[e] themselves from craftworkers into capitalists" may have disrupted the "traditional hierarchy of productive relations" within theater companies, they did not necessarily disrupt gender-based hierarchies within the economic unit of the thespian family, which persisted in the theater business well into the century.[15] As *Starring Women* demonstrates, the expanding, unregulated, and competitive theater industry of the early nineteenth-century United States created new entrepreneurial opportunities for women and new avenues to public renown and personal autonomy, even as the parameters of these women's lives remained highly constrained by the patriarchal structures and restrictive gender roles of the time.

Scholars' tendency to signify starring women mainly in terms of their aesthetic contributions to American entertainment or treat them as beneficiaries rather than agents of these changes reflects a larger bias in histories of women and capitalism critiqued by historian Ellen Hartigan-O'Connor. In her study of women's participation in the consumer economy of revolutionary America, Hartigan-O'Connor observes that much scholarship on economic changes in this period has "tended to reinforce the centrality of independence to economic motivation." For most free women, as for the enslaved, "political and economic independence were unrealistic aspirations," yet this hardly meant that women "were more 'traditional' or that they were isolated from the possibilities of commerce."[16] Women in commercial entertainment were among the most highly paid and visible women workers in the young nation, but even their relative prominence and importance to the economic success of theaters did not render them independent economic actors or able to make autonomous professional decisions like their male counterparts. Rather, starring women participated in innovations in the structure and content of American entertainment in the context of patriarchal family economies. For some, the starring system provided forms of professional mobility through which women subverted patriarchal structures, realizing new degrees of professional and economic autonomy and shaping the structure and aesthetics of the industry. The patriarchal family was a defining context of starring women's professional lives, but in ways that differed significantly from the narratives shaping their renown. These narratives nonetheless remain some of the most extant sources for opening up details about their lives and careers.

My use of professional terminology and naming choices reflects my dual effort to accurately capture the gendered structure of the industry without collapsing women's complex identities within patriarchal naming patterns (or narratives). In the entertainment business in the nineteenth century, men were actors and women were actresses, though both men and women were singers and dancers. Women who assumed management were occasionally described by the belittling gendered title of "manageress." In describing entertainers, I have followed the gendered terminology of actress and actor rather than defaulting to the gender-neutral "actor" for all thespians. The gendered language mapped the larger gendered structure of "lines of business" within companies, as well as gendered conceptions of a stage career.

I have chosen a more flexible strategy when identifying performers by name. Following conventions of the time, entertainers were identified with a gendered prefix and surname, as in "Miss Rock." Where I have been able to determine the performer's given name, I use this in place of the prefix except when quoting from primary sources. For players with the same surname, when my narrative allows, I refer to them by given name only, as Mary Ann and John instead of Mrs. and Mr. Duff. Except in rare cases, a woman took her husband's surname in marriage. I mark these changes of name, occasionally providing additional names for clarity, thus preferring Elizabeth Blanchard Hamblin to Elizabeth Hamblin or "Mrs. Hamblin," the name that reflected an actress's public role at a given moment. Through these naming practices, I attempt both to honor the complex life and identity of each of these entertainers and to highlight rather than subsume the family ties that drove the growth of theater.

Starring Women and Nineteenth-Century Gender Ideology

Though often treated as an exception to nineteenth-century gender ideologies, the lives, careers, and celebrity of female performers actually help us see the reach and contradictions of those ideologies. The starring system and the theater business generally exemplify a set of tensions in the history of America's market revolution, between women's vital productive labors, both paid and unpaid, and women's leisured domesticity as a marker of genteel social status.[17] It has become a commonplace understanding in women's history that for much of the nineteenth century, "women's entrance into public life was necessary, but always problematic."[18] Yet historians interested in the gender politics of public life in this period have shown little interest in women entertainers, perhaps assuming that the morally suspect status of the stage automatically kept women entertainers outside the bounds of genteel femininity. Because of the unique realities of a stage career as a form of paid and unpaid labor, as well as its representation in media, historians can learn much about how women may have navigated the lived contradictions of shifting gender frameworks. In a family grocery business, a wife's labors balancing the ledgers or overseeing the store were otherwise rendered invisible or collapsed into her other unpaid domestic duties. In the theater, women's labors were visibly essential to the family business and frequently involved them in executive decision-making. In other words, stage labor was unique among middle-class businesses in depending upon while making visible women's labors in ways that troubled the emerging separation of home from work so central to gentility. As a result, women's stage careers increasingly required a gender performance that rested on disavowing the real economic and cultural power women in entertainment could and did wield.[19] In entertainment as in other industries, both the institution of the family and gendered narratives of domesticity and redemptive womanhood framed women's waged and unwaged productive labor.

Scholars have identified the 1820s and 1830s as a period of renegotiation over the terms of women's involvement in public life as workers, consumers, reformers, and participants in politics.[20] Prevailing constructions of womanhood in this period emphasized whiteness, sexual purity, and an elevated moral sensibility that was grounded in woman's orientation toward the domestic and away from the public glare of the state, civil society, and the commercial marketplace.[21] White women who remained oriented toward civil society as educators, writers, and reformers consistently invoked woman's unique capacity to inculcate virtue in others as a way of preserving their class status.[22] This strategy, described by historian Barbara Cutter as "redemptive womanhood," encouraged a woman to "use her special moral, religious, and nurturing nature to redeem others."[23] This gender ideology also shaped the terms of female celebrity in the nineteenth century, emerging most prominently during the 1820s and 1830s as the height of women's involvement in the starring system encountered a new narrowing of women's public role.

Starring women in theater were not marginal to these shifts, particularly as the Protestant establishment continued to double-down on long-standing condemnation of theatrical amusements as morally suspect and particularly dangerous for society's moral avatars, genteel white women. But through their engagement with print and the development of new dramatic roles, starring women manipulated prevailing gendered ideologies to serve their professional ends. *Starring Women* plays with the space between women's performed private lives as framed and narrated in print celebrity and the skeletal biographies that can be constructed from these and other sources. Personal memoirs from female entertainers in this period are rare, personal papers even more so, particularly in comparison with star actors and actor-managers. Still, surviving records of women's movements and published histories written by men in the industry offer insight into women's careers and family lives, albeit contradictory and speculative.

By the 1830s, especially, the terms of female stage celebrity consistently played on sentimental narratives about family and respectability, in many cases deploying redemptive womanhood. Details about starring women's intimate lives were presented strategically, often defensively, in relation to a developing gender system that legitimated women's publicity through their careful negotiation of sentimental domesticity. This is comparable to what historian Mary Kelley has described, with respect to expanding print culture, as the practice of "literary domesticity," whereby women writers validated their labors for the commercial market in terms of their larger fidelity to a domestic ideal.[24] For thespian women, claims about artistic genius, a mainstay of theatrical celebrity, were framed by narratives of family that prioritized family as an affective unit while still acknowledging it as an economic one. Likewise, economic motives were often moralized as avenues to respectability. In sum, starring women's labors always took on significance that was connected in some way to the redemptive force exercised by women in their own and others' lives. Crucially, these strategies helped starring women appeal to an expanding middle-class market, even and especially as their performances stretched this narrow field of representation onstage.

It is no accident that the intensified respectability politics around stage performers aligned historically with a series of struggles from the 1820s over "sexual knowledge" that came to alight on the expanding urban sex trade and led to the rise of the moral reform movement.[25] Nineteenth-century female stage performers' proximity to prostitution within theaters did not mean that they were read as prostitutes; rather, actresses' vulnerability to moral decay was enhanced by their singular proximity to the world of vice. Likewise, female stage performers were less concerned with trying to convince their publics that they were not prostitutes than with conveying a shared rectitude and character with women who were neither actresses and most certainly not prostitutes. For the most part, thespian women attempted to align themselves with middle-class womanhood while maintaining a larger stubborn silence about public sexuality within theaters. They were too close to the world of sexual vice, too unstable in their claims to respectability to do otherwise. At least until the 1840s, starring women's popularity involved appealing *across* theater's socially diverse publics, encompassing the sporting men whose libertinage moral reformers deplored and the genteel white women to whom managers had begun marketing more purposefully by the 1830s.

It remains unclear the degree to which starring women during this period were in control of their celebrity, then becoming a profitable enterprise. In the late 1830s, print marketed to feminized, middle-class readers mobilized narratives about starring women to counter the equation of the theater and a stage career with moral dissolution and public disorder. This became part of a playbook used by aspiring stars, particularly Americans seeking to compete with foreigners. Meanwhile, the expansion of sensation journalism created a market for more salacious coverage as publishers sought profits through female celebrity. The availability of cheap print media undermined women's ability to control their image even as they worked to shape it, though accounts of starring women's lives and careers also betray ambivalence about the role of public intimacy in constituting stage celebrity. The expansion of female stage celebrity as a form of female publicity in the early nineteenth century reflected the multiple and at times conflicting investment of performers and industry figures in the profits of stage celebrity while marking a key shift in the gender politics of female celebrity.

The Gender Politics of Nineteenth-Century Stage Celebrity

The transatlantic theatrical starring system of the nineteenth century extended and reconfigured the transatlantic celebrity culture that originated in eighteenth-century England through the explosion of print and new forms of commercial leisure.[26] Scholars argue that unlike the premodern fame of monarchs or heroes, modern celebrity involved a way of "defining oneself, making oneself known, beyond the limitations of class and family," in other words, it became a commodification of the self that traded on what literary scholar Joseph Roach calls "public intimacy."[27] While the ability to produce a compelling "illusion of intimacy" intensified with twentieth-century forms of mass culture, these elements of celebrity were in place by the late eighteenth century.[28]

Scholars have mapped women's active participation in these developments as women used print and the expansion of the stage to participate in public life and embrace the possibilities of publicity.[29] British actresses in the 1750s and 1760s were at the vanguard of this emerging celebrity culture, as literary scholar Felicity Nussbaum has demonstrated, expanding the potential of the English stage to "mold a recognizable, though exotic, femininity in a public space." In so doing, they "revealed the performative nature of femininity even as they helped refine its margins" while still "offer[ing] bold, highly visible models for women."[30] Eighteenth-century actresses learned to maneuver within contemporary categories of femininity, a skill that was particularly challenging but important, given that their profession situated them outside of acceptable feminine ideals. They learned how to manipulate print, pictures, and dramatic roles to shape their public image.[31] The strategies for cultivating female stage celebrity were firmly in place by the dawn of the transatlantic starring system, though there is little literature that attempts to trace these developments into the early nineteenth-century United States.[32]

Starring Women explains the emergence of the frameworks and mechanisms of female stage celebrity through the American starring system of the early nineteenth century, arguing that female stage celebrity worked to resolve gendered questions about publicity that had shifted with the expansion of market society and evangelical Christian reform. The "fashioning" of women's celebrity was likewise at the forefront of efforts to counter Christian critiques of theater as a demoralizing amusement, particularly for women—though not always with success. But as proponents of theater grappled with questions about the public role that stage performers played and the implications of their social and cultural prominence, women especially were called upon to act as agents of uplift with the theater or at least demonstrate conformity to a narrow politics of respectability. They did so largely in terms of the politics of domesticity, first as daughters and then as wives and mothers.

However, in contrast to the actress celebrities of the eighteenth century, "fashioning" female celebrity in the nineteenth century involved drawing boundaries around women's private lives and interiority while carefully deploying markers of sentimental and domestic womanhood. This represented a significant departure from the culture of stage celebrity in England in the 1750s and 1760s, when an actress's renown was closely connected with her romantic intrigues and public deployment of her private self. Tragedian Sarah Siddons was a crucial transitional figure whose "maternal self-fashioning" succeeded in reshaping the terms of actress celebrity by taking advantage of the idealization of motherhood in the late eighteenth century. This provided her with a way out of the usual construction of the actress as prostitute and sexualized figure.[33] Actually, this self-fashioning involved "inventing herself as a rather different kind of public commodity," in which the line between the actress's self and the roles she played was redrawn. Deployment of Siddons's maternal identity did not require the revelation of her unique interiority.[34]

Starring Women argues that this redrawing of boundaries between the entertainer's self and her performance became crucial to female stage celebrity in the nineteenth century and was connected with efforts to counter Protestant critiques of theater and support claims that it was a moral and rational amusement. With the reestablishment of theater in the early United States, proponents contended that the theater could serve as a school of morals, improving a capacity for empathy. These arguments folded into the developing culture of sentimentality, also embraced by Protestant culture, which celebrated the cultivation of feeling as a moral and social good. The disagreement of course concerned the acceptable contexts for cultivating feeling. Defenses of theater as a school of morals shaped dramatic criticism and marketing of the theater and star entertainers.[35] Starring women, especially actresses, were called upon to support these claims by leading private lives that remained beyond reproach and conforming to proscriptive gender ideals, yet their very claims to respectability required that those private lives remain just that, private. As a result, starring women cultivated forms of "public intimacy" that involved the sentimental redrawing of boundaries between the private self and the publicized self, though the publicized self still rested on a claim to sincerity.[36]

Ironically, increased coverage of celebrities during the expansion of commercial print in the 1830s and 1840s made calibrating "public intimacy" to shared values between performers and their publics more difficult. A respectability politics seeking to redraw the boundaries between the public and the private existed in tension with an emerging celebrity culture that sought new forms of intimacy with public figures. The respectability politics surrounding female stage celebrity remained unstable. Scandals and silences speak to the disconnect between respectability politics and the structural realities of women's lives, as their pursuit of professional ambition often violated the very ideals they sought to exemplify onstage and off.

_____

Starring Women opens by charting the growth and expansion of theater and starring in the Northeast and mid-Atlantic regions from 1790 to 1830, showing the terms according to which women participated in the emerging starring system and the growth of US theater. Chapter 1, "Between Stock and Star: Theater and Touring in the United States, 1790–1830," charts the gendered realms of opportunity during the development of starring as English thespians began to explore the opportunities of the American market, some struggling and failing to maneuver from stock to star. Starring was gendered by genre in ways that have obscured the significance of enterprising women. Also, unlike men, women were rarely able to operate as if they were independent agents. Decisions about the allocation of women's labor were made in the context of the patriarchal family, as chapter 2, "(Dis)Obedient Daughters and Devoted Wives: The Family Politics of Stock and Star," demonstrates. This chapter shows the life cycle of starring actresses as they maneuvered in a geographically expanding market. But while these women and girls were "living one story," promotional and biographical materials mobilizing a gendered politics of respectability persist in "telling us . . . quite another."[37] New forms of publicity deployed starring women's identities as daughters, wives, and mothers in ways that both shield and hint at the messy family dynamics of starring and the theater generally.

Tension between the terms of starring women's celebrity and the structural realities of their lives emerged around Fanny Kemble. Chapter 3, "The Promise and Limits of Female Stage Celebrity: Fanny Kemble in America, 1832–1835," shows how journalists tried to mobilize Kemble's unique reputation as a literary actress to manage intersecting social and nationalist tensions in American theater. Meanwhile, Kemble's celebrity and popularity with genteel white women also animated questions about the legitimate parameters of women's participation in public life. Kemble's refusal to conform to some of these scripts drew fierce backlash, underscoring the narrow and contradictory terms of female celebrity.

Kemble's watershed tour reflected the growth of starring and celebrity culture over the 1820s and 1830s, which occurred in relation to the expansion of new regional markets. During the 1830s, starring women of varying stature explored and strengthened the economic viability of western markets. Chapter 4, "Bringing Female Spectacle to the 'Western Country,' 1835–1840," traces the national reach of "big stars" like Ellen Tree and Celeste Elliott while showing how their celebrity created the context in which an expanding cohort of women and girls pursued starring careers that featured an often controversial female-centered repertoire of breeches roles and spectacle melodrama. Even as they generated controversy, these entertainers ensured the economic viability of western theater.

Starring women frequently became the focus of competing ideas about what theater should be, tensions that played out around the celebrity tour of Viennese dancer Fanny Elssler, the focus of chapter 5, "Danger, Desire, and Celebrity 'Mania': Fanny Elssler in America, 1840–1842." "Elsslermania" manifested the possibilities of new forms of mass media and marketing while revealing contradictory things about American culture. Elssler was cast as a dangerous foreign influence on American society, disrupting republican manhood and threatening genteel white womanhood. Her draw with an expanding feminized middle-class public anticipated the gentrification of the theater by midcentury. The final chapter, "The American Actress's Starring Playbook, 1831–1857," examines the professional strategies of three American actresses, Josephine Clifton, Charlotte Cushman, and Matilda Heron, as they tried to compete with English stars in the context of intensifying respectability politics around the theater. Together, their professional strategies form a playbook of strategies actresses used to navigate the gender politics of the changing industry while shaping a viable celebrity. They appealed to nationalism, pursued original repertoire, and tried to align themselves with genteel white womanhood. These ambitious women discovered the necessity and pitfalls of having to negotiate an industry that still was largely controlled by male power brokers and in which appeals to respectability remained tenuous. Together, their stories demonstrate how the starring system made it possible for some women to pursue highly unconventional, independent lives for the time even as they strained to conform to narrow constructions of virtuous and sentimental white womanhood.

1 Between Stock and Star

Theater and Touring in the United States, 1790–1830

When Mary Ann and John Duff returned to Baltimore in November 1822, they were frustrated but hopeful. John's attempts to manage theaters in Boston had foundered. Meanwhile, Mary Ann had garnered notice for her improved abilities as a tragic actress. After closing Boston's City Theatre for good, John uprooted their family of six and traveled to Baltimore to join the company of the appropriately named New Theatre. This was a stepping stone. The Duffs hoped to obtain positions with the company, which was managed by partners William Wood and William Warren and performed between Baltimore's Halliday Street Theatre and the Chestnut Street Theatre in Philadelphia. They also would explore the demand for starring engagements featuring Mary Ann, or "Mrs. Duff." A decade earlier, John's talents had created opportunities for the family in Boston, then Baltimore, then Boston again, but now in 1822 the family prospects were attached to Mary Ann's acting. As the Duffs looked toward the future in a changing industry, they wondered whether Mary Ann's development as a tragedian could transform her permanently from stock to star.

The Duffs needed an ally. Mary Ann's acting had made a powerful impression on English star tragedian Junius Brutus Booth when he performed a starring engagement in Boston two years earlier, so they reached out, hoping to give Mary Ann another opportunity to play with him. Junius invited Mary Ann to join him in Philadelphia for his benefit night, which usually took place at the end of a starring run and during which the beneficiary took a percentage of gross receipts. It was a long-standing tradition in English theater that the beneficiary chose both play and cast.[1] Junius and Mary Ann selected Ambrose Philip's *The Distrest Mother*, an English adaptation of a French adaptation of a Greek drama and the very play that had drawn critical acclaim for Mary Ann in Boston. This was also a smart calculation for Booth, whose engagement had been a disappointment, receipts dipping as low as $167.62, which did not cover the management's expenses. The Booth-Duff benefit netted $493.35, from which Booth took home $404.51, or close to $9,000.00 today. Mary Ann and John Duff, meanwhile, were invited to open the Baltimore season in May with a starring engagement.[2] Maybe it would result in a position with the stock company, or perhaps Mary Ann's artistic development and popularity were the beginning of a new phase in her career as a starring itinerant. Everything depended on the size of audience they would draw into the theater.

Mary Ann and John Duff strategized professional advancement in a rapidly changing industry offering new opportunities for wealth and renown to actors from Great Britain. The Duffs were part of a transatlantic migration of English thespians hired to populate the stock companies of new theaters founded in eastern cities beginning in the 1790s. When Mary Ann traveled to Boston from Dublin in 1810 with her husband, pregnant with the first of ten children (seven of whom reached adulthood), the sixteen-year-old English actress was commencing a twenty-seven-year career in which she participated in the growth of residential theater in the United States and the development of starring. Mary Ann's career straddled a transformation in theater as an older artisan-based, waged system for producing theatrical entertainment that was reliant on elite patronage networks experienced new capitalist innovations through which actors and actresses, often in antagonistic partnership with managers, achieved greater professional autonomy and earning potential by touring as stars.

Manager William Warren did not mince words. After the Duffs' opening night performance on May 7, 1823, he wrote in his journal, "Duff & Wife play R&Jul't. . . . [S]he is a favorite—*he is done.*" In spite of her popularity, "Mrs. Duffs Bent As a Star!" was the only night when the couple actually made any money on their engagement.[3] The terms Warren worked out with stars dictated that they receive their portion of receipts only after the house broke even. According to a dramatic critic for the local mercantile paper, Mary Ann "played six nights *for nothing*" because the "estimated expenses of the house have not been cleared any one night that she has appeared." The receipts from her benefit alone determined whether she would "receive *any* compensation for it, or be a *loser* by her late engagement."[4] The benefit grossed $642, of which Mary Ann took $342 (roughly equivalent to $8,460 today).[5] This was six times the weekly salary of $56 that the Duffs had earned jointly as stock actors. Though this windfall saved the engagement for the star, the nightly returns were not enough for her to complete the jump from stock to star. The influx of performers from London theaters was more appealing to managers than an actress who had built her career in regional theaters. What these minor performers lacked in name recognition with theatergoers was more than compensated by the imprimatur of a London pedigree.

Popular interest in theater had grown in recent decades, with some theaters achieving economic stability through star engagements. From the 1810s on, starring transformed the structure and content of theater in the United States and fostered a transatlantic traffic in actors between England and the United States. This traffic had originated with strolling companies in the eighteenth century and then stock actors who populated resident companies when theater was reestablished in the 1790s. Experimentation with starring began in the early 1800s with leading stock actors Anne Brunton Merry and Thomas Cooper. In the 1810s and 1820s managers began sending agents to England to secure leading players from London theaters for starring tours—the Duffs came as stock performers in 1810, while Joseph George Holman brought his daughter, Agnes, to star with him in 1812. The 1820s saw a major shift in the number of English performers arriving as stars, mainly recruited by New York manager Stephen Price, who made his Park Theatre the first stop for star tours of eastern theaters. While some starring recruits returned to England rich from their tours, which had always been a risk, and resumed careers on London stages, many more remained in the United States to carve out American careers in a rapidly changing and geographically expanding industry.

Starring was an opportunity for performers to realize new levels of stature and wealth, as well as independence, yet these possibilities were realized and acted upon unevenly based on stature, geographic origin, and gender. Starring in the 1810s and 1820s was tied to a London reputation, though most of the women and men who came to the United States in this period were not at the top of the London theater world but actually trying to revive stagnant or flagging careers. In America's Anglophilic theater culture, a London reputation (however inflated) became essential to launching a successful starring tour. The familiar watersheds in the advent of the transatlantic starring system—the 1810 tour of George Frederick Cooke and the 1820 tour of Edmund Kean, both English tragedians—obscure the uneven and contingent development of the star-ring system, particularly as experienced by women, who pursued new professional opportunities within patriarchal structures of dependency. The spirit of enterprise in managers' arrangements with prospective stars simultaneously disrupted and rested upon women's status within acting families.

For actors in the United States, and even more so in Great Britain, capitalizing on professional ability, popularity, and reputation to become an independent contractor (an itinerant star) in the United States entailed different risks and rewards for women and men. With key exceptions, the performers most able to take advantage of starring, calculating the pro-fessional and financial risk of leaving a regular position to pursue profits and renown as an itinerant, were men and unmarried women, usually daughters trained and managed by ambitious fathers. While women be-came some of early American theater's highest grossing and in-demand stars, the advent of the starring system is a story of women's frustrated efforts to access these opportunities on terms commensurate with their abilities and ambitions. The uneven and consistently abortive starring careers of Anne Brunton Merry, Agnes Holman, Lydia Kelly, Clara Fisher, and Mary Ann Duff reveal the strategies actresses used to change the terms and trajectories of their careers in an industry controlled by male power brokers and in which women's professional opportunities were consistently tied to their duties as daughters, wives, and mothers.

Men dominated the advent of starring for structural reasons, though prevailing explanations have emphasized genre.[6] Actually, starring was gendered by genre in ways that have obscured the significance of en-terprising women: while the transatlantic star actors of the 1810s and 1820s were overwhelmingly tragedians, the star actresses who excited American audiences in the 1820s performed in comic and ingénue roles and thus did not receive the same level of sustained critical attention as tragedians in "legitimate" drama. Critics cultivating American tastes through the press were largely ambivalent about the very women who excited audiences most and appealed to the evolving tastes of American theatergoers.

Few of the transatlantic stars who came over in the 1820s, gender and genre notwithstanding, sustained long-term itinerant careers. For those who did not return to England after a season or two in America, realms of opportunity in American theater were also gendered. Actors who fled the intensifying competition at the top of the London theater scene to star in the United States remained and, often with the support of their families, experimented with theater management, becoming celebrated innovators in the American theater business. These opportunities were mostly closed to women. Actresses either returned to England or traded the relative professional independence of starring (an independence rarely reflected in their private or domestic lives) for the stability of stock positions.[7]

Beginnings

Starring began in a struggle. William Dunlap was trying to keep the brand new Park Theatre financially solvent. The novice manager and playwright eyed the Philadelphia company assembled in England by Thomas Wignell for the Chestnut Street Theatre, led by widowed English tragedian Anne Brunton Merry. Dunlap tried to entice Merry from her position in Philadelphia for his second season in New York, writing to her in early 1799, shortly after she was widowed, to inquire whether she planned to "return" to her "native land" or would "exert [her] talents . . . under my direction at New-York." "Is there any emolument that an American theatre can yield of a performer," Dunlap wondered, "sufficient to induce you to reside a year longer in the country?" In spite of the extravagant $60 per week salary Dunlap offered, equivalent to about $1,260 today, Merry demurred. She was happy with Wignell, who had "behaved to me like a man of honour and a sincere friend" since her husband's death in December, and expected to remain in Philadelphia.[8]

Two years later, Dunlap was still struggling to break even financially. He again tried for Merry, but with a different tack. He proposed to open the Park Theatre for a short summer season with the members of the regular company, who had no expectation of work, on half salary and offered Merry $100 per week, worth about $2,000 today, to star with English tragedian Thomas Cooper, whom Dunlap hoped to lure back to New York and retain into the winter. He offered Cooper $30 a week for the summer and $50 for the next season. Cooper agreed. Merry was a harder sell. Her doctor urged her not to travel, but reluctantly she agreed. It was a risk for both actress and manager that ultimately paid off.

In the remaining four years of his management, though Dunlap gave up trying to convince Merry to join his company, he continued to invite her up from Philadelphia for short engagements, usually supported by Cooper, which guaranteed Dunlap a bonanza. It was Cooper, periodically attached to the Park Theatre company, rather than Merry who developed the possibilities of the short-term engagement into the starring tour. While Cooper experimented with management and short-term starring engagements, commencing one of the longest itinerant careers in the

United States, Merry's career remained tied to the Philadelphia market through her successive marriages to actor-managers of the Philadelphia company, though she joined Cooper in periodic starring engagements. For this reason, theater historians have shown comparatively little interest in Merry even while recounting the innovative maneuverings of Dunlap and Cooper.[9] While both men produced a voluminous archive that scholars have mined to understand their professional ambitions and frustrations, Merry's relative silence makes her a comparative cipher. Of course, Dunlap's scheme and Cooper's opportunity were inconceivable without Merry, who continued to tour with Cooper until her untimely death in 1808.

In the 1790s, Anne Brunton Merry and Thomas Cooper had joined an Atlantic migration fueled by manager-recruiters like Thomas Wignell that built upon and transformed the patterns of touring and theater founding from the colonial period. Touring companies of actors had been a part of colonial life since the early 1700s, reaching a peak of popularity during the Seven Years' War, when the most successful of these outfits, David Douglass's London Company, "promot[ed] the theater as a patriotic spectacle."[10] The popularity of theater waned in the 1760s in the context of economic downturns and rising colonial tensions, though Douglass and his renamed American Company struggled on. The company moved in large slow circuits through the major towns of the colonies. They set up in converted warehouses, in the attic of a courthouse, or in hastily constructed theaters built in towns to which they planned to return the following year, like New York, where Douglass built the John Street Theatre in 1767.[11] During the War for American Independence, the Continental Congress passed resolutions to suppress all forms of amusement, from gambling to stage plays, which prompted a mass exodus of players. After the war ended, many of the English actors who had formerly circuited the colonies returned, joined by new troupes. Thus in 1785 members of Douglass's former company, now billing themselves as the Old American Company, were back in New York after a wartime stay in Jamaica. They did not settle in New York at once but continued as strolling players, moving between New York and other cities on the mid-Atlantic seaboard.[12]

This followed the model that had developed in England over the last century as companies of strolling players moved through regional circuits where permanent theaters were gradually established. Anne Brunton began her acting career in Bath in 1785 at age seventeen, then achieved a starring position in London, which remained the sun in England's dramatic solar system. It was the home of the patent theaters, which had the exclusive right to introduce new dramas approved by the Lord Chamberlain, thus limiting competition. Like other London thespians, she made periodic tours of provincial theaters. In 1792, however, the newly married actress abruptly retired to travel to France with her husband, poet Robert Merry, who was inspired to participate in the French Revolution. The adventure ended in disappointment and debt. The couple returned to London. Robert's efforts to secure a position for Anne at the Covent Garden Theatre fell through. In 1796, when Thomas Wignell approached the couple about his new theater in America, they jumped at the prospect. In September 1796 they sailed for Philadelphia with a few other recruits, including young Thomas Cooper, to open the new Chestnut Street Theatre.[13]

Wignell, Brunton Merry, and Cooper were participating in a new phase of theater founding occurring in the eastern seaboard cities in the 1790s as local elites in Boston, New York, and Philadelphia funded the construction of large-scale permanent playhouses with the support of local corporations.[14] The Chestnut Street Theatre in Philadelphia and the Federal Street Theatre in Boston opened in 1794, while in New York the money troubles of wildly speculating investors held back the opening of the Park Theatre for three years, until 1798. For the new generation of postwar elites who purchased stock in these vast economic enterprises, establishing theaters became a way of asserting social prominence, along with the creation of new economic institutions like exchanges and centralized banks. These theater venues were built as much for the conspicuous display of their stockholders as for the overall comfort of a growing population of theatergoers. Their founders hoped that the theater could also serve as a "school for Republican virtue," ideals novice manager and playwright William Dunlap shared. But this vision of theater as an edifying republican institution quickly foundered on a more complicated set of social and economic realities.[15]

The new playhouses of the early national period, which had a capacity of a few thousand patrons, demanded theatrical production on a scale that did not match the number of regular theatergoers, even in cities whose populations were rapidly reaching the tens of thousands. Managers charged with hiring a resident company, an orchestra, and a small army of laborers and arranging a season of entertainments, usually lasting from September to March, needed to appeal to a wider audience than stockholders, who enjoyed free entry. This meant that the theater's most regular patrons did not pay to support its regular upkeep. The weekly expenses of the Park Theatre, for example, were much higher than what it brought in. At this time, theaters played only three nights a week. In the acting company's first season, in 1798, the weekly salaries of about thirty people totaled $480, which was less than half of the theater's weekly expenses of $1,161. These costs included the orchestra, box keeper, prompter, dressers, laborers, doorkeepers, and constables, as well as cleaning, printing, scenery, wardrobe, and, finally, rent.[16] Under the stock system, the members of the company were hired to fulfill particular "lines of business," such as leading lady, first comedian, and old man.[17] Stock actors received their weekly wage and the right to one benefit performance per season, from which the headlining performer (or, in some cases, performers) received a percentage split of the net receipts. Dunlap was required to pay stockholders a percentage of rent on gross receipts, starting at $450 per night; hence, Dunlap and his first partner, John Hodgkinson, aimed to keep "nightly expenses" to $400.[18] But the theater receipts rarely rose above this threshold, which placed Dunlap and his rotating cast of partners in a tenuous position. A few seasons into his tenure in New York, Dunlap began to experiment with introducing English adaptations of melodramas by German playwright August von Kotzebue into the repertoire of British dramas and comedies dating back to the Restoration era. Attendance increased, pushing receipts over $450, which brought Dunlap a modicum of stability—when the city was not wracked by yellow fever epidemics.[19]

As managers in the early republic experimented with different ways of turning a profit, they discovered that engagements of leading actors did far more than even new repertoire to save the financial prospects of a season. While the "itinerant, visiting actor" had been a feature of theater in England for the past century, in the nascent, decentralized US market, first theater managers and ultimately actors and their agents began exploiting the economic potential of the starring engagement in new ways.[20] Initially, managers like Dunlap made arrangements to bring in actors for a short engagement at a higher salary with a benefit night. This did not fundamentally alter the overall economic structure of the business. While Dunlap was acting out of self-interest to rescue the fortunes of his theater, a starring engagement had different implications for Cooper and Merry. While Merry focused on strengthening her status within a single market, including through marriage, Cooper's comparative lack of family ties and competition with other actors led him to look elsewhere for wealth and stature. He exploited the enhanced earning power of the short-term engagement, which he preferred to a season contract.

Dunlap's 1801 summer season starring Merry and Cooper was a financial risk that more than paid off. They opened to $664 in receipts. Cooper stayed on with Dunlap, earning $50 a week. The manager repeated the feat the following April with even greater success, bring-ing in $1,000 on Merry's opening night and averaging $800 per night for the two-week engagement.[21] He might have done so indefinitely had Cooper not decided to return to London in 1803, chasing a position at the Drury Lane Theatre. When Cooper returned to the United States two years later, rather than engage with a resident company for a season, he instead made a series of short engagements with theater managers in the Northeast, including at Dunlap's Park Theatre. Cooper's rest-lessness was a product of his rivalry with tragedian John Hodgkinson, whose popularity in New York frustrated Cooper's ambition. Dunlap, in the meantime, found himself overwhelmed with debt and eager to get out of the business. He relinquished the management of the Park Theatre in 1805, then went back to work for Cooper, who took over in 1806 but did not want to be tied down. While Cooper toured, Dunlap served as his absentee manager.

In contrast to Cooper, and in spite of her periodic engagements, Merry remained attached to the Philadelphia market, though she clearly was also intrigued by the opportunities of management and starring. She had less reason than Cooper, however, to leave a market in which she had no rival. Merry remained unchallenged as the star of the Philadel-phia company. During the final years of her short life, marriages first to Thomas Wignell, with whom she had worked since 1796, and then to William Warren created both professional stability and opportunity. In 1803, barely two months after her marriage to Thomas, the pregnant actress again became a widow. Faced with the prospect of returning to England or "remain[ing] in the capacity of a leading actress only," "Mrs. Wignell" stepped into her husband's position as colessee and manager but waited a year to return to the stage.[22] She did not last in her new position. Anne navigated the economic vagaries of management in the context of a gendered struggle to establish authority over her company. As William Warren, who took Anne's place in early 1805, recalled, she "had been a good deal annoyed in the business of the theatre; some of the actors pressed their affairs with ungentleness." William attributed the failure of Anne's management to her "sensitive, generous and con-fiding" nature and clearly missed the interplay of gender politics with personality.[23] Anne Brunton Merry Wignell continued acting with the company but also took on starring engagements with Cooper in New York and then Boston in 1807, where the Federal Street Theatre was just beginning to feature stars, some from England and others attached to US theaters. In 1806 she married William Warren and became pregnant. The thirty-nine-year-old actress died on June 28, 1808, four days after the birth of her stillborn son, her multifaceted and expanding career cut short by the dangers of childbirth.

In his 1832 *History of the American Theatre*, William Dunlap joined a growing consensus among managers that starring could be blamed for what many agreed was a general "degradation of the drama." Starring shifted the focus of the manager away from the qualities of the stock company in favor of the financial needs of the star and his or her favored repertoire. Though as Dunlap noted in a sly allusion to the conflicts with John Hodgkinson, "Bringing in a *star*"—as he had done with Merry and Cooper—"can lessen the influence of a performer over the public," in turn "free[ing]" the manager "from an oppressive tyranny."[24] Still, Dunlap feared he had introduced a source of the drama's decline because starring increased the earning power and professional autonomy of the star actor over the manager. Over the 1810s and 1820s, as starring became more common in American theaters, the economic implications shifted as visiting actors and their agents made arrangements to receive a portion of the net profits during the nights of their engagements. Managers could get in on the speculation by demanding a cut of the actor's benefit night.[25] Managers who looked overseas to furnish their stock companies began to seek potential stars as well.

Cooke and the Holmans: Transatlantic Stars of the 1810s

Sustaining theater in the United States as an economically viable institution meant securing capable actors largely from English and Irish theaters. John Dickson, a failed actor who became joint lessee and manager of the Federal Street Theatre in Boston in 1806, "crossed the ocean upwards of forty times" over the next two decades in order to "engage talent" from England and Ireland for the theater's resident stock company.[26] Recruiters looked for players like Mary Ann Duff and John Duff of the Dublin Theatre, who showed promise but did not have prestigious or well-paying positions. The Duffs came to Boston with Dickson in 1810, the same year Thomas Cooper brought over George Frederick Cooke for a short-term tour, revealing the capacity of the American market to support celebrated London actors. The starring tours of George Frederick Cooke and two years later, Joseph George Holman and his daughter, Agnes Holman, established lasting patterns of transatlantic starring against the backdrop of stock recruitment. Both tours demonstrated that an American tour could revive an English actor's professional stature and generate considerable wealth while providing new entrepreneurial opportunities. For Cooke, the Holmans, and the Duffs, widely differing in professional stature and at different points in their careers, coming to the United States was a professional gamble that (mostly) paid off—Cooke got very rich, but then died suddenly. Their migrations reflect the cultural and economic gravitation of Atlantic entertainment in this early period: England remained the cultural center, producing entertainers who were drawn to the expanding and competitive promise of American markets.

Prior to Cooke's tour, there was no reason for a successful London actor to travel to the United States. Rather, managers of American theaters recruited actors like the Duffs from the smaller provincial theaters. These theaters had grown out of regional circuits traveled by strolling players in the early eighteenth century. Actors in the provinces dreamed of a London career. The provincial circuits made it possible for London actors to continue to work in the summer by making a series of off-season engagements and also to flee waning London prospects. Ultimately, London's patent theaters, Covent Garden and Drury Lane, known as Old Drury, remained the measure of success for actors in terms of stature and salary.[27] Recruiters like John Dickson offered provincial actors new professional opportunities overseas.

Dickson heard about John Duff from Thomas Cooper, who had seen Duff act at the Dublin Theatre during one of his recruitment trips. Interestingly, neither John nor Mary Ann came from an acting family. John had left his legal studies at Trinity College for the "allurements of the stage."[28] By contrast, Mary Ann's path was shaped by financial necessity following the death of her father, a man of dubious social status employed in the East India Company. Her widowed mother invested her limited funds in theatrical training for fifteen-year-old Mary Ann and her elder sisters, a more lucrative and sustainable living than the needle trades, for example. The sisters obtained positions with the Dublin Theatre, where Mary Ann rebuffed a proposal from poet Thomas Moore, one of Duff's old Trinity buddies. She married the twenty-three-year old Duff as he was being recruited for Boston's Federal Street Theatre. In July 1810 the pregnant sixteen-year-old and her husband sailed for Boston. Mary never saw her mother or sisters again, though the Duffs did return to England briefly in 1827 in an effort to improve their stature in America.

Cooke's 1810–11 tour was a game changer during a moment when the structure and business of urban theater in the United States were just stabilizing economically. Theater historians regard this as the first true starring tour in America—really the first blockbuster tour. Instead of coming over to take a regular position in an American theater, Cooke came over for a season, expecting to return to England with a fresh reputation and American profits. In 1810 Cooke's decorated London career was waning, his reputation and talents diminished by alcoholism, which made him susceptible, as the story goes, to Thomas Cooper's machinations. Cooper encountered Cooke after a demoralizing season at Covent Garden, but it is not clear how receptive Cooke was to Cooper's offer to come play in America.[29] Ultimately, Cooper exploited Cooke's drunkenness to serve his own ends, though the precise events that led to a signed contract and Cooke's departure on board the *Columbia* are not clear. Cooper expected to make a pretty penny for himself and his new partner in the Park Theatre, businessman Stephen Price, as well as for the English actor.[30]

Cooper's coup in securing Cooke was so unexpected that American theatergoers familiar with the major personalities of the London stage were incredulous. Some "even insinuated" that the man was "an imposter." As Dunlap noted in his 1813 biography of Cooke, "It appeared as impossible to many, that the great London actor should be removed to America, as that St. Paul's Cathedral should be transported across the Atlantic."[31] Newspapers published accounts of Cooke's unprecedented reception in New York, Philadelphia, and Boston, the crowds of ticket speculators, the ensuing fights, and the "pell-mell rush" when the theater finally opened, "the press violent and dangerous."[32] Dunlap's chronicle of Cooke's life, published shortly after the actor's sudden death in New York on September 26, 1812, from dropsy (no doubt exacerbated by liver disease), ensured that the American phase of Cooke's career would not be lost or downplayed.[33] Read in the context of Dunlap's commitment to the expansion of English theater in the United States, his *Memoirs of the Life of George Frederick Cooke* heralded the viability of the American market for speculative touring ventures by foreign performers after it had mainly served as an alternative labor market for regular actors.

Cooke's tour mapped the early geography of American theater, which would look very different within a decade. He played in New York, Boston, Providence, Rhode Island, Philadelphia, and Baltimore, Maryland. With the exception of Providence, these were the largest and most profitable markets and were also easily accessible via Atlantic packet ship and coach. No particular market dominated in these early decades. Philadelphia had a reputation for the strongest stock company, which after 1806 moved between theaters in Philadelphia and Baltimore (occasionally Washington) under the uncharacteristically stable managerial partnership of Warren and Wood. Philadelphia's Chestnut Street Theatre,

New York's Park Theatre, and Boston's Federal Street Theatre were all nicknamed "Old Drury," underscoring the decentralized character of the American theater industry and its English orientation. The devastating Richmond theater fire on December 26, 1811, severed whatever potential southern pull might have existed in this period. Cooke did travel once by early steamboat, but on an expedition to Albany, New York, and not to play—theater was established there only in 1813.

For a brief period in the 1810s, the economic model of "the tour" profited the manager more than the performer, though this changed over the 1820s. For Cooke's first ten nights in New York, during which he appeared three nights a week with one extra Saturday performance, Dunlap (who was employed to manage for Cooper and his new partner, Price) pulled in houses at the Park Theatre worth between $1,200 and $1,800. The star, meanwhile, earned a weekly salary and the entirety of receipts for his benefit night, a windfall of $1,875, equivalent to almost $40,000 today. However, his drunkenness and periodic lack of preparation could be costly. After forgetting his part during a benefit performance, receipts dropped as low as $467 one night.[34] Over the course of his two-year tour, Cooke continued to take in a salary and a clear benefit (or the entirety of receipts from his benefit night, with no portion reserved by the manager to cover costs). By one historian's estimates, the total receipts of Cooke's two years touring the United States were $250,000, worth almost $5 million today, of which Cooke received a mere $20,000, or about $395,000.[35] Even during Cooke's second year, when houses were smaller and Cooke was often idle, returns were larger than anything managers had experienced or could have anticipated.

Back in England, Joseph George Holman followed accounts of Cooke's success with interest. The forty-eight-year-old actor had played in theaters in London, Liverpool, Glasgow, and Dublin. In the 1790s he had been a "popular and serviceable actor" at Covent Garden but was hardly, as his letter of introduction to managers in the United States claimed, "the first actor in Covent Garden Theatre." He had also tried his hand at playwriting and briefly turned farmer, but his professional prospects shifted when he focused on developing the career of his nineteen-year-old daughter, Agnes, whose mother was Maria Hughes, formerly an actress with the Dublin Theatre and briefly Holman's common-law wife. Joseph left Agnes and another child in their mother's care, providing a small annuity. Hughes probably did train her daughter for the stage (she retired after marrying a lieutenant major), but it was Joseph who directed and profited from Agnes's early career. Agnes started appearing with her father in Glasgow around 1809. Shortly after her London debut in August

1811, Joseph announced that he planned to follow Cooke's example and tour America.[36]

In early July 1812 father and daughter boarded a British packet in Falmouth with two other passengers and, after a harrowing crossing caused by the declaration of war between the United States and Great Britain, docked in New York on September 11.[37] American theatergoers were eager for English entertainments, which continued in spite of wartime hostilities. On October 3 Agnes appeared at the Park Theatre playing opposite her father as Lady Townley in the Restoration comedy *The Provoked Husband*, her most popular and successful role. Agnes was not an experienced performer. Though the London papers covering her debut applauded her aspiration for the "opposite heights of tragedy and comedy," they agreed that her "powers had scarcely yet matured."[38] In the United States, however, Agnes rapidly eclipsed her father in celebrity and earning power. A New York critic declared that she was the finest actress to appear in the United States since Anne Brunton Merry Wignell Warren.

As the tour progressed, demand for the daughter supported the father, whose "success on the boards came to depend upon his daughter's abilities."[39] At the close of a "not splendid . . . yet respectable" Philadelphia engagement, for example, Joseph's benefit brought in $726, while Agnes's earned the highest receipts of the season, cresting $1,252.[40] Manager William Warren noted in his journal that "they don't seem to like Mr. H," but because of Agnes, the engagement made decent money for the theater and for Joseph.[41] By 1814 Agnes was earning $200 a performance (close to $3,000 today), an unprecedented salary for any actress in America. Technically, though, it was a joint salary, for as nineteenth-century theater chronicler Joseph Ireland wryly noted, it "included her father's volunteering his services."[42] Coming to the United States on the eve of war to launch a starring tour revived Joseph Holman's career because of the success of his daughter, who might never have reached a comparable stature in England.

After peace was restored between the United States and Great Britain in 1815, the financial and professional implications of a starring tour in the United States transformed the potential career trajectory of a London actor. Most stars of the 1810s and 1820s were frustrated in their ability to scale the London theater hierarchy or sought a way around it, as was the case, respectively, with Joseph and Agnes. Economic and artistic experimentation characterized US theater in the 1810s and 1820s. Managers intensified their overseas recruitment, sending agents to populate new theater companies and arrange starring tours with more known London players. Postwar nationalism and the disgraced collapse of the pro-British Federalists did not diminish excitement about English imports, though audiences were quick to discipline foreign performers who disregarded the will of audiences.[43] Meanwhile, some stock actors in America also tried to transform their professional prospects by trying out their draw as stars.

Growing overseas interest in the American market led to a shift in the financial terms of starring, which became a shared speculation, with stars requesting a share of the profits from their engagement rather than a fixed salary. As managers later complained, this shifted the risk to them: now managers were faced with paying theater expenses regardless of the audience turnout for a star engagement. Over the 1820s, as starring became more common among actors working out different kinds of terms, a hierarchy developed, with performers of different stature moving in regional circuits. The decentralized American market was reoriented by starring when Park Theatre manager Stephen Price pursued an aggressive system of London recruitment in the 1820s that turned New York into the major entrepôt for stars from overseas. Meanwhile, the city's expanding population fed a distinct and highly competitive theatrical culture, with high salaries for entertainers and avid critics able to make or break the reputation of a new performer.

"New Lions and Lionesses": Starring in the 1820s

In 1828 a satire in a new (and short-lived) dramatic weekly noted the now familiar cycle of starring as "new Lions and Lionesses arrive every day ... announced by the 'gratified' manager to the 'delighted' public with all the splendor of puff and play bill."[44] Over the last decade, the advent and popularization of the starring engagement grew theater in the United States and transformed its geography while effectively strengthening cultural and economic ties with English theater. English players looked to America as a viable market where they could make or remake their careers and possibly make a fortune, while American managers connected their prospects to recruitment of English talent, mainly relying on the pipeline of stars who arrived in America through Stephen Price's Park Theatre. Talented English players came to weigh the potential profits of a star tour in America against static London careers, and news of overseas profits also made transatlantic touring an appealing alternative to a provincial tour.[45] Initially, however, American theatrical agents had a harder time securing major female entertainers for starring engagements. Given the degree to which parental authority and family interests defined the terms and trajectory of women's careers, it is unsurprising that most star actresses came with parents or husbands.[46] Lydia Kelly, one of the most significant stars of the 1820s, was a comparative anomaly who proved the rule.

The careers of star actresses coming to America to tour also looked different in terms of both the critical attention they received and their long-term trajectories. Star actresses were more likely to popularize genres of which critics disapproved. Theater criticism in this period was in tension with the promiscuous tastes of American theatergoers. It was dominated by literary elites who positioned themselves as a check on the moral and aesthetic deterioration of the drama. Critics focused their essays, which appeared in mercantile dailies or their own (short-lived) literary and dramatic weeklies, on "legitimate" drama, with a bias toward English tragedy. They were more likely to deplore the roles popularized by star actresses like Kelly than provide serious criticism, yet the profusion of print culture associated with star actresses (not to mention box-office returns) is further indication of the popularity and cultural significance of these women.

Kelly was recruited by "King Stephen" Price, who managed the Park Theatre for two decades while becoming the dominant recruiter of London stars. His aggressive pursuit of monopoly over star imports altered the structure and geography of theater in America while strengthening ties between London and New York. Unlike the actor-managers who sought both greater profits and professional and creative autonomy by moving into theatrical management—albeit at great risk—Price was a lawyer and businessman. In 1808 Thomas Cooper brought Price into management, which he approached primarily as a business venture.[47] In 1816, after Cooper left the Park Theatre to focus exclusively on starring, Price brought in stock actor Edmund Simpson as a partner and explored new ways of growing the fortunes and stature of New York's "Old Drury." No actor close to George Frederick Cooke's stature had come to America since the end of the war, though managers of eastern theaters continued to replenish their stock companies with English immigrants. Price and Simpson hoped they might convince the leading players of London's patent theaters to visit America for a tour as Cooke had.

In early 1818 Simpson traveled to London to engage stock actors for the Park company, but his major sights were set on Drury Lane stars Eliza O'Neill and Edmund Kean. Although O'Neill's father met several times with Simpson to negotiate possible terms, pushing for a percentage of the profits on the arrangement, O'Neill elected to stay in London. She would marry in December 1819 and leave the stage, giving credence to rumors that she "dislike[d] her profession." Even if Simpson had been able to come to an arrangement with O'Neill and her father, he would have faced the same obstacle that kept Kean in London until 1820: the Drury Lane Theatre manager refused to release Kean from his season contract.[48]

Simpson also struggled to secure performers he considered suitable for the tastes and moral standards of American theatergoers. The diary of his 1818 trip is filled with curt dismissals of performers Simpson considered vulgar or ugly onstage or whose adulterous affairs, illegitimate children, and known drunkenness offended the manager and, he believed, would lead them to fail with American audiences. He managed to come to terms with a small contingent of provincial actors for the Park company and several lesser London actors for starring engagements: comedian Robert Campbell Maywood; James William Wallack, who was frustrated in his ambition to rival Kean; and Thomas and Mrs. Kilner. Simpson's predictions were not always accurate. He had been unsure about Maywood and found Wallack sloppy, but both had successful seasons as stars and stayed on in America as members of acting companies.[49] Within a decade, Maywood and Wallack were firmly established as managers of theaters in Philadelphia and New York, respectively, Wallack in direct competition with Price as partner in Charles Gilfert's new Bowery Theatre. In 1824 Kilner partnered with Henry Finn to manage the Federal Street Theatre in Boston.

Some of the hopes entertained by English performers were not borne out. Simpson chose not to engage Sarah Bartley, tragic actress at Covent Garden, and her husband, comedian George Bartley, in spite of their "determin[ation] to come to America." Though the "wife may do something," Simpson predicted that the husband "must fail in my opinion." The Bartleys decided to travel anyway, arriving in New York in November 1818 after the month-long crossing. The risk paid off: they debuted at the Park Theatre on November 18 and went on to tour theaters between Boston and Alexandria, Virginia, for two seasons, returning to England in May 1820.[50] Yet the New York press reported that their American tours had "not answered [their] expectations." The depression caused by the Panic of 1819 may have been a factor, for they complained of the "extraordinary change of the times, and the decay [of] patronage."[51] Still, as Philadelphia manager William Wood noted in his memoirs, the couple took home £4,000 from their two seasons, equivalent to £314,000 today, and resumed stock positions in London.[52]

Agents had more luck with recruitment as the decade progressed and English performers heard reports of the steady profits from American tours and the higher salaries earned by stock actors in American theaters. In 1819 Price traveled overseas to try for Kean again—and succeeded. Kean was the leading tragedian of the London stage, regarded as Cooke's heir. Like Cooke, Kean opted for an American tour when his popularity in London was beginning to falter. The tour allowed him to continue performing and potentially redeem his reputation. Kean was also a drunk, his performances unreliable.[53] Biographical sketches of Kean during his lifetime and after portray him as a Romantic hero, the emotionalism of his acting reflected in his tragic life, brought down by his personal vices and disappointments. Kean's celebrity was also associated with his dramatic style, which departed from the neoclassicism that had dominated English acting since the late eighteenth century and that was popularized by the Kemble acting family. In contrast, Kean followed Cooke in developing interpretations of tragic roles that registered emotional highs and lows rather than a declaratory continuity that favored the dramatic arc as a whole. Kean thus broke with conventions of characterization in exciting new ways. Edwin Booth, who hailed from a generation of American actors and actresses inspired by the Kean tours of the 1820s, recalled how the tragedian's interpretation of Shakespeare's Othello conveyed both "exquisite tenderness, as well as his sombre and fiercer passions."[54]

Kean arrived in the United States in November 1820. His tour would rival Cooke's in acclaim and cold hard cash. For his first fourteen nights in New York, houses brought in averages of $1,000, out of which the managers paid Kean a nightly salary of $222 and half of the gross from his two benefit performances. Historians estimate that Simpson and Price took in a profit of $7,000 from this first engagement, while Kean earned $4,300 (almost $100,000 today). Arrangements with other theaters varied but were consistently profitable for star and manager alike: Kean performed on sharing terms in both Boston and Philadelphia, where he took home $5,747 (worth $124,000 today) for his sixteen performances.[55] When attendance dropped off toward the end of the season in 1821, Kean became picky, in Boston refusing to perform to a paltry house. This would come back to haunt him in 1825, when he returned for another star tour. Meanwhile, the success of the Kean venture prompted Price to use his London theater connections more aggressively. Over the decade, the Park managers monopolized the circulation of actors from the London theaters, securing their debut engagement at the Park Theatre, then booking them with managers in theaters along the East Coast. In 1826 Price set up shop in London, taking over as manager of the Drury

Lane Theatre, but he continued to send performers to New York, where he maintained a financial stake in the Park Theatre.

In contrast to Kean, whose tour built upon and reignited his London fame, Lydia Kelly was not in fact a "*star* of foreign growth." Her "popularity" was "purely American," but it was built upon familiarity with the Kelly name through her elder sister Fanny Kelly's London stardom.[56] The popularity and wealth the younger sister realized in the United States may not have been available to her in England. Her elder sister Fanny had been prepared for the stage by their uncle, composer Michael Kelly. Fanny then trained Lydia, who debuted in Glasgow in 1810 when she was thirteen. In 1824 Lydia was a successful comedic actress performing alongside her sister in the Drury Lane company, had made circuits of the provincial theaters as a headliner, but was undeniably in Fanny's shadow. Price's offer to bring Lydia to America transformed her career, and she in turn explored the geographic capacity of the American market. She toured the United States from 1824 until 1831, circulating northeastern seaboard cities and also following the expansion of English theater into the Deep South, arriving in New Orleans in 1826. She returned to England in 1831 with a fortune of £5,000 (worth about $587,000 today), married, and retired from the stage.[57]

Kelly's repertoire encompassed English comedy, German opera, and new forms of spectacle melodrama. During her first season touring, she starred in American debuts of the German Romantic opera *Der Freischutz*, which terrified audiences with its supernatural special effects and disappointed critics who deemed German opera inferior to Italian. She also popularized the Orientalist spectacle melodrama *Cherry and Fair Star*, in which she played the youth Cherry, a breeches role. Her engagements drew record houses and compared favorably with George Frederick Cooke's, yet critics were divided. Some remained silent out of "gallantry" rather than deliver public censure.[58] "There must be some merit," a Boston editor wondered in November 1824, "when opinions so entirely opposite are formed."[59] Some of this silence was a function of genre. In reflecting on the season, the *New York National Advocate* noted Kelly's "conspicuous part" in the "melo-dramatic spectacles" that dominated the season. These were "only as far tolerable as they occasionally renovate the public mind from the utmost bent to which comic or tragic excellence push it." Dramatic critics preferred Kelly in "genteel comedy," for "what is superior to her Beatrice?"[60] However, Kelly's penchant for stretching the boundaries of femininity in performance made elite male tastemakers uncomfortable, particularly given her draw with women.

Figure 1. A commercial engraving of Lydia Kelly as Beatrice
in Shakespeare's *Much Ado about Nothing* from a painting
by American artist John Neagle. The image appeared in
the Acting American Theatre edition of the play published
in Philadelphia in 1826. Used by permission of the Folger
Shakespeare Library.

Women flocked to see Kelly's racy interpretations of both genteel
comedy and spectacle melodrama. A New York "Sojourner" marveled
at the "triple tier of ladies" assembled for *Cherry and Fair Star*, which
drew his attention away from the performance.[61] The "Sojourner" was
delighted that Kelly's popularity made it possible to ogle women offstage
and on. But when her performances called out and mocked gender hierarchies, others complained. "Jacques," writing for Philadelphia's *United
States Gazette*, was representative of critics who disliked that Kelly
opened her engagements with Hannah Crowley's *The Belle's Stratagem*.

This eighteenth-century comedy of manners inverted gender conventions, following Letitia Hardy's attempts to regain the attention of her indifferent fiancé through a course of bad behavior, transforming from "hoyden" to "lady."[62] "Jacques" preferred Kelly as the "shrew" Catharine in *Catharine and Petruchio*, an eighteenth-century adaptation of *The Taming of the Shrew* and as Beatrice in *Much Ado about Nothing* (fig. 1). Kelly's comic intensity matched critics' conceptions of those roles, in which the female protagonist's transgressions are satisfactorily disciplined, in contrast to Crowley's Letitia Hardy. Kelly was also at the vanguard of popularizing breeches roles, which critics rarely reviewed without some censure. Though Kelly's Rosalind in Shakespeare's *As You Like It* was one of her most popular roles with audiences, her performance when disguised as the youth Ganymede tainted the piece for critics who could not "bear to see a female usurp the breeches."[63]

During her second year touring, Kelly continued to draw huge houses. Her popularity with women took on additional significance in relation to Kean's return in late 1825. Kean was fleeing an adultery scandal and faced additional public censure in the United States over his imperious treatment of American managers and audiences back in 1820. Theater riots disrupted his initial New York and Boston engagements. Both the prospect of rioting and Kean's morally compromised reputation made attending his performance socially unacceptable for genteel white women. In Philadelphia, Kelly's engagement provided an opportunity for women to reclaim their place in the theater audience. The "ladies" who had "been prevented from visiting the theatre during Kean's engagement" displaced men from theater boxes to cheer Kelly.[64] Her string of engagements at the Chestnut Street Theatre in February and March 1826, directly on the heels of Kean, pulled in nightly averages of $610, culminating in a $1,111 house for her benefit performance in *As You Like It*.[65] The theater was so crowded that night that poor "Jacques" complained he could not see the stage. After manager William Wood announced that Kelly would stay on for another five nights, overlapping with Thomas Cooper, enthusiasm drowned out Kelly's performance in the afterpiece.[66]

Kelly's stardom established a pattern around female stage celebrity shaped by the narrow gendered tastes of dramatic critics. While breeches acting remained extremely popular with American audiences over the 1820s and 1830s, Kelly and other star actresses in this line did not benefit from the kind of sustained, ecstatic critical attention as actresses in tragedy, which was considered a higher form of histrionic art. The popularity of breeches performance, while rarely treated seriously in criticism, was tacitly accepted so long as it occurred within "actress-as-boy" conventions, especially in fairy-tale contexts like *Cherry and Fair Star*.[67] Because Kelly failed to realize critics' ideas of genteel comedy, she rarely received the lavish critical attention, let alone the hero worship, that surrounded male tragedians like Kean. Kean's stature aligned his gender with his gendered repertoire. He was feted by the same men who chronicled his accomplishments in their papers. In 1820 Kean's debut New York engagement concluded with a testimonial banquet by New York "gentlemen" who delivered toasts celebrating the values these "friends of the drama" wanted to see in the theater. They toasted a shared transatlantic culture and conviction that "*Genius*" was "the birthright of no country;—the common property of all." They hoped "common admiration of the same merits and talents" would "cement a friendship" between the nations.[68] Kelly did not fit within this transnational imaginary and probably disappointed the tastes of some of those very gentlemen even as she packed the theater.

In 1827 Price and Simpson arranged a tour for sixteen-year-old star Clara Fisher, who had been acting in Great Britain for a decade. She was their most significant coup since Kean, and, much like it had for Kean, a transatlantic tour gave Fisher the opportunity to reinvent herself during a transitional period. In 1817, at age six, Fisher began appearing in infant productions, part of a larger cohort of child stars celebrated for their precocity who performed a range of characters, especially in multirole or protean dramas that showcased versatility. Her father also coached her to deliver monologues of Shakespeare's Richard III and Shylock. The appeal of an "infant phenomenon" like Fisher operated through a tension between the Romantic idea of the natural child and an awareness of the "studied precision" necessary for demanding parts like Richard III. Critics in England marveled at Fisher's "ability to persuasively embody roles for which she was terribly miscast."[69] As Fisher aged out of this category, she adopted ingenue leads in legitimate drama and comedy such as Juliet, but she continued to play protean farces like *The Actress of All Work* that gave actresses more expressive opportunities beyond narrow dramatic lines. When the sixteen-year-old Fisher arrived in the United States, her career as an infant "prodigy" continued to shape the terms of her celebrity.

While the tour earned incredible profits for the star, managers discovered that they could not always predict audience behavior. Fisher's fortunes in Philadelphia reveal the uneven benefits of the starring system for managers. By the end of the decade, the number of star nights in a season were double those of stock nights, when the regular company performed unassisted. Starring was profitable for both manager and star so

long as the stars "were attractive enough for their houses to equal twice
the manager's expenses," but unfortunately, "many stars did not draw
the $300 to $400 per night that it took . . . to operate."[70] Frequently, stars'
return engagements saw a drop in gross receipts, but houses also suffered
when stars with similar repertoire followed in close succession because
of bad scheduling. Managers felt the loss more than the performers and
came to see themselves as double victims of the "fickle . . . public mind"
and greedy, grasping stars.[71] Such was the case during Fisher's first American season. A Philadelphia manager recalled that her first Philadelphia
engagement in February 1828 "averaged upwards of seven hundred dollars per night, out of which she received nearly four thousand dollars," a
take-home of over $100,000 today, but "when she returned, all curiosity
to see her had subsided," and her engagements were no longer "profitable to the treasury of the theatre."[72] The engagements continued to be
profitable for the Fisher family, however, leading Clara's mother and de
facto agent to approach Simpson about arranging a southern tour.

By the mid-1820s expanding southern markets beckoned. Since 1815
the theater had been reestablished in Virginia and South Carolina, usually
by itinerant companies that performed short seasons in regional circuits,
as well as in Kentucky and Tennessee and in the Deep South among the
boomtowns of Mobile, Natchez, and New Orleans. Fisher's tour mapped
these expanding markets. After her Park Theatre debut in December
1827, Fisher circuited Boston and Philadelphia, then traveled south to
Baltimore and Washington. During her second year touring, she moved
south from Baltimore on a six-day journey to Charleston, then into the
Southwest. Fisher recalled, "After four or six nights in one place" they
traveled to another, much of the "time . . . passed in stage coaches or on
the river steamers." Clara's head rested in her mother's lap as they jogged
along rocky turnpike roads "to Pittsburgh and St. Louis, and back again,
or else to Natchez and Memphis, New Orleans, Nashville, Vicksburg, and
Mobile," always returning for a "longer stay at New York and Boston"
and "perhaps a visit to Canada."[73] These expanded markets sustained
almost continual touring until Fisher's marriage in 1834.

New print industries developed around the starring system, extending the reach of women's celebrity. Whereas early stars were marketed
by local theater bills and paid newspaper advertisements and puffs (promotional pieces inserted by management), Fisher's American celebrity
was accompanied by extensive marketing and use of her name and image by new commercial industries. Lithographers sold portraits of Fisher
and other performers, while sheet music publishers also marketed songs
sung by Fisher, as they had with Lydia Kelly. A portrait of Fisher in 1828

by American painter Henry Inman in the "attitude . . . when singing the 'bonnets of blue'" became a mass-produced engraving (fig. 2).[74] The sheet music for "Bonnets of Blue" sold in music and stationery stores long after Fisher introduced the song in 1827, as did her commercialized portrait. Both painting and the mass-produced engraving featured signifiers of Fisher's celebrity. She wears a medal awarded her by New York theatergoers, part of the developing rituals of public adulation around stars, as well as a bracelet with a medallion portrait of George Frederick Cooke, of whom her father was apparently a "great admirer." The Cooke portrait also helped situate Fisher's American celebrity by making a connection with Cooke's historic tour.[75] Images of celebrated performers appeared in a range of print media. In 1826 actor-manager Francis Courtney Wemyss began publishing "editions of the most popular plays," each with "a Portrait of some eminent performer," an obvious selling point.[76] *Much Ado about Nothing* featured Lydia Kelly, while other editions included

Figure 2. Photomechanical print of an engraving of Clara Fisher by Bourne after Henry Inman's 1828 painting. Rare Book and Manuscript Library. University of Illinois at Urbana-Champaign.

portraits of Mary Ann and John Duff and others, the engravings based on paintings by American artist John Neagle (see figs. 1 and 3 in this chapter and fig. 4 in chapter 2).

These commercial images expanded a star's reach beyond theatergoing publics while simultaneously mediating theatergoers' exposure to starring women. Commercial images thus both "substituted for . . . a social relationship" with celebrities and promised a close scrutiny of their physiognomy seldom possible in a crowded theater. Yet as portraits proliferated, they often looked less and less like their original, although they still featured a recognizable iconography, as with Fisher's cropped hair and face-framing curls.[77] Meanwhile, a burgeoning celebrity consumer culture beyond print "worked to unfix" the names of stars from the "body," now connected to a spectrum of objects, including fashions. "Fashionable ladies under twenty-five" imitated Fisher's "delicate but natural lisp" and the "rolls or puffs" of hair that Fisher wore "on her brow" (but apparently not the "closely cut" hair "on the back of [her] head," which suited the boy roles prominent in Fisher's repertoire).[78] English actor Joe Cowell cataloged the widespread use of Fisher's name, attached to "ships, steamboats, racehorses, mint-juleps, and negro babies." In Cowell's telling, "negro babies" were a curiosity object, yet this naming practice "suggests that some audiences saw in her the promise of a brighter future for their children."[79] Cowell's reference to African American naming practices also points to marginalized publics within the theater audience who drew their own meanings from its entertainments, as well as the expanding reach of stage celebrity through commercialization.[80]

The unprecedented earning potential of foreign stars became another object of public interest as editors used their privileged relationship with theater managers to report box-office totals. Reprinting practices extended the reach of these items, which provided a decontextualized glimpse of the sums stars brought into theaters (or not). This became a public way of measuring the "relative attraction" of different stars and publicized foreign women's significant earning power. Reports originating in the *Charleston Mercury* in 1830 listed the "amounts received by . . . performers" in recent engagements at the Charleston Theatre, comparing Thomas Cooper's $1,212.75 for fifteen nights with Fisher's $1,197.43 for eight nights, and the smaller returns of several other English stars. The appearance of the item in Augusta, Georgia, papers overlapped with Fisher's engagement there, then reached Philadelphia and Massachusetts papers a few weeks later.[81]

These numbers would have juxtaposed starkly with contemporary reports of the depressed state of women's wages. While actresses remained a minority of female wage earners in American cities, they were the highest earning and the most visible laboring women of the era, with stock actresses earning far more than women anywhere else in the nineteenth-century labor market. For example, in 1827 salaries for stock performers at the Boston Theatre started at three dollars per week for walking ladies, a weekly take-home equivalent to seventy-nine dollars today. The pay scale crested at fifty dollars, the joint weekly salary earned by the managerial partners and their wives. These earnings had to cover room and board and stretch into summers of unemployment. Stage performers also furnished their stage wardrobe from their salary but could count on additional income from their seasonal benefit night. In comparison, weekly wages for outwork and factory jobs ranged "between 75 cents and $1.50 a week," today equivalent to twenty dollars and forty dollars per day. Servants' wages were similar, though they had greater stability and could save more if they lived in with their employers.[82] Mill operatives in the New England textile industry fared somewhat better, averaging sixty cents per day in the 1830s.[83] New England teachers, who came from the "most propertied backgrounds" of wage-earning women, earned only $1.25 per week but usually received free room and board, many living with family. Compared with mill operatives, domestic servants, and industrial workers generally, teachers enjoyed the "lengthiest periods of wage work." Most women's employment was seasonal, characterized by chronic instability and overwork. Women usually had to furnish room and board out of their wages. Even as industrialization expanded wage-earning opportunities for women, their wages remained depressed and hovered below subsistence in hypercompetitive urban markets. Depressed wages were also a factor in women's increased practice of prostitution in this period.

The stage, in comparison, was a highly specialized form of skilled labor that afforded women tremendous earning potential. These were well-paying positions with some job security, given the specialized skill set required. Women had the potential to move up the professional hierarchy, earning equal pay for equal work. Though women started with the lowest salaries, half of the women in a theater company, including married women earning a joint salary, ultimately made at least ten dollars per week. The fifty cents per night earned by a New York supernumerary was for "relatively light work and few hours" compared with the factory worker's thirty-three cents per day and included a clear path to higher stature and earning potential.[84] Whether women were raised by thespian parents or chose the stage, they entered a specialized but competitive and socially marginal profession with significant earning potential. Over the course of the 1830s theatrical apprenticeship became appealing to some American-born women, and foreign stock perform- ers and stars continued to make the transatlantic passage. But even for women with established stage careers, like Mary Ann Duff, ascending from walking lady to leading lady was difficult and from leading lady to itinerant star even more so.

Mary Ann Duff: Between Stock and Star

The Duffs came to the United States on John's potential as a versatile lead actor. A decade later, Mary Ann emerged as the key to the family's professional mobility. In their early years in Boston, John's contract al- lowed him to travel for periodic starring engagements, which he did in Providence, New York, and a new theater in Albany. Mary Ann, mean- while, labored in the stock company and oversaw the instruction of their expanding family. New family limitation practices that were reducing family size in the United States in this period seem not to have disrupted the Duffs' robust fertility. Mary Ann was also barred from exploring her dramatic range by existing casting practices.

Lines of business and casting practices that favored the most estab- lished players with the company, especially wives of theater managers, pre- vented Duff from developing her abilities as a tragedian. In her first decade on American stages, Duff played ingenue and pantomime breeches roles, which were plentiful and favored young, attractive actresses like Duff, whose "beautiful figure enhanced the charm" of her "boys and pages."[85] In the Philadelphia/Baltimore company that employed the couple in the 1810s, Juliana Westray Wood, wife of manager William Wood, monopolized leading "heavy" parts, or roles in high tragedy. During these early decades, before starring took off, the marriage partnership at the head of a theater company could be crucial to its success and contributed to the greater stability of theater in Boston, Philadelphia, and Baltimore compared with New York. Westray Wood might also have played a less visible part helping run the company, much like Anne Brunton Merry Wignell had. This expe- rience made it possible for Anne to step into management after Thomas Wignell's death, and she probably continued to be involved in the busi- ness once William Warren took over management and they married. The importance of a woman's executive labors to the financial success of her husband's managerial ventures also shaped professional decision-making, making it unlikely that a leading actress married to a manager would try itinerancy rather than continue at the head of the company. Also, in this early moment of the 1810s, the difficulties of travel and the uncertainty of new markets made itinerancy less appealing. Mary Ann Duff's trajectory might have looked very different had John been more successful as a manager. Instead, she matured as an artist in the context of his decline as a star and his managerial disappointments and then began to explore her draw as an itinerant star.

When the Duffs returned to Boston in 1817, Mary Ann began playing ingenue roles in tragedy, like Ophelia and Cordelia, often opposite star tragedians. But it was during Kean's 1821 engagement that Boston critics first identified the actress's "new powers." When "Mrs. Duff" played with "Mr. Kean," she "burst from our dramatic constellation like a celestial stranger."[86] A piece of Kean lore surrounding Mary Ann Duff's emergence as a tragedian associated her "new powers" with his influence while revealing her evolving sense of herself as an actress. During rehearsals, the star "requested [Duff] to play with less force and intensity or her acting would throw him into the background; to which she replied that, though she honored his rank and position in the profession, her duty to herself and the public would constrain her always to play to the best of her ability."[87] The retort was also a tacit rebuke to the prevalence of starring. Kean was yet another English tragedian whom Mary Ann was called upon to support. Duff answered to her publics, however, not to Kean's glory. And perhaps she also imagined glory and profit of her own.

As newspapermen close to the theater world tried to account for Mary Ann's new tragic powers, they associated her transformation with the needs of her family. They told a story of a desperate wife anxious to compensate for her husband's languishing talents—or worse. As William Clapp, Boston critic turned theater chronicler, explained, "For years . . . a third rate actress," Duff "threw off the languor of indifference . . . as if touched by a magic wand." The "sudden . . . change" was a matter of "necessity" as the actress grew "fearful that she might at any moment be thrown upon her own resources."[88] John's popularity was waning at this time, the family had growing debt, and he may have shown signs of the illness that led to his death in 1831. Mary Ann and her husband were both experimenting with new styles of dramatic acting associated with Kean and his imitators; however, her powers were understood as forged from necessity. Journalists saw John as the serious thespian whose abilities shaped the family's professional direction. Nonetheless, he was losing his touch. In 1826 the Boston *Ladies' Port Folio* censured John Duff for an unfortunate new "habit" of "ranting" and producing "harsh, unmeaning and discordant sounds . . . in a style" that "outrages decency, good sense and order."[89] Where he failed to adapt to changing styles and tastes in tragic acting, his wife succeeded. The engraved portrait from

Figure 3. Engraving of Mary Ann Duff from a painting by John Neagle depicts her as Mary in the 1824 melodrama *Superstition* by American playwright James Nelson Baker. Library Company of Philadelphia.

John Neagle's painting of Mary Ann Duff (fig. 3) captures the actress's dramatic intensity with the unusual choice of a direct gaze, which Joseph Ireland, who reprinted the portrait in his 1882 biography of the actress, assured readers "gives but a faint idea of the beauty of the lady, as it represents her in the Mad scene of the play."[90]

Mary Ann Duff may have acted better during Kean's engagement than ever before, but it was proximity to Kean that cast her emerging powers into relief and generated the critical assessments that survive today. Mary Ann's local popularity and critical acclaim outlasted the Kean engagement, but they did not immediately translate into solo engagements or even greater control over the terms of her career. John maneuvered himself into the managerial partnership of the Federal Street

Theatre in 1822 but was pushed out after a scandal over Kean's refusal, when he returned to Boston in early 1822, to perform for an insufficiently large crowd. The following summer, John opened the small City Theatre, probably counting on his wife's attraction. It was a disaster and cost the Duffs their place in the Boston entertainment market. When they arrived back in Baltimore and tried to launch Mary Ann as a star, she could not bring large enough houses to secure engagements. By 1822 London performers were a better calculus for managers hoping to fill theaters than a vaguely familiar stock actress, in spite of her reputation as the "American Siddons."

Mary Ann's lack of a London pedigree was probably the most significant factor in her inability to move from stock to star. In spite of having started her career in the Dublin Theatre, Mary Ann was seen as an American actress. The increased traffic in London stars, on the other hand, provided Americans with the experience of London theater, allowing them to share in a transatlantic theater culture. When American critics called Duff the "American Siddons," they placed her within a symbolic artistic lineage that traced back to English tragedian Sarah Siddons, then still living but retired from the stage. (Stylistically, Duff actually showed the influence of Kean's Romanticism, but as an actress, Duff would not have been seen as an American Kean.) National origin and stylistic lineage notwithstanding, Duff had never performed in London and thus could not offer theatergoers the connection that had become fundamental to the American starring system.

Between 1823 and 1827 the Duffs moved between various theater companies, trying out different managers and markets. Mary Ann occupied an intermediate position, between stock and star, hired on a season contract and used like a star but without the mobility and autonomy of one, let alone the earning potential. The ambiguities of the evolving industry for popular stock actors emerged in an 1827 breach of contract lawsuit over the Duffs' efforts to change theaters in New York. One of the managers who testified explained that Mary Ann's "principal value to a manager would consist in her appearing seldom" while she was with the company; meanwhile, the manager would "[send] her at times to Philadelphia or Boston."[91] In 1827 Mary Ann played a series of starring engagements in eastern theaters, but though she was "the best actress in our country" and the "Siddons of the American stage," she did not bring in houses that were comparable to those of London imports.[92] In December 1827 the Duffs and their seven children booked passage for Liverpool. They would try to reshape their American careers through a London engagement. If Mary Ann could get a position or a debut at one of the patent theaters, they might return to the United States with the imprimatur of a London reputation and perhaps rise out of the rank of stock actors for good.

———————

The US theater industry had changed significantly since Mary Ann and John Duff came to America in 1810. In 1827 Mary Ann occupied an unstable position in a shifting professional hierarchy, her highly regarded powers as an actress unable to translate into regular independent starring, which was dominated by foreign performers who offered Americans a taste of the English theater scene. In the Duffs' first years in the country, John was a beneficiary of the early experimentation with starring by managers and performers. Over the 1800s and 1810s the American starring system grew from the willingness and desire of English actors and actresses to explore different ways of earning a profit in the expanding but still quite new residential American theater market.

This experimentation was gendered. The transatlantic starring system began with experimentation by relative outsiders like Thomas Cooper and later the Holmans, with opportunities—and interests—varying by gender. Cooper's frustrated ambition and professional conflicts pushed him to try for short-term engagements as he used starring to maneuver around professional roadblocks. Still, his early opportunities are inconceivable without Anne Brunton Merry. In contrast, Merry found professional and personal security within a single market that was strengthened by her successive marriages. As American theater managers and their agents aggressively pursued English entertainers over the 1810s and 1820s, they had the most success with and in some cases preferred to engage men—especially unattached men. As we will see, the structural factors shaping women's lives actually made transatlantic itinerancy less desirable. Meanwhile, some of the most popular starring women who came over in the 1820s, like Lydia Kelly, are not as visible in histories of American entertainment because their performances did not align with the vision of theater championed by male journalists. Even as actresses were barred from forms of celebrity associated with the heroic male tragedian, emerging commercial mechanisms extended the renown of stars like Kelly and Clara Fisher, who clearly appealed widely to American theater publics.

Access to starring was also shaped by nationality. Starring in the 1820s was associated with the London stage. It gave American theatergoers new access to English culture. Mary Ann Duff's abortive attempts to maneuver from stock actress to star map these boundaries. In order to have a chance, Duff believed she needed a London debut, which unfortunately never came to be. In the 1830s, after her husband's death, she became part of a second tier of itinerants who accessed expanding southern and western markets.

Rescuing Duff from comparative obscurity was the impetus for Joseph Ireland's 1882 biography, *Mrs. Duff*. She never attained the stature he believed she deserved, so he crafted a biography to honor her contributions to American theater. In so doing, Ireland grappled with the question of ambition, a gendered problem that shaped female stage celebrity across the nineteenth century. In *Mrs. Duff*, Ireland cast Duff as a reluctant star who was pushed by her husband and the economic necessity of supporting their large family rather than pulled by her own creative and professional ambitions. Explaining how and why women did or did not become stars and understanding the nature of transatlantic starring for the women who *did* come to the United States requires a closer look at the gendered terms of their lives and careers.

2 (Dis)Obedient Daughters and Devoted Wives

The Family Politics of Stock and Star

In her 1897 autobiography, written when she was eighty-seven and delivered before the enthusiasts of the Dunlap Society of New York, Clara Fisher Maeder recalled that she had been "greatly pleased at the idea" of coming to America to tour.[1] Clara's stage labors had supported her family since her early childhood, beginning with her formal debut at age six in an infant production at the Drury Lane Theatre in London. An American tour both created an opportunity for the sixteen-year-old actress to transition to adult repertoire and provided new professional opportunities for the other Fisher children. Mindful of the public function of her memoirs, Fisher Maeder tried to satisfy her auditors' interest in her as a relic of early American theater without exposing too much about the family dynamics surrounding her career. However, the structural realities of her career, directed by her parents, in company with parents and siblings, then later husband and children, meant that the private could not help but intrude.

Peeking through the warm nostalgia of Fisher Maeder's 1897 memoir are hints about the costs of her early labors and the struggles over the terms of her career, which continued into her marriage. Fisher Maeder recalled that though ostensibly she was the family breadwinner, when the family came to America in 1827, the sixteen-year-old actress was still "regarded as a mere child."[2] Fisher's acting career was a product of her parents' decisions to train her and her siblings for the stage. During her six years touring the United States, Clara recalled that she was "almost perpetually on the stage" either in rehearsals or in performances. It was a punishing schedule. Itinerancy intensified the physical and psychological costs of "long and severe rehearsals" and the "constant study" required to keep up with the "daily change of programs."[3] Marriage was one of the few avenues for girls to break from parental control before they reached the age of majority, twenty-one.[4]

Clara's marriage to musician James Maeder in 1834 at age twenty-three made it possible for her to adjust the intensity of her stage career, which was also affected by motherhood. Though historians casually attribute Clara's decline in touring after her marriage to diminished appeal from losing the allure of girlhood, Clara faced other pressures. She bore seven children in these years, which may be one reason she shifted permanently from touring to stock work in 1840. There were also clear conflicts within her marriage over the allocation of her labors. In a rare admission of marital discord, Fisher Maeder noted in 1897, "Mr. Maeder always preferred I should teach [elocution], but I was 'fond of the footlights,' and always glad to get back to them."[5] In the theater, as opposed to other male-dominated trades to which female family members contributed their labor, it was not possible to "[confine] female members to non-executive participation in the family business."[6] Delivering private instruction in elocution was an imperfect solution for their family. This may have reflected pressures of childrearing and James Maeder's investment in gendered ideals for his family, preferring his wife to devote herself to private domestic labors. Even as Fisher Maeder continued to act, she positioned her career in relation to her maternal role. For an 1841 benefit night, she delivered verses by her friend Ann Stephens that surveyed Fisher Maeder's long career but concluded in a sentimental portrait of her role as wife and mother. Fisher Maeder proclaimed to her public that

> all the glory of my first eclat
> Was not more dear than that soft word 'mama,'
> With which an infant group will rush to meet
> The first faint sound of returning feet.[7]

While continuing her executive labors in the family acting business, Fisher Maeder connected them to an increasingly sentimentalized maternal vocation.

Even as the starring system enabled stage performers such as Clara Fisher Maeder and other girls and women from Great Britain and the United States to elevate themselves from waged laborers to speculative

contractors, the terms and proceeds of these arrangements were not necessarily theirs to determine, let alone control. The gender politics of the
family economy shaped the career trajectories of girls and women in distinct ways. The early United States carried changing English legal under-
standings of childhood into its own laws, which increasingly emphasized
parental authority over labor and over marriages involving children under
the age of majority.[8] Children from theatrical families began informal
training from infancy and were regularly put to work both onstage and
backstage at the same age that Clara became an infant phenomenon.
Parents controlled and benefited from their children's labor in the theater as elsewhere, even after their children assumed regular positions
of their own. Parents had a particular interest in controlling children's
labor as stars. Many girls assumed stock positions in their teens, often
in the same company with their parents, at least until marriage. With
marriage, girls and women became the legal property of their husbands,
though they had more recourse to divorce in the United States than in
Great Britain. Nor did women's unique potential to earn equal pay for
equal work in the theater mean that they controlled their earnings or
the terms of that labor.[9] The overall practice of hiring women as part of
family groups headed by men had the potential to alienate women from
their earnings.[10] Yet the number of widows who managed theaters in Britain (and in the United States) "demonstrate[s] the structure of joint utility that may have operated in many businesses credited to husbands."[11]
The highly restricted legal parameters of women's lives with respect to
their ability to control their own earnings, own property, exchange their
labor, or enter into any form of contract do not actually tell us about
women's executive role within the acting family, that is, about the ways
professional decisions were made. The appropriation of women's labors
within the family economy was constant for both the skilled labor force
of stock actors and the elevated class of touring stars, though starring
created unique possibilities for personal and financial autonomy. With
key exceptions, men expected to control and supervise the labor of their
children and wives. The degree to which women practiced personal and
professional autonomy varied considerably but is difficult to determine
from available sources.

Unfortunately, few star actresses left extant personal papers, though
fragmentary correspondence survives in archived papers of theater managers. Much of what we know about these women's lives and careers comes
secondhand, from memoirs of managers and critics eager to preserve the
history of the stage, construct a taxonomy and genealogy of greatness,
and demonstrate that actresses could preserve their womanly character

in spite of their profession. These accounts by journalists and managers remain the most prominent record of women's lives and careers. It is only by close reading to unpack the ideological frameworks of these narratives that it becomes possible to tease out the structural parameters of women's stardom. Family was fundamental to their lives and careers but in ways different from those conveyed in these sources. While actresses were "living one story," biographical sketches invested in gendered politics of respectability persist in "telling us . . . quite another."[12] Often, their public reputation mobilized starring women's identities as daughters, wives, and mothers in ways that both shield and hint at the messy family dynamics of the starring system and the theater more generally.

Mapping the gendered contours in the lives and celebrity of the women who became itinerant stars, first in Atlantic seaboard markets and a bit later in the trans-Appalachian West and South, over a life cycle of childhood, marriage, and motherhood (or not), as well as widowhood or divorce, reveals common gendered features of the starring system for girls and women. Girls enhanced the professional stature, fortunes, and opportunities of parents and siblings. Their marriages, often in their late teens to other members of the profession, were a vital professional calculation that could expand or constrain their careers. If marriage was, for some, a risky bid for professional autonomy, improvements in transportation made it more common for unmarried women to pursue itinerancy and resist the pressures of the intensely promarital culture, though widows were more prevalent than unmarried adult women. Unmarried women may have been uniquely vulnerable to physical assault and professional disrespect, yet itinerant starring offered new professional opportunities and success for femes sole. While divorce was rare in the profession, as theater markets expanded west and south, a legal exit from marriage could allow for professional reinvention.

However, the gendered frameworks through which contemporary biographers recounted women's careers consistently distort or conceal their degree of personal and professional autonomy or experiences of exploitation and abuse. In a significant historical shift, nineteenth-century stage performers increasingly tried to present themselves as sharing the values of an expanding middle-class business culture (also a growing market) that aligned respectability with Christian domesticity and looked upon wage-earning women with both sympathy and suspicion. This is why nineteenth-century actress biographies consistently "strain to represent the actress as not naturally a worker and wage-earner," even though the contours of actresses' lives suggest a much more complicated story.[13] By the 1830s, as print industries devoted more attention to the lives of public figures, ghostwritten promotional materials in the United States (as in Great Britain) were used to establish the legitimacy and significance of a woman's career by aligning stage performers with domestic femininity, mobilizing the hyperrespectability of their private lives in support of their public roles. This literature assured publics that an actress's womanly character remained inviolate (or perhaps less violated), showing how it was possible for a respectable woman to labor perpetually before the public to earn a living. Consistent narrative and rhetorical patterns highlighted genius, usually discovered by a parent, or subsumed a girl or woman's ambition (or reticence) within the needs of the family economy. Girls and women are portrayed as serving other forces in their lives, even though many may have been just as driven and self-promoting as star actors whose biographies frequently emphasize youthful ambition with a tinge of rebellion. In contrast, narrative conventions that managed tensions between shifting gender ideals and the visible realities of actresses' labors concealed much of the realities of girls' and women's intimate and professional lives and the nature of their personal ambitions.

(Dis)Obedient Daughters

For the majority of stage performers acting in Atlantic theaters, the family economy was the founding context of their careers. Theater was or became the family business. The new resident theater companies assembled from immigrant actors in the 1790s, like the strolling companies of the colonial period, were dominated by married couples contracted jointly and paid a joint salary over a season. These family ties formed the webs upon which the industry grew, creating and reproducing a skilled labor force of actors who populated companies in the expanding United States. This pattern persisted into the trans-Appalachian West after 1815, when small theater companies composed of family groups ventured west and south along the Ohio and Mississippi Rivers, offering seasons of eight to ten weeks in a regional circuit before constructing full-scale permanent theaters through local investors. In America, as in Britain, "kinship networks sustained the exploitation of much human and investment capital and kept a combination of key personnel consistently together."[14] Both daughters and sons could enhance a family's earning potential, especially as they entered their teens. Parents determined children's education, directed their labor, and profited from it. Training of future actors was a form of unpaid labor largely overseen by mothers on top of their duties as thespians.[15] Effectively preparing children for the stage could enhance a family's overall earning power and their professional and geographic mobility. Of course, not all thespians were born to parents in the profession. In such cases, marriage was a vehicle onto the stage, a way to achieve professional legitimacy and training.

While family figured prominently in narratives about the professional rise of distinguished players, increasingly over the nineteenth century, changing conceptions of family and childhood that gained purchase throughout the Anglo-Atlantic world began to shape thespian origin stories, especially of starring women. From the late eighteenth century on, romantic ideas of childhood as a distinct and consequential stage of life led to a greater focus on early childhood education. Fiction and didactic literature, also strongly influenced by Christian evangelicalism, reimagined the family as a sympathetic unit in which key lessons might be instilled and the unique qualities of children be developed, also placing a new emphasis on the role of mothers. Family limitation practices also contributed to an intensified focus on the maternal relationship. In the United States especially, proponents of education, founders of maternalist associations, and writers of didactic literature connected the "success of America's republican experiment" with the "ability of parents to implant checks and balances in the moral character of future generations."[16] Architects of stage celebrity and chroniclers of the stage offered origin stories of prominent players that reframed professional genealogies within sentimental tales about the family.

During the early nineteenth century, the stories about the rise of starring girls and women mobilized changing ideas about the family. While thespian parents continued to train daughters for the stage, actress origin stories reimagined family as an affective unit in which a daughter's genius would be discovered and nurtured in appropriate ways rather than a productive unit in which girls and boys were trained for the family trade. Family simultaneously became more important to explaining girls' stage careers even as the nature of its role shifted to emphasize either extreme necessity or a dramatic genius that could not and should not be contained within the domestic sphere. This was the debutant daughter plot, which mobilized assumptions about the gendered paths of sons and daughters and, tellingly, had no male equivalent. A girl's stage career represented a deviation from the arc of a woman's life and disrupted a family's imaginary path to respectability. The debutant daughter story solved two related problems, explaining either why a successful family of actors would continue to train their daughters for the stage and jeopardize their social mobility or why a respectable family would allow their daughter to be put on the stage, thus drawing the family into the profession. The plot rested on an affective father-daughter relationship. While discussion of dramatic genius did provide an indirect vehicle for exploring girls' ambition, in these stories, fathers discover, nurture, and direct a girl's talent in legitimate ways.

The shift in Anne Brunton Merry Wignell Warren's origin story after her death illustrates how changing conceptions of the family were mobilized around thespian women through the story of the debutant daughter. A collection of "green-room" tales published in England in 1795 portrayed her father, John, as transparently ambitious through his daughters, "whom he intended to introduce on the Stage, [taking] great delight and pains in their instruction." Six of his fourteen children became stage performers. He aggressively promoted their careers and during Anne's London debut "was indefatigable in sounding her panegyric."[17] After the actress's death in 1805, theater chroniclers rewrote her origins as a sentimental story that downplayed her father's mercenary approach. Though six of actor John Brunton's children had careers on the stage at the time of Anne's 1785 debut, nineteenth-century readers were led to believe that John "had no intention of preparing [Anne] for the stage."[18] Anne had merely been taught "Shakspeare as a means of mental improvement" but shocked John when he overheard the precocious fifteen-year-old "reciting" Calista from Nicholas Rowe's *The Fair Penitent* and discovered that "she was perfect in the part"—among other tragic ingenue roles. Her genius compelled him to prepare her for her career. She debuted the following week on the Bath stage, which secured a coveted invitation to Covent Garden Theatre in London.[19]

While nineteenth-century chroniclers softened John Brunton's brute economics motives, they still recognized the connection between Anne's powers and her family's fortunes. Boston journalist William Warland Clapp put a sentimental spin on the story in 1853 that was also reminiscent of the narrative surrounding the 1829 debut of another English actress, Fanny Kemble. According to Clapp, "The father, who had battled hard to obtain the means of subsistence for his family, saw that a mine of wealth had long been concealed in his own family, under modesty and reserve, and at once determined to encourage the talent which had lain dormant, and bring his daughter before the public."[20] The daughter's career was a last resort, not a design. This had been the case for Kemble. In 1829 the twenty-year-old daughter of bankrupt Covent Garden manager Charles Kemble (and niece of Sarah Siddons) suffered a jarring shift from a life of genteel domesticity and her boarding school education when she had to help bail out her father. In neither Kemble's nor Brunton's case was the daughter's ambition seen to be a factor in her stage debut. Rather, the narrative explained not only how but also why a daughter's genteel education and upbringing might be turned into valuable capital through a stage debut, implicitly disrupting the family's bid for social mobility. Whereas Fanny's memoirs substantiate this account of her reorientation from private life to stage career out of financial necessity and reveal her deep ambivalence about her short-lived profession, the absence of Anne's voice from the historical record makes it impossible to consider her own ambitions relative to her father's.[21] The pleasures, ambitions, and strategies of girls and women pursuing or resisting a stage career are crowded out in these narratives by their obligations to others.

Dramatic genius remained a constant but frequently appeared as a force outside a child's own agency in narratives that again downplayed the messier realities of child labor. This was the case with Clara Fisher's early stage career, which was framed by English constructions of natural genius and changing ideas about childhood, the professional and financial motivations of her parents and siblings downplayed. When Fisher debuted in 1817 at the age of six, her early celebrity mobilized emerging Romantic ideas of childhood that emphasized innocence in place of older beliefs in innate depravity, thus supporting arguments for early childhood education. The apparent precocity demonstrated by Fisher and child stars of the era tapped into contemporary questions about children's natural capacity for learning. Fisher debuted after a wave of child stars, when public interest seemed to be waning; however, qualities of her performance seemed different from those of her predecessors. According to one paper, "There is a *mind* about [her performance] which proves that it is not the mere offspring of imitation." Critics who grappled with whether Fisher and other child stars revealed "a precocity of genius" or were mere "plastic creatures" and "*automata*" were considering the nature of childhood itself.[22] Whether genius or imitation, these performances still rested on hours of study and practice.

These frameworks also shaped Fisher's celebrity while she was touring in the United States, when she was aging out of the category of infant phenomenon but continued to appeal to audiences by performing girlhood and showcasing her dramatic virtuosity. Much of the material about her published during her tour came directly from the English press. According to these narratives, Fisher's dramatic career, prompted by her childhood genius, seemed outside her overt agency. The child was drawn to dramatic art rather than mobilized by a desire for a dramatic career, which presented itself as a possibility almost in spite of her parents' wishes or the child's intentions. Ultimately, the child became a star through parental regulation, which was treated as a beneficial rather than an exploitative force. A piece in the February 1828 issue of the *Souvenir*, a magazine published in Philadelphia, reprinted from the London *New Monthly Magazine*, detailed the infant Fisher's performances for family and friends in the private drawing room. Two years later, news of the precocious young Fisher produced invitations from men attached to the London stage who were anxious that Mr. Fisher allow his daughter to perform. At long last, "the objections which Mr. Fisher had to Clara's appearing as an actress, at so early a period of life, were ultimately overruled."[23]

Of course, the narrative concealed important realities, beginning with Clara's father's frustrated theatrical ambitions. The eldest child, Jane Fisher, born in 1796, was appearing in the provincial circuit around the same time that Clara debuted in *Lilliput* at the Drury Lane Theatre. By 1817 the stage had become the family business through the Fisher children. The Fisher parents reoriented their lives and made a lot of money in the process. In spite of their unique and highly visible labors for the family economy, girl stars remained subject to patriarchal authority and consistently failed to disrupt those prerogatives. They are rarely allowed a voice in these records.

Still, some daughters clearly did attempt to gain control over their lives and livelihoods, mainly through marriage. By the end of the eighteenth century, the strengthening of "parental custody" and belief that individuals under twenty-one were less able to exercise "individual choice" meant that parents began to serve as "guarantors" of marriage contracts for children who had not reached the age of majority.[24] Anne Brunton, Clara Fisher, and Agnes Holman, whose starring careers were each instrumental to the family's earning potential, married within only a few years of attaining the age of majority. Brunton married in 1791 at twenty-two, and in the United States, Fisher married in 1834 at the age of twenty-three and Holman in 1815 when she was twenty-two. Parents' interest in controlling the labor of their children, especially within the theater, explains why these starring girls married comparatively late. Age consciousness had increased by midcentury, reducing the number of youthful marriages of females to 22 percent in the North but only 40 percent in the South and trans-Appalachian West. Still, scholars conclude that it was parents' vested interest in retaining the labor of children more so than their concerns about youthful marriage that may have fueled resistance to a daughter's marriage before majority.[25] This was certainly true in Agnes Holman's case.

Agnes Holman came to the United States with her father in 1811 when she was eighteen. Her popularity sustained her father's career in these years, though by various accounts, she was not happy with her professional and family situation. In 1815, having reached majority, she contracted what manager William Wood considered a "hurried" and "ill-judged marriage" to a German musician, Charles Gilfert in order to get away from her "auster[e]" and "almost cruel" father, Joseph, whose "severe treatment" had exhausted the young star.[26] Still, their careers remained closely tied. Joseph moved into management, opening a theater in Charleston. Agnes and Charles joined the company. There were clearly problems in the marriage as well. Joseph supported Agnes in a lawsuit against her new husband for control over the "income and profits of her profession." The father who had rebuilt his career and fortune on his daughter's stardom now helped her protect her earnings from her husband's profligacy. After Joseph's death in 1817, Agnes supported Charles as he tried to establish a dramatic circuit in the South and in 1826 entered into a partnership to open a new theater in New York known as the Bowery Theatre.[27]

Over the 1810s and 1820s, as the "talent raid" of English actors by American managers and their agents picked up, family ties structured these arrangements, often acting as a constraint on agents' abilities to hire women. This was a source of frustration for Park Theatre manager Edmund Simpson. In an attempt to avoid being drawn into family politics or pressured to engage entertainers with less appealing qualities, he broke with the practice managers had used for decades to assemble stock companies and actually tried to avoid engaging families altogether. Family ties also proved a more significant obstacle with the female performers whom he was anxious to book. Simpson complained, "Miss [R.] Penley is a very pretty girl & . . . comic actress—her father will not let her travel."[28] He wanted to secure Catherine Leesugg and her younger sister but without having to engage the entire family, for he felt that her parents would be meddlesome and "by their manners would disgrace any Theatre, they came into."[29] He wrote to the father offering eight guineas a week for the two girls but was turned down.[30] In a comedy of miscommunication (or was it strategy on the elder daughter's part?), Leesugg called on Simpson the following day, professing not to know of her father's decision, and explained that "it was her wish to accept" Simpson's offer.[31] Simpson insisted that she "consult with [her father] and let me know on Saturday." Simpson would meet with both father and daughter again, separately, ultimately engaging the actress for a three-year contract.[32] The elder girl was twenty-one and had reached the age of majority, yet Simpson was reluctant to make any arrangements without the father's approval.

The close networks that structured the industry may have kept daughters like Catherine Leesugg and Agnes Holman from obtaining the professional independence that was their legal right and personal desire. Stage performers relied on parents, siblings, in-laws, friends, and associates in other markets to inform them of new openings and opportunities, provide letters of introduction, or negotiate for them. Simpson wanted to cultivate networks in the English theater world, not gain a reputation for luring children away from their parents. Consequently, the majority of female performers who sought work on American stages, whether as salaried stock actors or as touring stars, came either with husbands or with parents who were themselves employed actors. Agents may have seen unmarried girls and women as a liability where they saw unmarried men as an advantage. It was also dangerous and difficult to be a woman alone and unmarried navigating the industry and its unfamiliar networks in a foreign country.

Feme Sole, Part 1: The Actress (Un)Protected

There were far fewer unmarried women among the English actresses who crossed the Atlantic to tour in the 1810s and 1820s compared with unmarried men and married women accompanied by their husbands. The higher moral standard and greater scrutiny that fell upon women explain why we see far more women starring as part of acting couples, like Sarah and George Bartley, or traveling with an older relative who was functionally a chaperone and business partner. Consider the case of the sisters Wallack. On his 1818 recruiting trip, Edmund Simpson met with all four of the Wallacks, who were themselves descended from English actors. Simpson engaged both James and Henry, who came with their actress wives, though only Fanny Jones Wallack, married to Henry, had a successful stage career in the United States. Simpson found "Mrs. Pincott & Child"—Elizabeth Wallack and her thirteen-year-old daughter, Leonora—to be "very clever & very useful but I cannot engage her [as] her character is bad." Likewise, Mary Wallack, or "Mrs. Hill," as she was then known, "wants to go to America," and though "she is very clever," Simpson was in "the same predicament—cannot if I wished."[33] Simpson was similarly anxious about drunkards and ruled out performers whom he considered too "vulgar."[34] But whereas he refused to consider women who had run off with lovers or had illegitimate children, he showed no scruples about engaging Robert Maywood, who "has parted from his wife."[35] There were divorced and widowed women in this period whose touring allowed them to support dependents and others who flouted respectability entirely: Frances Alsop was a notorious opium addict, and Philadelphia-born Mrs. Henry had divorced her first husband, also an actor. But women clearly faced greater pressure to perform respectability as part of their bid for public patronage, which placed unmarried women in a more vulnerable professional situation.

In contrast, actors often ventured overseas for a few seasons without their wives, if they were married at all, or brought actress wives who did not star with their husbands. Mrs. James Wallack traveled to New York with her husband in 1818, giving birth to their son Lester in 1819. She seems never to have acted on American stages, though manager William Wood recalled engaging the couple for his 1821 company, at least until Wallack broke his leg and suspended his season and also his wife's.[36] The most successful starring actors of the period, all of whom actually spent most of their careers in the United States, including James and Henry Wallack, Junius Brutus Booth, Charles Matthews, and Robert Maywood, did not star as part of a family unit. Some actors saw touring as a way to escape an unhappy marriage—or start a new one. In 1821 Junius Brutus Booth left England with his pregnant lover, Mary Ann Holmes (whom he may have married in a legally questionable ceremony), leaving his estranged wife and child behind, and established a home for Holmes and his new family on land he ultimately purchased in Maryland.[37]

Given the intensifying respectability politics around the theater in this period, men who failed to shield illicit relationships from public view also jeopardized their careers, though women remained far more vulnerable. This is illustrated by the outbreak of violence during Edmund Kean's return to the United States in 1825. This time, he was fleeing an adultery scandal and divorce. When he returned to the United States, opponents drew connections between the lack of personal honor in his private life and his past professional conduct, recalling how he had refused to play for a small audience in Boston at the end of his first tour. Rioting publics stopped Kean from performing in New York in November 1825, and in Boston the rowdies made short work of the theater, tearing up benches, lamps and chandeliers, windows, and box doors. Managers during Kean's tour hired extra police on the evenings when he was to appear.

While managers feared destruction of their property for engaging Kean, women acting with him faced slanderous attacks, as did the lone female spectators who risked violence and public censure to see him play. Kean's sexual peccadilloes with the infamous Charlotte Cox, his adulterous lover, made his leading lady in New York, Ellen Johnson Hilson, the target of audience jibes during the New York riots. Calls of "Alderman

Cox" directed at Kean were joined by shouts of "Mrs. Cox" as Hilson took the stage in the part of Lady Anne opposite Kean's Richard III. Her husband "rushed upon the stage, and carried Mrs. Hilson . . . behind the scenes."[38] When news of the riot made regional papers, Baltimore's *Federal Gazette* rebuked Hilson for performing with Kean, shocked that an "actress whose character we have always esteemed so much, should . . . have consented to perform" with Kean. The editor applauded Thomas for "carrying his wife from the stage," thereby "remov[ing]" her from the "contact of pollution" (and from physical harm as well).[39] Kean's flagrant disregard for sexual morality threatened the delicate webs of respectability that actors were trying to construct around their profession. Women were key markers and agents of that respectability, onstage and off, and thus much more vulnerable.

Mary Rock's attempts to navigate the shifting terms of the American theater business and maneuver from stock to star demonstrate the independence possible for women in the starring system, on which Lydia Kelly also capitalized, while highlighting the challenges unmarried women faced. In September 1827 "Mr. Rock and Miss Rock" arrived in Boston from Liverpool with others engaged for the Federal Street (or Boston) Theatre.[40] No subsequent mention of "Mr. Rock" appears. Various theater chroniclers agree that "Miss Rock" was an orphan. According to the most extant biographical sketch of the actress, from a 1901 history of theater in Montreal, Rock was an English orphan adopted by a wealthy aunt in Dublin and raised in wealth and "society" until "reverses" took her to Edinburgh, where she studied for the stage and debuted, all by age twelve.[41] Rock may actually have begun her career in Dublin at the Crow Street Theatre, acting with her uncle, Anthony Rock, who served as deputy manager. After his death, Anthony Rock left £500 to his son and a sizable £1,000 to his niece, Mary. However, the money was to come from repayment of a loan from the manager of the Crow Street Theatre. Mary never saw the legacy but successfully sued the managers for her salary before leaving the company.[42] If this was the same Mary Rock who traveled to Boston in 1827, her companion may have been her cousin James, who had also been cheated out of his inheritance but shared Mary's sense of adventure, leaving with her for America.

However, five months into a promising American career, Mary Rock faced down a breach of contract suit and the censure of the Boston public. She navigated this delicate juncture by both appealing to and defying patriarchal lines of authority. On February 4, 1828, Rock published "A Card" in several Boston papers defending herself against accusations by the managers of the Boston Theatre that she was in "violation" of her contract by engaging for three nights with the rival Tremont Theatre. Though Rock expressed "extreme reluctance" at "appear[ing] in person before the public in self-justification," she clearly feared the consequences of the Boston Theatre's campaign, which tacitly urged theatergoers to boycott her forthcoming Tremont appearance. In the card, Rock defended her moves. During a midseason change in management, she had "sent in [her] resignation" and considered her contract with the theater void.[43] When she joined the Boston Theatre company at the start of the season, she was earning a weekly salary of $35.52 (about $970 today), the highest individual salary in the company, in the same wage bracket as most of the joint salaries (except for the manager partners and their wives, who each earned $50 per week).[44] The stock actress had since "become a votary of the starring system," a Boston paper noted snidely if accurately. This was all a "game" being "played by skillful hands."[45] Rock was making a calculated risk to further her professional stature, but it could founder on public opinion, as well as on legal judgment.

Rock said no more in the papers, though the "facts" she promised clearly got into the right hands, shaping a public debate in the city papers during and after her Tremont Theatre engagement. The debate turned on Rock's right of contract in her attempts to turn star and fixated on her relative vulnerability as a woman. "Amicus" urged the theatergoing public to consider Rock's status as an "unprotected female" and foreigner, lamenting that the "community" appeared determined to "blight the reputation of a deserving [female] in a strange country, and far from home."[46] Another paper echoed this stance in its plea to readers to stop sending "public animadversion." These editors did not consider it appropriate to "assume . . . the air of opposition" where the "reputation of a female is involved."[47] This benevolent paternalism operated uncomfortably at the intersection of Rock's gender and marital status and her professional stature, however.

The woman addressing the Boston public in February 1828, championed as an "unprotected female" who was "far from home," was actually an accomplished actress and businesswoman of twenty-eight with at least sixteen years of theater experience—and the veteran of a lawsuit. But successfully appealing for sympathy and patronage required a deployment of female reticence. Shortly after the Rock incident, another kerfuffle broke out between the managers of the Boston and Tremont Theatres over the correct dates for the star engagement of Amelia George, who traveled with her sister Mrs. Gill, also an actress. Here the matter was clearly between the two theaters, so George escaped censure and did not have to compromise her modesty, unlike Rock, by "appealing to the justice of a liberal public."[48] Rock's appeal reflected her professional vulnerability to public opinion, especially because she was relatively unusual, in the profession, as a woman "unprotected."

Rock also clearly took care not to appear like another unmarried Englishwoman scandalizing American publics at the time, the free-thinker Fanny Wright, then on a lecture tour, or like American travel writer Anne Royall, who aggressively marketed her books while continuing to travel the country. "Fanny Wrightism" would quickly become a term of opprobrium for women who pushed against emerging Christian frameworks of pious, subservient, domestic womanhood.[49] Royall's success as a travel writer and later as editor of her own weekly paper occurred in the context of her notoriety for flouting an increasingly rigid gender ideal. In July 1829 she was tried and found guilty in Washington, DC, of being a "common scold": she had been charged mainly for her strong anticlerical views and was issued a fine. However, over the early 1830s, a period in which women became more involved in publishing but aligned with domestic themes, Royall distanced herself as a known figure from the newspaper she published, which ceased to be regarded as a platform for her political views.[50] Wright and Royall offered extreme models of mobile, opinionated, and economically successful unmarried women who flouted emerging gender norms and quickly came to exemplify all that women should not be. Fanny Wright became an epithet used well into the century to police forms of women's activism. Given this context, it became imperative for women employed in a public and socially marginal profession to take care in their forms of public address and observe gendered professional hierarchies. Rock's careful stance and her allies' deployment of her gender did not protect her from public censure. But in spite of the "slight *hiss* of *serpent* malevolence" during her Tremont engagement (perhaps a reference to a rowdy claque in the theater), Rock's proponents boasted that the $1,200 in receipts (close to $33,000 today) for her Tremont Theatre benefit were *"greater than on any benefit night ever before in Boston!"*[51] Rock's calculated risk had paid off handsomely.

Rock continued to tour, remaining unmarried for at least another decade. According to the Montreal account, in 1843 she wed Captain Sir John Murray, a gentleman rather than an actor, which reflected her stature as an established and successful star. She did not leave the stage, rare for actresses who married outside the profession, though not for actors. Rock's wealth may have been the key motivating factor for Murray. Shortly after their marriage, Murray traveled to England "for the benefit of his health," a trip funded by his wife's "hard earned means" and jewels, but he never returned.[52] Ironically, Mary Rock seems to have done very well for herself professionally until her marriage to a scoundrel.

Feme Covert: Wives and Husbands

Choice of marriage partner had significant professional implications for women and men in the theater. Given the enduring custom for married couples to engage together at the same theater, earning a joint salary that reflected their respective lines of business, a marriage partner carried implications for employability and preparation of children for the profession. Marriage could transform the trajectory of a player's career or restrict it, as clearly occurred at varying points in Mary Ann Duff's career. While the decision making that occurred within professional marriages is nearly impossible to view, a comparison of the marriages and professional trajectories of English thespians Elizabeth and John Johnson and their daughter, Ellen Johnson (Hilson), underscores how choice of marriage partner transformed professional trajectories, yet presumptions of patriarchal authority within marriage made it far more difficult for wives to challenge or subvert a husband's decisions about the family's career trajectory. This had real implications for how women were able to explore the possibilities of the American starring system.

In 1798 Park Theatre manager William Dunlap hired Elizabeth and John Johnson to lead his new company, the husband playing first old men roles, while the wife performed leading business in both comedy and tragedy. The Johnsons had come over from England in 1795 shortly after their marriage when the actress was sixteen, John twenty-six. Dunlap explained in his 1832 *History of the American Theatre* that the actress looked up to John as someone who "could protect and instruct her," though it was clearly an advantageous match for him. The actress was a "tall, elegant beautiful young woman, whose taste in dress made her a model for the belles" of New York and a lucrative draw for the Park Theatre. She also took in a higher portion of their joint salary, twenty-five dollars (or about $527 a week today) to John's twenty dollars. While Dunlap understood the marriage through a paternalistic lens, John clearly benefited professionally and financially from his wife's abilities and popularity. But he was also frustrated with being overshadowed by other actors in the company. In their spring 1798 benefits, Elizabeth filled a house worth $832, while her husband drew a dismal $416, failing to cover rent or expenses. The next day, John announced to William that they planned to return to England.[53]

Dunlap's diary offers a rare view of Elizabeth Johnson's place in these negotiations. After the disappointing benefit, John announced to Dunlap that he was "much dissatisfied & says he will go to England." While still awaiting replies from England, he had "in part engaged his passage." Dunlap wrote that Elizabeth "seems down-cast." He called on the couple and found a distressing scene. The "low-spirited" wife "choked & burst into tears." Dunlap tried to work out a provisional arrangement for the next season. The husband agreed, but a week later Dunlap had a "terrible shock." John had received word from London that managers there had "heard of Mrs Johnson, that she may [have] a situation at either house." Dunlap noted with resignation, "I should not oppose his determination." That evening, he went for a walk with his own wife and daughter. He said no more about Elizabeth, for he had promised not to interfere.[54]

Professional decisions made by husbands and fathers had the potential to alienate women's professional agency in order to serve particular conceptions of family interest. John Johnson leveraged his professional connections back in England to secure a coveted London position for his wife, a rising talent. This also extricated him from a market in which his professional advancement seemed limited. She, however, was reluctant to make this move. While the material and professional benefits of a London position for Elizabeth Johnson were indisputable, they exacted a clear personal cost. Her daughter Ellen's professional trajectory was likewise altered by marriage and shaped by her husband Thomas Hilson's professional interests, though the shifting cultural context elevated Ellen, posthumously, into a model of devotion to family. While Dunlap's diary offers a rare window into Elizabeth Johnson's frustrations, biographical sketches that celebrated Ellen's life situate her negotiation of marriage, motherhood, and acting within a simplistic narrative of sentimental domesticity.

Ellen was born in London in 1800. Her family made two more Atlantic voyages before Ellen was six, then chose to remain in England for the next decade, presumably to provide their daughter with better schooling. It is likely that her parents felt that Ellen's future as an actress would be enhanced by connections with the London stage. In 1816 the Johnsons returned to New York, where Ellen took a position at the Park Theatre. Ellen quickly replaced her mother as the family breadwinner following Elizabeth's retirement in 1817 and John's death two years later.[55] In 1826, when Ellen was twenty-six, she married Thomas Hilson, a popular comedian fifteen years her senior who had been acting on American stages both with stock companies and in starring engagements since his arrival from England in 1810.

Elizabeth Johnson and Ellen Johnson Hilson participated in shifts in the family occurring over this period as women led a revolution in family limitation practices connected with changing ideas about motherhood and family. Though uneven, the shift away from the eighteenth-century culture of procreation and the corresponding reduction in family size, supported by new ideas of virtuous self-control and the maternal-child bond, had significant implications for a woman's professional trajectory in the theater.[56] It is no accident that many starring women of the nineteenth century had small families, in contrast to their predecessors. While Elizabeth's youthful marriage at age sixteen was not unusual for the time, Ellen delayed marriage until the age of twenty-six while working as a stock actress in New York, but each woman had only one child during her marriage (Ellen's lasted a decade). This striking similarity in

Figure 4. This engraving of a John Neagle painting captures Ellen Johnson Hilson at her professional height in 1827 performing a role from the seventeenth-century English drama *A New Way to Pay Old Debts* by Philip Massinger. Rare Book and Manuscript Library, University of Illinois at Urbana-Champaign.

family size increases the likelihood that Elizabeth shared family limitation strategies with her daughter, though both women may also have
suffered from miscarriages or fertility problems. In contrast, Ellen's contemporary Mary Ann Duff married at sixteen and gave birth to thirteen
children over her reproductive life, seven of whom lived to adulthood.[57]
Ellen's delayed marriage and single child made a touring career with her
husband possible, while Mary Ann was unable to fully take this risk as
she supported a growing family. While Ellen Johnson Hilson and Mary
Ann Duff were from the same generation, they had very different experiences of marriage and family, experiences that determined each woman's
professional trajectory.

Marriage to Thomas Hilson created new professional opportunities
for Ellen, who joined her more successful and popular husband in a series
of starring engagements in Boston and Philadelphia in 1827, followed by
a more extensive tour of the South and West after her mother's death in
1830 (fig. 4). The Hilsons were accessing the secondary starring circuit
that developed in the 1820s and 1830s as managers filled dates between
the arrival of foreign stars by engaging performers of lesser prominence,
some of whom had built careers as leading stock actors in American theater. However, this ended abruptly for the Hilsons in 1834 when Thomas
died from apoplexy while playing in Louisville, Kentucky. Their tours
had been lucrative: according to Philadelphia manager William Wood,
Thomas left "considerable property" upon his death.[58] Ellen returned to
New York with their infant daughter, Maria, where she acted until her
untimely death from scarlet fever in 1837.[59] She would have had many
reasons for returning to stock work. Her husband had been the main draw
in their starring days, and she could not create demand alone. She may
have been ambivalent about becoming an itinerant. Acting in the stock
company of the Park Theatre provided a good income and the support of
friends in the profession, which the widowed mother desperately needed.

After her death, Ellen became the subject of a profile in the *Ladies'
Companion*, one of a growing number of literary monthlies marketed to
genteel white women. This article paired matrilineal biographies of "Mrs.
Johnson" and "Mrs. Hilson" that had very different emphases, reflecting
a shifting culture of female celebrity emerging in the 1830s. Women's periodicals had to tread carefully when covering theater culture and stage
celebrity so as not to jeopardize the growing alignment of genteel white
femininity with Christian reform culture. Periodicals like the *Ladies'
Companion* and, to a lesser degree, *Godey's Lady's Book* used stage biography to mobilize new ideals of womanhood, showing how actresses
modeled these gendered ideals, yet these magazines still grappled with

the implications of their subjects' continuing labors.[60] While the profile of "Mrs. Hilson" featured criticism from Johnson's London debut to
showcase her attainments as an actress, it passed over Johnson Hilson's
acting career to discuss her significance as an avatar of virtue even while
laboring in the theater. The "salutary example" of the "Late Mrs. Hilson"
revealed that the stage could harbor virtuous womanhood, evidenced by
her devoted maternity and subordination of her career to the interests
of her husband and child. It celebrated the emerging affectionate family
ideal, centered on the mother-child bond, recounting how, after Hilson's
death, Johnson Hilson spurned suitors, her "whole soul . . . wrapped up in
the recollection of that man" and "his child," for whom she "only live[d]
now," vowing to "devote [her]self" to the child's "education" and continue
acting only as the "child's interest requires it."[61] The significance of her
career ultimately turned upon details of her private life, her identity as a
professional actress subordinated in a story of sentimental maternalism.

While the *Ladies' Companion* hoped, with this and similar pieces,
to challenge "objections" commonly raised "against the stage as an occupation . . . for females," the continuing social marginalization of stage
performers and elevation of a new domesticity meant that, with few exceptions, women hoping to continue their stage careers married fellow
stage performers. A distinct set of expectations about life trajectory coalesced around starring women due to their visible wealth and prestige.
An 1827 profile of Lydia Kelly from a "Ladies' Literary Gazette" that was
reprinted widely in regional newspapers from Albany to New Orleans
expressed dismay that an actress with such "unblemished character . . .
in private life" showed no signs of retirement. The author wondered how
such a "fine woman, fitted for an exalted sphere," could prefer to "display her person lightly before any audience" or "submit with indifference to . . . the repetitions of allusions not always delicate." Kelly clearly
possessed a "heart . . . divided." The author hoped that "speedy acquisi-
tion of *fame* and fortune" would allow Kelly to retire, thus granting her
"freedom" from the "fatigues and perplexities of a dramatic career."[62]
Some stars, including Kelly, did marry out of the theater. In 1834 English
star Fanny Kemble chose Pierce Butler, heir of a Georgia planter family,
out of both genuine attraction and her desire to leave acting and pursue
writing. In his memoir, actor-manager Noah Ludlow noted with regret
that star actresses seemed to choose wealthy suitors who turned out to
be "heartless adventurers" when these women might have remained
"independent, pecuniarily, for life."[63] Such were the social pressures on
women to marry, in the case of stars, not in spite of but because of their
wealth and independence.

In contrast, actors who married out of the theater usually maintained their stage careers. These marriages were often a bid for respectability and social stature, if still controversial. In these cases, marriage allowed these men to realize a white male ideal that connected their social mobility with the ability to restrict their wives to domestic labor. Whether an actor married outside of the theater was also the factor that most determined whether his children entered the profession, underscoring the importance of maternal instruction to a child's professional trajectory. Two years after he emigrated from England, actor Francis Wemyss married "Miss Strembeck, the youngest daughter" of the city sheriff. She moved with him between Philadelphia and Baltimore, fulfilling Wemyss's ideals of companionate marriage. As he recalled nostalgically, "The annoyance of the theatre was forgotten in the comforts of home."[64] None of his children entered the profession. Star tragedian Thomas Cooper married twice, both women from the New York gentry. Cooper's wealth and renown gave him entry into the world of New York elite who lived and entertained in the mansions of Park Row. His second wife, Mary Fairlie, was a society belle descended from old Dutch ancestry whom Cooper met through writer Washington Irving. Mary raised their seven living children in lavish splendor in a mansion on the Delaware River in Bristol, Pennsylvania. Only one of Thomas's children entered the profession. In 1833, inspired by the success of Charles Kemble and his debutant daughter Fanny Kemble and facing declining finances following Mary's lingering illness and death and Thomas's own poor health and waning popularity, the actor trained seventeen-year-old Priscilla for a stage debut. She toured with her father from 1834 until her marriage in 1839 to Robert Tyler, son of John Tyler, the former governor of Virginia and later president of the United States, thereby bringing her acting career to an end.[65]

Though it was less common for men to marry into the acting profession, as opposed to actresses who married out of it or actors who married for social mobility, the case of Catherine Leesugg and James Hackett shows just how readily a woman's executive labors could be reshaped by her husband's ambitions. At the time of their marriage in 1819, James was a struggling merchant, though he had also been part of an "amateur association" in his hometown of Jamaica, New York, and played briefly in Newark, New Jersey, in a traveling company under an assumed name, a sign that his family would not have approved of this path.[66] Catherine was at the "very height of her popularity" on the New York stage.[67] But she finished the season, moved with her husband to Utica, New York, and retired from the stage. Six years later, James was again facing "business troubles."[68] The couple returned to New York and Catherine to the

New York stage.[69] James debuted opposite his wife several months later and developed a career as a starring comedian, though Catherine retired in 1832. Few sketches of the actor give more than passing reference to the role that his marriage played in securing the professional capital for his stage career. Nor do they speculate about Catherine's influence on this shift. Perhaps she convinced her husband that returning to the theater would be a savvy move for both of them. She may have been disappointed in her retirement. Conversely, James may have pressured Catherine to relinquish her life of private domesticity to transform the family's earning power. James Hackett's biographers had little interest in his wife, either way.

Women's labors as actresses also kept them tied to theaters in which their husbands worked, especially theaters their husbands managed, sometimes at the expense of other professional opportunities. Frances Denny Drake's professional trajectory, from amateur to partner in her husband's family theater circuit to itinerant star, follows the expansion of English theater into the trans-Appalachian West in the 1810s. Small, family-based companies played to a growing population of migrants who speculated, squatted, and purchased land that the US government had recently obtained from Indigenous peoples in brutal land cessions. These actors brought the social values of northeastern culture with them, though such values were often difficult to realize. Women and girls were both more vulnerable to exploitation and more able to break from family and social strictures. Frances was an eighteen-year-old amateur when she joined the Drake family acting company in 1815. She was the daughter of immigrants, one of thirteen children. Her widowed mother owned the boardinghouse down the street from the Green Street Theatre in Albany, New York. English actors Samuel and Mary Drake, recent immigrants to America, had come to Albany in 1813 with their five children, then between the ages of eleven and eighteen, all trained for a life on the stage. After the sudden death of his wife, Samuel decided to try a new venture. Facing difficulty finding professional actors willing to venture west, he hired Frances Denny and another local amateur, Noah Ludlow.

Denny parted ways with the company shortly thereafter. She traveled east, acting in Montreal between 1818 and 1820 and then for a season at the Park Theatre in New York, where she obscured her western origins, appearing on the bills as a new actress "from the Boston Theatre."[70] Her comparative lack of experience relative to the English actresses who dominated eastern stock companies prevented her from playing leading business. The fragmentary record of her early seasons in the East suggests a popular and promising young actress whose status as a novice and comparative lack of ties within the profession hampered her advancement. In 1821 she decided to join the Drakes in Cincinnati and married Alexander Drake, who had been taking a greater role in managing the circuit of theaters established by his father.[71] It was an advantageous marriage for both. For the next seven years, Frances and Alexander played between Albany, Cincinnati, and the Kentucky circuit. Frances had four children, pregnancy her only periods of absence from the stage. She became a vital partner in the Drake business. Her developing dramatic abilities and popularity with western audiences were a steady draw.

However, Denny Drake seems to have been torn between opportunities to star in other markets and the financial demands of maintaining and improving the Drake theaters to draw in a growing migrant population who expected style and comforts resembling eastern theater. Over the 1820s she established a reputation from Albany to New Orleans as a leading tragic actress, but her dramatic abilities remained harnessed to the family circuit in the Ohio River Valley. In 1824 and again in 1828 Frances and Alexander traveled to New York for engagements based on Frances's acting abilities and connections. She also played in New Orleans and Natchez, Mississippi. In 1828, however, the *Cincinnati Daily Gazette* reported that Denny Drake had turned down a "most advantageous invitation to New Orleans and Mobile" in order to "tend the aid" of her "powers" to some "new pieces which have been gotten up by her husband" in Cincinnati.[72] Her executive labors in the family theater business were too vital to permit her taking starring engagements elsewhere. She finally made it back to New Orleans for a starring gig in 1829. Her husband would have joined her but was barred from leaving the state by the debts he had incurred updating the theater. Alexander died a year later. Frances was a thirty-two-year-old widow with four children to support and her husband's debts to manage. Out of personal tragedy, Denny Drake remade her career as an itinerant star. She looked to touring as a way to both keep her finances solvent and support her family. The best income Frances could earn as an actress was to be found on the road.

Feme Sole, Part 2: Widows and Divorcées Navigating the Road

Frances Denny Drake and Mary Ann Duff became widows within a year of each other. They met, probably for the first time in their careers, when they played overlapping engagements in Philadelphia in September 1831. What conversations might these two women have had about the changing contours of their lives? Thirty-two-year-old Frances had five children to support. Mary Ann was thirty-seven when John died on April 28, 1831, leaving seven children, four under the age of ten.[73] She was helping prepare her eldest, Mary Duff, born in 1810, to go on the stage. In the preceding decades, both women had developed reputations as celebrated tragedians, each at various points referred to as an "American Siddons." Both had experiences with itinerancy but then pursued itinerant starring more purposefully in widowhood.

Comparison of the stories of widows Drake and Duff with Elizabeth Blanchard Hamblin, who commenced divorce proceedings against her husband, Thomas Hamblin, in 1832, highlights the push and pull of itinerancy for mature actresses. For these three women, professional ambition and economic needs were bound up together. Denny Drake eagerly seized new opportunities to inhabit the role of an "American Siddons." She preferred itinerancy to managing the Drake family theater circuit. Blanchard Hamblin's divorce jeopardized her career because it contained terms barring her from acting in New York, but expanding theater markets gave her an avenue to remake her career. She ultimately aspired to manage, like her ex-husband. In contrast to Denny Drake and Blanchard Hamblin, Duff is portrayed by surviving sources as a more reluctant itinerant star. Itinerancy fit uncomfortably with her commitment to her family. She also struggled with depression and drug addiction. Both Blanchard Hamblin and Duff ultimately enhanced their personal and professional security by contracting second marriages. In all three cases, itinerancy was a professional phase that offered mature thespian women professional autonomy and earning power, even in the more competitive field of the 1830s.

Denny Drake was transparently ambitious. For her widow's benefit, she published notices in Cincinnati papers that framed her deservedness for public support in terms of both her professional sacrifices and her ambition. The *Cincinnati Daily Gazette* reminded the "Cincinnati public" that "Mrs. D." had not received a "salary for many months" during the recent "ruinous" season "in order to keep the company together." The notice also explained that the widowed actress was "anxious" to "place her five interesting children, in a situation to enable her to devote her time to that profession"—that is, tour—and even spend "a year or two in Europe."[74] Patronizing Denny Drake's benefit would help her family become financially solvent, in turn furthering the actress's professional aspirations.

Few actresses remained in widow's retirement for long. The financial costs were too dear. Two months after Alexander's death, Frances returned to the stage to finish out the Cincinnati season, then traveled to St. Louis to take an engagement in a theater managed by her old friend Noah Ludlow. As she traveled east, Denny Drake sought letters of introduction that could convince eastern managers and critics who were skeptical, as a Philadelphia paper put it, of the "appearance of any thing like genius from the far west." She left a Washington engagement with letters from "General Jackson, Henry Clay," and Daniel Webster. Regional chauvinism notwithstanding, the Philadelphia press concluded that the "lady from beyond the mountains" was "worthy" of patronage.[75]

By 1833 Frances Denny Drake was being hailed in Philadelphia as the "Siddons of the West."[76] As she toured, she tried to appeal to her audiences in comparison with English star Fanny Kemble, who debuted in New York in September 1832; however, Denny Drake avoided directly competing with her in the same markets. Denny Drake chose to play roles popularized by Kemble, including Bianca in *Fazio* and Julia in *The Hunchback*, a play written for Kemble's 1829 London debut. Meanwhile, Frances emphasized her American identity, a strategy embraced by other thespians in the context of Jacksonian nationalism. For example, English manager Thomas Hamblin renamed the Bowery Theatre the American Theatre in 1831. "I will try what Yankee Doodle can do pitted against Old England," Drake wrote to William Duffy, manager of Philadelphia's Arch Street Theatre.[77]

However, Frances could not compete successfully with English stars, who continued to saturate the American market. She recognized that playing in London could transform the terms of her American career and thus promoted her plans for a European trip while also playing into a new nationalist politics around the theater. In puffs for engagements, she asked "her countrymen" to support the *"American Siddons"* before her "professional visit to England" and even announced an "engagement at Drury Lane."[78] She continued to solicit letters of reference, approaching Washington Irving, who addressed an agent with the American embassy in London. A letter from American actor and playwright John Howard Payne to an English MP identified her as the same "Mrs. Drake of the Western World" who had been praised by travel writers Frances Trollope and Karl Bernard, duke of Saxe-Weimar-Eisenach, in their recent memoirs. Payne noted that Denny Drake of was "one of the few among us . . . allowed by Mrs. Trollope to possess first-rate talent."[79] Drake must have secured something from Trollope, whom she had known in Cincinnati.

In spite of this preparation, Denny Drake did not embark for Liverpool in 1833 as planned—or ever. This was probably due to the demands of supporting her children. Drake calculated the prospects of entering the high-stakes London market relative to her family responsibilities.

In 1839 she returned to Louisville to take over management of Samuel Drake's theater. In 1840 she married George Washington Cutter, a lawyer, a poet, and, briefly, an Indiana state legislator. But the "marriage . . . was evidently an unhappy one," and within a "matter of months . . . they separated and were divorced."[80] Undoubtedly they benefited from the more liberal divorce laws in western states, which considered desertion, cruelty, and adultery as grounds for divorce. Through the itinerant starring system, Drake performed her way to professional success and economic self-sufficiency. She did not need to remain in an unhappy marriage.

Divorce was comparatively rare in the profession. This may seem surprising, given that actresses, as women who had a form of "financial independence outside of marriage," fit the description of women most likely to succeed in early nineteenth-century divorces. While husbands were more likely to simply leave a marriage, practicing "customary forms of self-divorce" through desertion, wives had a greater interest in a legal end to the marriage, particularly because they sought economic benefits or because they hoped to protect "their own trades, businesses, and property." Thus women were disproportionately represented as plaintiffs in this period.[81] But while female stage performers did earn disproportionately high salaries compared to other wage-earning women, their careers remained dependent upon male-dominated professional networks. The close family and professional ties upon which their careers were based may have mitigated against women's desires to get out of abusive, exploitative, or unhappy marriages.

The 1832 divorce of Elizabeth Blanchard Hamblin is the exception that proves this rule. Her husband, Thomas Hamblin, though regarded by his peers as a reliable businessman, was a known adulterer who consorted with prostitutes and entered into sexual relationships with actresses he trained and employed. New York allowed divorce only on the grounds of adultery (increasingly, other states included desertion and cruelty in their fault-based divorce statutes). Still, divorce was a socially ambiguous remedy relative to the intensifying ideology of domesticity to which many thespian couples also subscribed. For to "succeed in divorce was tantamount to a more fundamental sort of failure" of a woman to "exert her moral influence" over a "roving" husband.[82] While Blanchard Hamilton was forced to own this failure publicly by divorcing her adulterous husband, her motivations were clearly also professional. Her attempts to regain control over her career through divorce were fiercely resisted by her husband and came at a professional cost.

Elizabeth Blanchard Hamblin emigrated from England with Thomas in 1825. Stephen Price had engaged him as a star. Thomas toured while Elizabeth acted in the Park Theatre company and raised a daughter and son, the sole surviving children of seven pregnancies.[83] In 1830 she helped her husband establish himself as manager of the Bowery Theatre. The following year, while Elizabeth traveled to England to secure new recruits for the company, Thomas maneuvered to replace his wife at the head of the company, first with Josephine Clifton and then with Naomi Vincent, whom he trained and introduced as stars. Vincent became widely known as Thomas's mistress. When Elizabeth returned in 1832 and discovered this state of affairs, she filed for divorce on grounds of adultery. As sensation journalist Mary Clarke recounted in her 1837 exposé, which rested upon Clarke's claim of intimacy with the actress and thus drew heavily from Elizabeth's recollections, "As Miss Vincent continued to be the favorite of the Bowery audience Mrs. H. had the worst. . . . [A]ll their money was at his command, and she was penniless."[84] Thomas's novel strategy for competing against the starring system by training in-house debutant talent jeopardized Elizabeth's professional position but offered her no alternate outlet.

They signed articles of separation in September 1832, and the divorce was finalized two years later. Thomas admitted to adultery but attempted to use the conditions of the divorce to force Elizabeth to retire from the stage. As he later reported to the *Evening Star*, a paper sympathetic to him throughout the public scandals surrounding the divorce and continuing acrimony, Thomas offered Elizabeth "$1200 . . . per annum if she would quit the stage and live as a private lady," but this "being rejected, $600 per were settled on."[85] According to the settlement drawn up in June 1832, Elizabeth retained custody of the children, who were placed "at an approved Boarding school," with Thomas to pay Elizabeth $200 and thereafter a yearly alimony of $500 "in monthly payments." Elizabeth, in turn, was allowed to "pursue her profession," but she was barred from New York and ultimately required to "retire" from the city as her place of residence.[86] Thomas was also barred from remarrying under New York law, though he ultimately lived openly with the new "Mrs. Thomas Hamblin," Naomi Vincent, who died in childbirth on July 30, 1835.[87] Though Elizabeth was prevented from continuing her trade in New York, the dominant East Coast market, divorce did make it possible for her to continue pursuing her "profession."

Over the next five years, both Thomas and Elizabeth used the press to shape their claims to sympathy. Thomas cast Elizabeth as a vengeful

and greedy liar, while Elizabeth presented herself as a wronged wife. Elizabeth was a key informant for journalist Mary Clarke, who published *A
Concise History of the Life and Amours of Thomas S. Hamblin* in 1837
after the sudden death of a third Hamblin protégée, Louisa Missouri
Miller. Though sympathetic to Elizabeth's plight and anxious to chronicle
Thomas's many crimes, Clarke ultimately faulted Elizabeth for failing
to protect Naomi Vincent. Clarke deployed a framework of domesticity
that may have prevented other similarly frustrated actresses from seeking separation and divorce. According to Clarke, Elizabeth's "action for
a divorce" was clearly a "wrong measure."[88] Clarke felt that when faced
with Vincent's rivalry, it would have been "wise" for "Mrs. H" to "have
renounced the stage, and retired to domestic life . . . thereby changing the
rival [Vincent] to a servant" while reigning as "lady of the house." Clarke
believed that Blanchard Hamblin could not inhabit woman's true role as
moral guide to her husband and guardian of female virtue so long as she
continued her stage career. Though Clarke's account "remind[ed] readers of married women's vulnerability," she believed that had Elizabeth
fully embraced her domestic responsibilities, she might have realized
marital "peace" and prevented Thomas from straying.[89] This reflected a
larger view of divorce as representing a woman's failure, even when she
had been wronged by her husband.

In defiance of such judgments, Elizabeth rebuilt her career on the
road. She shored up her reputation with puffs that delicately alluded to her
misfortunes as a wronged woman but reiterated her more relevant claims
as a talent. She focused on expanding southern and western markets,
touring as a headliner and in 1834 organizing a strolling company that
traveled between the languishing theaters of Richmond and Petersburg,
Virginia. However, Elizabeth wound up deeply in debt from her management in Richmond, as had her predecessors in this unreliable market.
The actress-manager returned to New York in 1835 to renegotiate the
terms of her divorce to a one-time settlement of $2,500 (about $73,500
today) and in so doing regained access to the New York market, which
served her managerial ambition.[90] Over the next three years, Elizabeth
directly challenged Thomas in the New York market, performing star
engagements and managing a rival theater. In 1836, while Thomas surveyed the devastation of the Bowery Theatre fire, Elizabeth opened the
Richmond Hill Theatre, which had recently hosted a circus, managing it
(with periodic interruptions) for two seasons.[91] Thomas fought back and
accused Elizabeth of adultery when she was in England years earlier with
actor James Charles. Elizabeth, who may well have been guilty, married
Charles in 1838 after countersuing Hamblin for libel. In 1839 she was

acting in New York as "Mrs. Charles" and continued her trials as a manager, now in partnership with her second husband. In 1840 they opened a variety house in Brooklyn. Touring had allowed Elizabeth to continue earning a living and to rebuild her reputation so that she was well positioned to return to the New York market in 1835. Few actresses were as daring—or desperate—as Blanchard Hamblin. While divorce made it possible for her to reanimate her career, her second marriage to a fellow actor is a reminder that marriage partnerships remained an important foundation for women's professional aspirations. Women's careers were indelibly shaped by family ties—and their dissolution.

Mary Ann Duff, in contrast to Blanchard Hamblin and Denny Drake, found the lack of a marriage partner deeply destabilizing. Even prior to John's death, she struggled to find clear direction and financial security. Like Denny Drake, she understood that she needed a London reputation to compete with English imports. In 1827 the Duffs brought their seven children to London to strategize Mary Ann's debut at the Drury Lane Theatre, which Stephen Price was managing. But conflicts over salary, which was not enough to support the large family, compounded by John's chronic health problems, led them to shorten their stay to a mere five months.[92] The Duffs were on surer financial, professional, and personal footing in Boston. In 1828 Mary Ann was hired at the new Tremont Theatre for an unprecedented fifty dollars per week, worth about $1,370 per week today.[93] She occasionally traveled for starring engagements. John Duff returned to the Federal Street Theatre, probably earning much less than his wife, but continued to chase his managerial ambitions. In 1830 he partnered with Junius Brutus Booth to build a new theater in Baltimore in 1830, ultimately relocating the family to Philadelphia.

John's death on April 28, 1831, left Mary Ann as sole provider, transforming the stakes of her evolving career. The widowed actress grappled with whether she should pursue the security of a weekly salary at a small New York theater or attempt the uncertain speculation of touring in new markets. Puffs for her widow's benefit reported that a recent southern tour had been "profitless" and that she was also "in feeble health."[94] Her return to the stage in late May, scarcely a month after John's death, folded readily into a narrative of financial need. Duff was clearly undecided about the best direction for her career. That spring and summer, she played star engagements in Philadelphia, Boston, and New York and oversaw her daughter Mary's acting debut. She then took a position with the company of the Richmond Hill Theatre, the small uptown New York theater. Critics who looked down on this venue bemoaned the waste of Duff's talents, asking why "the first female tragedian should not have the doors of the principal theaters open to her."[95] However, Richmond Hill was a secure job, and Duff was the chief attraction. The manager convinced her to stay on instead of trying to make money with a tour of the South. But in April 1832 Duff left New York to tour. Her 1833 return to Richmond Hill was not a success.[96]

Mary Ann Duff's career was not over, but she was floundering, hounded by her husband's creditors, struggling with bouts of illness, depression, and opium addiction. She contracted two marriages, looking for the partnership and possibly also the financial and legal assistance she desperately needed. In 1833 she married another actor with the Richmond Hill company, Charles Young, and then promptly "disavowed and repudiated the act" and filed for an annulment. She explained that she was suffering from depression and the effects of opium when she accepted his proposal. As a friend with a Philadelphia theater recalled, "Mrs. Duff was overwhelmed with debts accumulated by the extravagance of her family." Young offered to settle on her some of his own legacy to help her out. He was probably also hoping to improve his reputation by association with the "American Siddons." After the marriage, his "large property in England" was revealed as fiction.[97] After the annulment, Duff returned to the road, and though she pieced together various engagements, money troubles hounded her.

Around 1836 Mary Ann married again. Joel Seaver was her attorney and had been helping her handle her family's debts. As her children assumed the acting positions for which their mother and father had prepared them, "Mrs. Seaver" withdrew from the stage and settled with her husband in New Orleans. Perhaps she wrestled with her husband's expectations for his wife's proper role. Perhaps she was glad to leave the stage behind. She survived all but three of her children. In 1854 she settled in Texas with her surviving daughter, Mathilda, who had not become an actress. Three years later, Mary Ann Duff died of cancer.

When theater critic Joseph Ireland began to work on his biography of the actress, he imagined it as a project that would "suggest her greatness in the dramatic art, and to reproduce her identity, by reflecting the impression that she made upon the times through which she lived." He chose this approach rather than "writ[e] an exclusively personal portrayal and analysis of his heroine." Ireland thus reproduced the division of the public from the private through which actresses in the early nineteenth century were understood by their publics. Still, much of what we know about Duff's "personal" life comes from Ireland's account.[98] Perhaps she was the ambivalent star portrayed by Ireland and subsequent chroniclers. But reluctance was also a compelling explanation for why this "American

Siddons" never seemed to achieve lasting success outside of stock work. It is not without irony that in his refusal to overshadow his conception of Duff's greatness with diversions into the "personal," Ireland shielded key aspects of her life that defined the contours of her career.

———————

Tempting though it may be to read the expanded professional opportunities of the starring system as an avenue for women's personal and professional autonomy, the reality was far more ambivalent. Enduring professional networks that drew upon the nuclear family, which remained a key institution training new theater professionals, kept women's careers yoked to family interests. Yet women could and did break from parental control. While marriage was the safest and surest avenue for girls to do so, some did resist marriage to serve their own professional ambitions. Given this larger context, a woman's choice of a marriage partner and his professional designs had real implications for her career, as did the number of children she bore.

Still, the negotiations within a marriage remain opaque, and women were as likely to embrace new professional opportunities of starring as to prefer retirement, particularly when they had labored as child performers. Narratives about women's careers mobilized frameworks of domesticity to appeal to a shifting culture that elevated women as avatars of companionate domesticity and motherhood. Where possible, hagiographers connected women's professional choices to their responsibilities as dutiful daughters, companionate wives, and devoted mothers. Women's studied silence about their lives may have been a function both of these gendered frameworks and of the structures shaping their lives and careers.

The shift in the terms of Fanny Kemble's celebrity, from her sensational American debut in 1832 to the scandal surrounding the 1835 publication of her journal after she had married and retired from the stage, revealed cracks in these frameworks. While Kemble's private education and literary ambitions distinguished her from many of her peers in the profession, the story of her American celebrity and the ensuing scandal not only describes an exceptional figure but also suggests how other women in the theater may have strained against and manipulated gendered expectations to serve their own professional ends—and far more than the source record allows us to see.

3 The Promise and Limits of Female Stage Celebrity

Fanny Kemble in America, 1832–1835

In January 1835, pages from Fanny Kemble's journal, which was to be published later that year, were leaked to the press. The Americans who had celebrated, scrutinized, and applauded the English actress now rushed to preview Kemble's account of her 1832–34 tours. "The spirited and popular lady seems to have placed herself in rather an awkward predicament," a New York paper proclaimed. Kemble's account "ill corresponds with the polite attentions bestowed upon the niece of John Philip Kemble and Mrs. Siddons."[1] The leaked excerpts did not fit the celebrity persona cultivated by Fanny's father, Charles Kemble, and the literati he courted during their tours. Instead, the actress emerging from the journal more resembled another English travel writer, Frances Trollope, whose *Domestic Manners of the Americans* generated outrage in 1832 just ahead of Fanny's and Charles's arrival.

Kemble had kept the journal intending to use its publication to support her beloved Aunt Dall, Adelaide De Camp, who had traveled with the Kembles. Aunt Dall's death in April 1834 following complications from a coach accident had immediate ramifications for Kemble, who was hoping to retire from the stage and focus on writing. She was also exploring a romantic attraction. In June Kemble married Philadelphia scion Pierce Butler, heir to a Georgia planter fortune, and retired from the stage. She remained committed to publishing her journal, hoping to develop her reputation as a writer. After a second pass of editing by Butler, the journal finally appeared in print in May 1835. Americans crowded local booksellers, anticipating the pleasures of their own outrage. The scandal mobilized nationalist tensions over the relationship between America and Great Britain while showing how narrow were the gendered expectations surrounding female celebrity. These gendered nationalist tensions had been in play during Kemble's tours, but now her violation of scripts governing foreign female celebrity were more on display.

The journal's content and style violated gendered expectations because it revealed a persona that had not been in evidence (critics felt) when they first met the actress. Critics, overwhelmingly male, agreed that Kemble's journal made for a lively read but were shocked at the "vulgarity" of her language and commentary. Her "easy, slip-shod, flippant style" revealed that Kemble was not the lady they imagined but merely a common actress.[2] The journal confirmed that no individual was truly immune from the deleterious effects of life on the stage. Where formerly men had heralded the actress as the "promise of the drama," there was now a "blot . . . upon the name of Kemble." She may have "sold her book, but she has bartered away with it, the good opinion of a community, and the affectionate regard of those whose esteem is above all price."[3] Kemble's journal exposed elements of her character hidden from view. Critics were also embarrassed to see their culture and society satirized by a woman whom they had praised and feted. While her pedigree as niece of lionized English actress Sarah Siddons allowed Kemble to begin her career with an elevated reputation further enhanced by her accomplishments as a poet, in 1835 male critics in America seemed to take pleasure in tearing her down and thereby policing the boundaries of female publicity.

The 1832–34 American tour of Charles and Fanny (Frances Ann) Kemble, which followed closely after Fanny's London acting debut in 1829, formed a watershed in a growing culture of transatlantic stage celebrity in America. A widely reprinted profile of "Miss Kemble" that appeared in early September 1832 heralded her as "the most interesting woman living" and saw the "arrival of her and her father in this country" as representing "an era in our dramatic history" that would "produce a complete revival of the legitimate drama upon the American boards."[4] The tour underscored the continuing importance of the American market for English performers, but the meanings of this traffic were shifting in the context of a struggle over the content and ownership of American theater. The Kembles arrived in a country poised on the brink of a culture war over theater that was playing out at the intersection of class and nationalistic politics. Journalists connected the Kembles' tour to a politics of dramatic uplift, mobilizing their celebrity in relation to aesthetic and social tensions in American theaters.

Journalists celebrating the Kemble tour as a "revival of the legitimate drama" used this category to draw boundaries of taste, establish themselves as cultural authorities, and push back against the market desires of an expanding public of urban laborers. On the one hand, "legitimate drama" referred to the canon of Shakespearean and Restoration drama, which was expanding to include new domestic dramas, often historicist, coming from English playwrights. "Legitimate drama" was also defined by that which it was not: melodramas and paratheatrical entertainments that elevated the sensationalistic and scopic pleasures of theatrical performance and that were often championed by expanding urban working-class audiences. Champions of Fanny and Charles Kemble believed the Kembles could help reestablish the popularity of styles of acting and types of dramas that were falling out of public favor. The Kembles' draw would elevate the theater as a vehicle of intellectual and moral instruction and reestablish elite dominance. The Kemble tour thus offered critics and "fashionable" publics the opportunity to affirm and celebrate their vision of the theater both aesthetically and socially.

This project encountered nationalistic tensions that increasingly mapped onto class, becoming a vehicle for growing social tensions in American theaters. The Kembles debuted in New York's Park Theatre a year after the Anderson theater riot, sparked by English singer Joshua Anderson's alleged insulting remarks about Americans, and within a few months of the publication of Trollope's *Domestic Manners*, which created an intense national debate about American society. Even while British culture continued to dominate American culture, Anglophobia was increasingly becoming a vehicle for expressing social tensions in American urban life. As Fanny Kemble unwittingly discovered, she was a cultural ambassador during a tense geopolitical moment, her actions closely scrutinized both as a woman but especially as an *English*woman. As a celebrated public figure, Fanny became an unwilling touchstone for these intersecting questions about the content and ownership of entertainment culture, nationalist cultural politics, and woman's public role.

Fanny Kemble was a new kind of celebrity, an actress who brought together existing forms of public womanhood during a period of fierce contestation over the terms of women's engagement with public life. During the 1830s, as theater competed for publics in the face of rising Christian reform culture, women entertainers faced the increasingly difficult task of positioning themselves in relation to middle-class standards of domestic Christian womanhood. Kemble's genteel upbringing and reputation as a woman of letters was an argument for her ability to act as a vehicle of uplift in the theater and help restore its aesthetic potential. As the dramatic heir of her aunt, English tragedian Sarah Siddons, Fanny was a link to an idealized dramatic past. But even more importantly, in contrast to star actresses who preceded her, Kemble bridged distinct spheres of female accomplishment, the world of letters and the world of theater. She offered a model of female genius that could mark drama as a literary art and the stage as a legitimate sphere of female genius.

Kemble's celebrity and her powers as an actress also resonated with genteel white women, who flocked to see her perform. Both onstage and off, Kemble dramatized questions animating their lives about the terms whereby genteel white women could engage with public life while realizing ideals of white Christian womanhood. Ultimately, Kemble's celebrity offered contradictory answers, suggesting that an educated and virtuous woman could elevate any world she chose to enter, even the theater, without compromising her sterling character. It also revealed some of the real costs of that public career. Kemble's performance of gender both onstage and off was very circumscribed, requiring performances in private life that the actress despised. When Kemble disrupted these expectations, the backlash was swift and vindictive. In her refusal to conform to the contradictory scripts expected of her, Kemble exposed the constructedness of her celebrity and was punished for it. Heralded as the "most interesting woman living," Kemble became a lesson in the narrow and contradictory terms of female stage celebrity.

"The Rising Hope and Promise of the Drama"

The news that Stephen Price had made arrangements for Charles Kemble and his daughter Fanny Kemble to tour the United States came to New York during a cholera epidemic. Charles, Fanny, and Aunt Dall learned of the scourge when their packet ship approached Long Island in early September 1832. They had seen cholera in London earlier that year. The transatlantic packets that English performers sailed to reap the profits of the American market had brought the disease across the Atlantic, and it then spread to the American interior. New York papers noted the Kembles' departure from Liverpool in July while tabulating the growing number of cases. While the Kembles' fellow passengers approached the city docks "in terrible anticipation of the worst . . . where they had left their loved ones," Fanny and her father feared the effect the outbreak could have on the size of their audiences.[5] They needed theaters to be open and houses to be full.

Charles Kemble was relying on the profits from this tour to dig himself out of bankruptcy following his failed management of London's Covent Garden Theatre. Three years earlier, Charles and his wife, Maria Theresa, had taken their eldest daughter out of boarding school and prepared her for a stage debut in October 1829 as Juliet. Fanny drew full houses and critical acclaim, acting in London at her father's theater, followed by summer tours of provincial theaters. She gained access to an exciting new social world of aristocrats and literati and became an adored celebrity object. However, Fanny's continuing successes were not enough to salvage Charles's management, let alone his finances. In 1832, as Charles dodged his creditors, he finalized plans for an American tour, hoping his daughter's transatlantic celebrity could allow them to recover. Charles was aging and ill. Though Fanny despaired at having to separate from her family and "go off to that dreadful America," the twenty-two-year-old recognized that her family's prospects depended upon her success.[6]

In New York the cholera had abated and theaters were reopening for the fall season as the Kembles disembarked September 4, 1832, after a month at sea. Two weeks later, on September 17, Charles debuted at the Park Theatre as Hamlet. Fanny performed the following evening in a play unknown to American audiences, Henry Hart Milman's *Fazio*. The houses both nights were "very fine indeed, in spite of the intolerable heat"—what New Yorkers "considered mild autumn weather."[7] Fanny's "heart ached with anxiety" for her father's performance, and though the play "got off very well," Charles would never be a popular success like his daughter due to his age and his more understated, cerebral style, which was falling out of favor.[8] After her own debut, Fanny wrote to a friend that she "looked and acted well" but detested her costar, Mr. Keppel, "a poor man under a strong mental delusion [for] he cannot act in the least."[9] Kemble tried to be "realistic" about the matter of her success: "My dislike to the stage would really render me indifferent . . . but that I am working for my livelihood; my bread depends upon success."[10] Fanny struggled, throughout her two years touring, to reconcile her intensifying "dislike" of her profession with the manifold expectations placed upon her as an actress and a celebrated public figure.

During their first season, Charles, Fanny, and Aunt Dall moved between engagements at New York's Park Theatre and Philadelphia's Chestnut Street Theatre, bringing in huge houses. Nightly receipts for their first twelve nights in New York averaged $1,235, more than double the nightly averages for the rest of the season (and at least $37,000 today).

Their performance together in *The Hunchback*, a new English play written for Fanny by playwright James Sheridan Knowles, drew a record high of $1,561, or $43,000. Over the course of their first season in America, the Kembles played a total of five engagements in New York, bringing in "aggregate receipts" of more than $56,000, or $1.7 million today, of which they took a percentage.[11] In early 1833 their tour extended south to Baltimore and Washington, returned to Philadelphia and New York, then concluded the season with a long-overdue engagement in Boston, delayed due to a contract dispute.

Later, readers of Kemble's journal would discover how much she detested touring. She was homesick for England, for stability, and for the privacy and comfort of the life of gentility that she had grown up expecting to enjoy. After their first jaunt from New York to Philadelphia in late 1832, Kemble was already complaining in her journal that she was "sick of the road."[12] Travel between these cities was a daylong affair involving steamboats, the occasional train, and cramped public stagecoaches that jerked along muddy roads, the discomfort of which was exacerbated by the social drain of impertinent traveling companions. Fanny considered all of it the "perfection of misery."[13] She was particularly aggrieved by the expectations attached to her celebrity. Fanny struggled to find society that met her own social and artistic expectations; meanwhile, she was pressured to meet the approval of a parade of journalists courted by her father because he recognized that they were vital to the Kembles' success.

The editors and correspondents of the competing New York literary and dramatic weeklies, the *New York Mirror* and the *Spirit of the Times*, which also covered the sporting world, were among the visitors traipsing through the Kembles' rooms in the American Hotel. This new generation of newspapermen offered themselves as informed mediators between the proliferation of entertainments in American theaters and what they considered an ignorant public easily taken in by French ballet and acrobatic troupes, female breeches performance, equestrian dramas, and new melodramas. Poet George Pope Morris, who established the *Mirror* in 1832, and its contributors, novelist Theodore Fay and poet Nathaniel Parker Willis, practiced dramatic criticism to cultivate cultural authority. William Porter, founding editor of *Spirit of the Times* in 1831, though often at odds with the *Mirror*, advocated for the respectability of the theater while trying to position his paper as *the* arbiter of "legitimate drama" in New York. These men used their amusement columns to defend the theater as a valuable moral and intellectual institution, shape what appeared on American stages, and elevate their own literary reputations—goals that often conflicted, given the close ties between the press and theater managers. Cultivating social ties with visiting stars both enhanced journalists' social capital and generated copy.[14]

These journalists attached significance to the Kemble tour in the context of recent imports they considered in poor taste, degrading to the drama, and an embarrassment for the nation as a whole. This type of coverage was also strategic, part of a larger appeal to publics whose patronage could uplift the theater. The *Mirror* lamented that the popularity of "rope-dancers," as it called the Ravel family of acrobats, had delayed the return of "the *regular* drama" to the Park Theatre until early September.[15] Its editors were proud to see such crowds for Fanny's debut later that month because they indicated that a "young country like ours" could appreciate "all that is most exquisite in art."[16] Such discourses reflected continued sensitivity to British opinion of American culture and society, with critics reading patterns of patronage as signs of national taste and progress. They positioned themselves as critical consumers of foreign imports, discerning the implications of different types of entertainments for America's younger and more impressionable culture. After the Kembles' initial New York success, printer and journalist William Leete Stone used his literary weekly, the *New-York Spectator*, to reflect on what he considered the alarming deterioration of the American stage, which had "sunk . . . far beneath what it ought to be, and what it once was." No longer "a school of morals where lessons were taught by holding the Mirror up to Nature, and exhibiting vice in its own image, and virtue in its own likeness," American theater had been taken over by "Kick-shaws and German Extravaganza . . . Elephants, and Rope Dancers" at the expense of the "sterling old English drama." Stone hoped that the Kembles would reignite a love of English drama.[17] These writers positioned New York theatergoers within a transatlantic imaginary in which New York tastes reflected on the nation as a whole and had real implications for the contours of the transatlantic starring system.

Actually, Kemble refused to confine herself to the more narrow dramatic repertoire expected of a young actress. Though the ingenue Julia in Knowles's *The Hunchback* earned Kemble her most consistent and lofty praise, she regularly acted outside the ingenue line. She adopted dramatically challenging and morally ambiguous characters like Bianca in Milman's tragedy *Fazio* and Lady Macbeth from Shakespeare, a part associated with Sarah Siddons. To the irritation of some critics but to the delight of theatergoers, Kemble performed popular German melodramas by August von Kotzebue like *The Stranger*. In comedy, she acted not only Shakespeare's Beatrice from *Much Ado about Nothing* and the ever-popular Lady Teazle in Richard Brinsley Sheridan's *The School for Scandal* but also Bizarre in the racy Restoration comedy *The Inconstant*, by George Farquhar. This diverse repertoire was a rare privilege enjoyed by star actresses, and even then, Kemble's broad repertoire was unusual. However, Kemble never performed breeches roles, even when venturing into comedy. This repertoire would have jeopardized her association with the "legitimate drama." While Kemble's reputation as an intellectual actress made it possible for her to develop a controversial character in a historical drama like *Fazio,* acting a breeches role or even playing opposite a breeches Romeo, as she had done in London, was a professional risk neither Kemble nor her father was willing to take.

Critics expected the classical acting of the Kemble school, but Fanny also surprised them. Charles's acting was too quiet and stylized for American audiences, but his daughter burst forth with passions described by the *New York Mirror* critic as *"Kean-like."* She had mastered her father's more declamatory style, but she also projected an emotionalism associated with Charles's leading English rival, Edmund Kean. Though her father's influence could be found in the "monotonous delivery of elaborate passages," critics marveled at Fanny's ability to "[depict] tenderness, jealousy, hate, and despair with a truth that now melts the soul, now makes it tremble." This, they argued, reflected acting of *"mind."* "Only the highest intellect and the most warmly affectionate nature," the *New York Mirror* believed, "could conceive the illustrations of thought and feeling which constitute the charm and glory of this young girl's acting."[18] A Philadelphia critic called Fanny's New York debut "one of the finest exhibitions of dramatic skill . . . ever . . . witnessed" in that city.[19] The contrast between stylized restraint and "Kean-like" passion became evidence of Fanny Kemble's intellect and skill, which extended beyond her dramatic abilities to encompass her reputation as both a woman of letters and an actress.

Fanny Kemble was probably one of the most accomplished actresses to perform in America to date, but she was also a figure of interest for those very qualities that distinguished her from other women in her profession. Kemble had not been raised to the stage but instead had a boarding school education and a genteel upbringing "amid a most refined and accomplished circle." She had even developed a reputation as a poet and historicist playwright.[20] In February 1831, during Fanny's second season on the English stage and long before an American tour was conceivable, the *Mirror* introduced her to American readers as the "rising hope and promise of the drama" and later described her as the "poet-actress, who so early in life has astonished and rivalled the finest . . . poets of her day."[21] For Porter of the *Spirit*, Kemble was an "angel" who "united . . . the most immutable fascination of an actress, and the lofty endowments and unchallenged pre-eminence of the poetess." Kemble's role relative to the drama was defined—rather, mythologized—by the title "Priestess of the Temple."[22] Porter framed Kemble's accomplishments in terms of her "great prototype and aunt," actress Sarah Siddons, then explained that Kemble had also "eclipsed . . . her sex" as an authoress by "[giving] to the world the most perfect tragedy of modern times," the play *Francis the First*, which debuted (to mixed reviews) in London in February 1832.[23] Editions of the drama were made available by booksellers before the Kembles landed on American shores, and Fanny's reputation as a poet continued to drive her celebrity in the United States.

Kemble's reputation as a woman of letters drew together shifting standards of female publicity in the United States. Since the 1790s, advances in women's education corresponded with women's increased engagement in civil society as writers and speakers, but during the 1820s and 1830s, a larger gendered backlash reshaped women's involvement in education and print culture.[24] This backlash had to do with both the expansion of white male suffrage, which increased suspicion of women's participation in politics, and an expanding Protestant establishment, which was fueled by religious revivalism and which encouraged women to align themselves with the church. Even as women continued to engage in a broad range of social organizations and activities outside the home, including reform activism, framing this activity in terms of a feminized sphere became an important strategy for protecting it. Female education and forms of female publicity were reoriented toward the domestic, while motherhood experienced a historically unprecedented level of idealization.[25]

These dynamics were especially visible in print culture. While women had long participated in transatlantic print culture around diverse social and political issues, by the 1830s women were restricting their writing to domestic themes. The domestic "construction of female authorship" simultaneously allowed women to expand their participation in print industries while reflecting the larger redrawing of boundaries around women's engagement with public life. This played out through poetry as well, with the publication of women's verse that increasingly fixed on domestic subjects, their output sanctioned within the categories "sentimental" and "moral."[26] Kemble's poetry exemplified the "genteel lyric" that English and American women poets adopted, espousing a domestic sentimentality even as many of these poets did not actually restrict themselves to the domestic.[27] For Kemble, then, writing genteel, sentimental verses was of a piece with her manifestly public role.

She epitomized the sentimental, domestic feminine from her unusual stature as a celebrity actress, her literary output one of the few aspects of her publicity that she was able to shape. At times celebrity pressures also dictated her literary production.

Like the girls and women who preceded her, Kemble actually had little control over the terms and marketing of her celebrity. Kemble's name was affixed to new fashions like bonnets and other consumer goods. Reproductions of her portrait by English painter Sir Thomas Lawrence sold in shops alongside illustrations of Kemble in various famous roles. While Kemble's appearance varied across these images, they produced an increasingly recognizable iconography of the actress, always shown with a low, heavy brow and dark hair in a simple center part. These portraits offered publics, including those who might never see Kemble perform, the opportunity to read the actress's character and genius in her physiognomy.[28] Portraits of Kemble as various dramatic characters also offered a close look at intricate costumes, inspiring Kemble-themed fashions (fig. 5).

Unlike that of her contemporaries, Kemble's literary reputation involved additional pressures to produce for the literary marketplace and perform the role of poetess. Kemble's writing was commercialized, solicited by editors who used it to sell their papers. On the Kembles' second full day in New York, Fanny wrote, "My father asked me, this evening, to write a sonnet about the wild pigeons welcoming us to America; I had thought of it with scribbling intent before, but he wants to get it up here, and that sickened me."[29] The following week, the *Mirror* solicited a poem. "Autumn. Written after a ride by the Schuylkill, in October" was reprinted widely. Connecting Kemble's claims as an actress to praise for her abilities as poet and "authoress" widened the possible reach of her celebrity to publics unlikely to attend the theater. Stone published "Autumn" in the *New-York Spectator* as a way of introducing Kemble and her father to readers unfamiliar with theatrical personalities and ambivalent about the theater generally. Stone explained that while Charles deserved notice due to his superior character as a gentleman, "his daughter . . . is no ordinary woman." Her reputation was not merely "factitious," a function of her birth, the "fascination of her manner, or the practiced *duperie* of the stage." To obtain a true measure of her worth, "let her poetry speak for itself."[30] Critics less credulous than the *Spectator* agreed that Kemble's poetry served as a true measure of her merits as an artist and proved that an elevated sensibility supported her powers as an actress.

Kemble bristled at the contradictory pressures her celebrity invited because they increasingly made her unable to be both a private person

MISS F. KEMBLE,
AS BELVIDERA.

Figure 5. Commercial engravings of Fanny Kemble in her various roles (here as Belvidera in *Venice Preserved*, a Restoration-era drama by Thomas Otway) circulated in England and were most likely also reproduced in the United States. Rare Book and Manuscript Library, University of Illinois at Urbana-Champaign.

and a public figure. The distribution of her image made her known, exposing her to address from shopkeepers and "unceremonious questions" from strangers, to which she had been unaccustomed in England.[31] After Americans "abused" Lawrence's portrait, which Kemble felt actually "paint[ed] me as I am," she tried to refuse future sittings. "My physiognomy, that they shall certainly not have with my own good leave," she proclaimed, but her father insisted, recognizing the importance of circulating her image widely.[32] Kemble would ultimately sit for multiple portraits with Philadelphia artist Thomas Sully. While the originals remained in private hands, engraved reproductions rapidly entered the commercial marketplace. And though she disliked being asked to produce poems on command, Kemble continued to provide sonnets when asked. Public interest in her verses increased the possibility that the woman of letters could ultimately replace the actress. (This desire led Kemble to marry scion Pierce Butler over Aunt Dall's concerns and retire from the stage just months after her death. The public and private fallout from the 1835 publication of Kemble Butler's journal kept her from publishing anything for a decade, until she sued for divorce.) As her tour progressed, Kemble's Englishness became an increasingly unstable feature of her celebrity. Surging nationalist tensions repeatedly asserted themselves in theaters where she performed and focused new levels of scrutiny on Kemble's conduct in private life, threatening her reputation and her family's livelihood.

"Heiress of Mrs. Trollope"

Six months into the Kembles' American tour, Fanny Kemble found herself facing down an outraged Philadelphia audience armed with handbills that asked whether Philadelphians would "continue to pamper the heiress of Mrs. Trollope."[33] Charles Kemble interceded with the crowd while the terrified actress waited in the wings, "crying dreadfully with fright and indignation."[34] Fanny had not suspected that a private aside made in a Washington, DC, stable two weeks earlier would threaten her return to Philadelphia. But Americans were "an unhappily sensitive community."[35] Actually, by virtue of her celebrity, Kemble had become a touchstone for intersecting social and nationalistic tensions playing out in American theaters.

Kemble arrived in America during a national debate about the nature of American society recently ignited by English travel writing. This debate exacerbated an intensifying culture war over audience behavior and dramatic taste. Captain Basil Hall's 1829 *Travels in North America* and then Frances Trollope's 1832 *Domestic Manners of the Americans* sold well even as—and perhaps because—they upset many with their cutting portrait of the young nation's rough, ill-mannered society.[36] Trollope's descriptions of American manners were considered particularly offensive because she presented caricatures as if they were distinct features of American society but ignored signs of gentrification and culture. She also failed to note that similar behavior was characteristic of English society, too. In the Cincinnati theater, Trollope complained, men sat in their shirtsleeves, lounged with the "heels thrown higher than the head" or perched on the front of a box, "the entire rear of the person presented to the audience" (also the subject of a cartoon accompanying the text). The audience's "cries and thumping" and calls for "Yankee Doodle" disrupted the performance.[37] New York theatergoers were no better but showed "a general air of contempt for the decencies of life." Men kept up a steady stream of tobacco spitting, and Trollope even observed a woman in the lowest circle of boxes "performing the most maternal office possible."[38] Though white women did attend the theater, Trollope felt the right kind of female society was absent. Trollope observed that American women preferred the church to the theater and unfortunately had to endure distasteful manners when they attended plays. For Trollope, Americans' lack of manners reflected their broader lack of culture. Trollope's criticisms in turn prompted outrage from Americans and calls for reform (some more serious than others), but ultimately they suggested that English visitors were incapable of appreciating American culture on any terms except cultural chauvinism.

The debate animated by Trollope's 1832 travel narrative tapped into a new nationalism in American society and politics connected with the 1828 election of Andrew Jackson to the presidency. Jackson was a western war hero and was championed by various constituencies as an avatar for the common man who would fight against tyranny and corruption, though Jackson's opponents saw him as hopelessly corrupt. Jacksonian politics were often overtly anti-British, which made pro-British sentiment politically volatile throughout the 1830s and 1840s.[39] While much of American society continued to avidly consume British culture, especially theater, the convergence of a new nationalism in American politics and America's continuing saturation with English culture contributed to more calls in the 1830s and 1840s for the development of a national literary culture. Nationalism also began to play a larger role in efforts by managers and performers to compete in dense commercial markets like New York, where Anglophobia frequently became a vehicle for expressing class tensions.[40] In spite of this, British perceptions of America continued to matter, whether as an object of outrage or a source for correction.

Foreign commentary like Trollope's played into social tensions over the standards governing public life and sociability. When on the evening of Kemble's New York debut a man in one of the theater boxes turned around in conversation, exposing his back to the pit and the stage and allowing his coattail to dangle indecorously over the front of the box, the incident, occurring as it did during the debut of a celebrated English actress, became a flashpoint for competing behavioral standards among America's socially diverse theater audiences. Audience members seated in the pit responded to the oblivious gentleman with "hissings . . . and then bleatings."[41] According to English lieutenant Edward Thomas Coke, who published his own travel memoir in 1833, the "murmur . . . presently burst forth into loud cries of 'Trollope!' [']Trollope!' 'turn him out,' 'throw him over.'"[42] While Coke did not want to identify himself with Trollope's stinging criticisms of American manners, he did feel her observations would "do good amongst a certain class of people." He interpreted the scene at the Park Theatre in September 1832 as a sign of "reform." When the fellow finally resumed his proper seat, the theater burst into "four rounds of applause."[43]

The incident at Kemble's debut dramatized diverging cultures of sociability at the intersection of class and gender. Many New York papers described the scene in the service of their own social commentary. Some connected it with their ongoing calls for reform, while others delighted in the reversal of rowdy patrons in the pit disciplining elites in the upper tiers, "civilization dawning on the savages of the land of Knickerbocker." Still others pointed out that elites misbehaved too, levying complaints about bonnet-wearing women in the front rows of the boxes or patrons who "turn the lobby of a theatre into a promenade," their noise carrying into the theater boxes.[44] The incident exposed a developing clash between a thriving urban male sporting culture and a rising feminized Christian middle-class culture trying to reshape elite attitudes toward the conventions of theater culture. These included the sale and consumption of alcohol, solicitation by prostitutes in a theater's third tier, and rowdy publics who periodically incited riots.

Theater riots were a recurring if extreme manifestation of the culture of audience sovereignty that was the rule in Anglo-Atlantic theater. In American theater riots of the 1820s and 1830s, the public sought to discipline managers and performers, especially foreigners. In such cases, rioters acted on shared conceptions of national pride, "enforc[ing]" a "code of behavior" that foreign visitors had violated, as with the 1825 riots protesting Edmund Kean during his second American tour.[45] However, the prominence of a more visible and vocal working-class public in theater riots troubled elites, who were coming to see riots as a challenge to their own social and cultural authority. In October 1831, when riots disrupted the Park Theatre in retaliation for disrespect shown by English singer Joshua Anderson, divisions quickly emerged between popular and elite publics that played into growing tensions over the social ownership and culture of the theater. This was the kind of incident that Kemble feared would arise in Philadelphia in response to the handbills.

The 1831 Anderson riot began in response to rumors that Joshua Anderson had insulted Americans prior to his arrival in New York. It rapidly came to be about the nationalistic and class politics of New York theater. After audiences disrupted Anderson's debut with shouts and projectiles, the singer published an apology in the city papers, but threats of rioting carried into the weekend. During Anderson's return performance, crowds turned on manager Edmund Simpson when he tried to intercede on Anderson's behalf. Elites like Philip Hone were disgusted by what they saw as an excessive plebeian overreaction to a minor offense by a minor player. Hone described the rioters as "venge[ful] sovereigns" who "would not be pacified."[46] After dark, crowds attacked the theater's exterior, prompting Simpson to hang tricolored bunting from the windows in a show of patriotism. The riot thus shifted from being about one performer to being about the Park Theatre as an institution that failed in its responsibility to defend popular conceptions of national pride. In spite of their disgust, elites like Hone and most city journalists still framed the riot within the very transatlantic context that produced nationalistic sensitivity. They feared, however, that such "manifestation of national vanity" did nothing to "contribute to our respectability."[47]

Having further exposed social tensions at work in New York theater, the Anderson riots also created an opening for the articulation of a new set of nationalistic values around the stage. The English manager of the rival Bowery Theatre, Thomas Hamblin, saw an opportunity in this frenzy of "national vanity." He announced that the Bowery would henceforth be called the American Theatre. Hamblin was accused of gross opportunism. Hone even repeated a rumor that the boys who instigated the rioting on Saturday night were acting on Hamblin's orders. Hamblin, meanwhile, pointed out that in spite of his English nationality, under his watch, the American Theatre would distinguish itself from the Park by serving as a vehicle for native talent.[48]

The Anderson riots became a useful fulcrum in Hamblin's efforts to compete against the Park, which controlled access to transatlantic stars. When Fanny Kemble debuted at the Park Theatre, Hamblin advertised two homegrown stars, Josephine Clifton and Naomi Vincent, American girls whom he had trained and whose careers he carefully controlled. He cast Josephine Clifton in the same roles Fanny Kemble was popularizing, then asked Charles Kemble to coach Clifton. Shortly after his daughter's debut, Charles received a letter from a "cabal . . . forming by the friends" of Clifton and Vincent—"(native talent!)" Kemble wrote dismissively— who threatened "to hiss" the Kembles "off the New York stage" or "send people in every night to create a disturbance."[49] The threat of patriotic plebeian riot came to nothing, perhaps because of services that Charles rendered to Hamblin behind the scenes. Hamblin, meanwhile, successfully appealed to the value system of the Anderson rioters, launching an alternative business model that incorporated but was not dependent on foreign imports.

In Philadelphia, Fanny Kemble discovered that during this moment of nationalism and patriotic sensitivity, her everyday actions had serious ramifications for her career. No conversation in which Kemble engaged was entirely private, even in a Washington, DC, stable. Her disparaging comments about the quality of her American mount (and possibly the horsemanship of her American companions) became the "town talk,—fields, gaps, marshes, and all, rang" with reports of her "evil deeds and evil words." The news traveled the halls of government, where Kemble had recently been an invited guest and traded barbs with President Andrew Jackson. "Not less than *fifty* members of Congress" spoke of the matter to John Quincy Adams, who called on Charles to inform him of his daughter's mistake. "Fifty old gossiping women!" Fanny sputtered in the pages of her journal. It was "the greatest piece of blackguardism."[50] Kemble expected to be hissed in Washington but performed without incident. Her relief was short-lived. The gossip traveled ahead of her to Philadelphia and appeared on the incendiary handbill. Charles's public apology from the stage turned the crowd in his daughter's favor, but Fanny also gained new appreciation for her vulnerability before demanding and volatile publics. Her gender intersected with her national identity, transforming readings of her behavior.

Kemble discovered that her social identity as an elite white Englishwoman did not protect her as she felt it should. Instead, Kemble was forced to "stand,—as no woman ought to stand,—the mark of public insult."[51] This comment also betrayed her intensifying frustration with the contradictory pressures of having a private self and presenting a public face. Kemble was not able to separate what it meant to be a woman in private life from her role as a public figure not only because she was an actress but also because she was an Englishwoman in America during a moment of surging nationalist tensions with respect to England. Her gender did in fact protect her, but not to the degree that she expected. While Kemble believed that her gender should have shielded her from public scrutiny of her private life, an increasingly intrusive celebrity culture that elevated her as a figure of interest *because* of her gender did the opposite. Her private life became a public object. A developing culture of American stage celebrity was changing women's experience of a public stage career even as American culture was drawing and policing more clear restrictive boundaries around women's engagement with public life. In spite of her growing distaste for the stage, it remained one of the few places where Kemble was able to play with different ways of being a woman in the world. This contributed to her fascination for her female publics.

Kemble's "Fine Pieces of Acting"

On a Tuesday evening in April, Anna Quincy waited anxiously in her Cambridge home for her brother to return from Boston with tickets for the Kembles' performance of *Fazio*. Quincy "was wild" to see Fanny Kemble act but despaired about the tickets.[52] Scenes at the box office of the Tremont Theatre were frenzied. Kemble, who observed the tumult from the window of her rooms at the Tremont House, described crowds lying in wait that exploded into a "rush" of "thumping and pummelling," with "yelling and shouting as though the town were on fire." The "low" men who lined up to buy checks for the boxes "smear their clothes with molasses" to keep the better sort, "whose clothes are worth a cent, from coming near the box-office."[53] They then sold the checks to wealthier men for a steep profit. Anna's brother may have been a beneficiary of these tactics. That evening, the Quincy siblings were among the fortunate squeezed into the boxes overlooking the "overflowing" Tremont Theatre.[54]

Later, Anna wrote in her journal that Kemble "entirely equalled—indeed passed my expectations." She praised Kemble's "grace, the expressions of her countenance," and marveled at the "great power of her attitudes, & her expressions," her "*shrieks*, her starts," and "her *laugh* of agony & insanity," which was "truly horrific." Quincy described Kemble's acting in terms of the emotional journey theatergoers experienced. Quincy and her companion, Mrs. Hodgkison, were "over set" with tears at the end of the play, all the while paying close attention to how Kemble elicited this response from her audience. Anna noted that when Bianca's condemned husband, Fazio, is led to his execution, "she stood, I should think five moments—a perfect statue—and the death like stillness that reigned over the crowded audience, every person seeming to hold their breath . . . until the bell tolled again—at that sound the full sense of her wretchedness seemed to write upon her mind—and nearly to destroy it—she gave a start, which every one seemed to feel, & with one of her thrilling screams of agony rushed from the stage."[55] Quincy's interest in Kemble, then, joined the affective experience of the performance itself with an analytical exercise involved in distinguishing the way Kemble created this effect.

Diaries of elite theatergoers like Quincy capture the ways theatergoers responded to Kemble while also revealing how criticism shaped public reception. Anna Quincy was no stranger to the theater in Boston, though she was hardly a habitué. Quincy was a member of Cambridge's elite, daughter of Josiah Quincy, a former mayor of Boston and currently president of Harvard University. Attending the theater and dances with family and friends was among the many amusements with which she filled her days, including extensive social visits, concerts, and lectures in both the city of Boston and her hometown, Cambridge. She saw William Charles Macready, another celebrated English actor, during his Boston debut in 1826.[56] Kemble's Boston run between April and May 1833 looms large in Quincy's diary of that year. Quincy returned to the theater at least four more times between April and May to see Kemble perform her most celebrated roles, as Mrs. Haller in Kotzebue's melodrama *The Stranger*, as Belvidera in Thomas Otway's *Venice Preserv'd*, and as Beatrice in *Much Ado about Nothing* opposite Charles Kemble. Throughout this cycle, Quincy wrote highly detailed entries about the performances and about her encounters with Kemble in Boston society. Her assessment of Kemble's acting was undoubtedly influenced by the coverage in the American press and by Quincy's position as a member of Boston's social elite.

While male journalists evaluated and shaped Kemble's celebrity through their sense of social and cultural authority, genteel white women like Quincy brought different meanings to bear on Kemble's prominence as a public figure. Women and girls were conspicuous publics both inside and outside the theater. When Kemble left Boston in May 1833, Boston critics laughed at the "seri-ludicro, and tragico-comico" scene outside the Tremont House hotel. Girls lined the street bearing bouquets for the actress and clutching mementoes from her performance. They craned their "swan-like necks" to catch a glimpse of their idol, then sighed *"She's gone!"* with "tear[s] of disappointment."[57] Male critics had trouble taking public adulation by young white women seriously, but clearly Kemble's celebrity carried distinct gendered meanings for them. As Quincy's diary reveals, Kemble's celebrity both legitimated their presence in theater audiences and spoke to questions animating their lives concerning shifting standards of genteel white womanhood. And Kemble's performances were frankly thrilling.

Questions about the relationship between Kemble's character and her dramatic abilities dominated both published and private reflections about Kemble in part because she chose controversial roles and repertoire that did not always fit her celebrity persona. Actresses were more likely than actors to be associated as individuals with the roles they played. For example, critics connected Mary Ann Duff's powers interpreting Hermione in *The Distressed Mother* with her identity as a mother. Even as theater reformers increasingly mobilized the private character of stage celebrities to argue that the theater was not a morally corrosive profession, they never really got rid of the idea that there was some essential connection that made it possible for a thespian to successfully interpret a role. In attempting to reconcile contradictory elements of Kemble's stage celebrity, critics emphasized the intellectual skill involved in her acting, granting her powers of mind usually associated with celebrated actors. This helped support the controversial, morally ambivalent roles through which Kemble stretched the terms of her career in ways both artistically and personally fulfilling.

Acting, it seems, literally allowed Kemble to try on different ways of being a woman in the world. While Kemble might not have become an actress if she had had the choice, she clearly achieved feelings of agency through the roles she played. In January 1831, a little over a year after her London debut as an actress, Kemble wrote to her friend Harriet St. Leger about her upcoming appearance as Bianca in *Fazio*. "Do you know the play? It is very powerful, and my part is a very powerful one indeed. I have hopes it may succeed greatly."[58] Kemble chose *Fazio* for her New York debut and repeated it in all the cities she visited in the United States, although the play was controversial for its moral content. It tells the story of a manipulative seductress, Aldabella, an adulterous husband, Fazio, and a spurned wife, Bianca, who turns vengeful in her pain and jealousy. Bianca leaves her children in the pursuit of vengeance, exposes Aldabella and Fazio's adultery, and arranges for her husband's execution.[59] Though her remorse at the occasion of his death is one of the crowning emotional moments of the play, audiences and critics were troubled by the character's active pursuit of vengeance. Kemble had no patience for such objections. In her 1835 published journal, she defended the role of the "wild woman Bianca" in terms that acknowledged and celebrated the power of strong emotions and motivations. The "excess" of "mighty passions" cannot be compared with "the base, degraded, selfish, cowardly tribe of petty larceny vices," Kemble wrote. "Great crimes" are "in their very magnitude, respectable," which is exactly what makes them, in their "evil grandeur," worthy of representation on the stage.[60]

Unlike the majority of Kemble's roles, Bianca was not known or acted in America prior to 1832. The *New York Mirror* noted the risk Kemble took in coming before her first American audience on September 18, 1832, in an unfamiliar play. *Fazio* remained controversial, turning as it did "upon the avarice of a profligate and the arts of an unfeeling, mercenary, and meretricious coquette," the lady Aldabella. It generated mixed reactions from critics and publics who struggled to reconcile the turns and lessons of the plot against the clear power of Kemble's performance. In contrast to the suffering heroines of most popular tragedies, Bianca was no passive jilted wife. Theatergoers did not know what to make of the crucial role she played exposing her husband. While the play and part might "shock" the "sympathies," critics agreed that they certainly gave an "actress of genius" the opportunity to showcase her powers.[61] While Philadelphia's *Saturday Courier* judged *Fazio* "entirely deficient in incident and situation" and imagined it would be incapable of moving an audience in "common hands," Kemble was no "common" actress. Her success became "triumphant proof of her superior powers."[62] Kemble continually moved theatergoers, Anna Quincy among them, to tears over the misfortunes and despair of the deserted Bianca.

Girls' diaries suggest that they connected more directly with Kemble's shifting performances of womanhood onstage and relished the emotionalism of her performances. Like Quincy, twelve-year-old Katherine, or Kate, Sedgwick, niece of writer Catharine Maria Sedgwick, experienced strong emotional identification and catharsis during Kemble's performances. For Kate, Kemble's powers as an actress and reputation as an accomplished Englishwoman combined to form an object of fascination and desire. After seeing Kemble play *Venice Preserv'd* in New York in 1833, Kate Sedgwick explained to her father how during the scene in which Belvidera pleads for her life "a cold chill runs through you." Belvidera is a loving wife sacrificed to the lusts of her brother's dishonorable compatriot in order to support a plot to overthrow Belvidera's father, an unjust ruler. Like Quincy, Sedgwick was deeply moved by Kemble's expressions of agony, such as when "she utters three piercing Shrieks, which make your blood curdle."[63] While both Quincy and Sedgwick clearly drew on the discourses in newspaper criticism to articulate and signify their affective experience of Kemble's performance, for these girls, Kemble's choice of roles did not violate their sense of what was natural and appropriate. If anything, Kemble's biography not only legitimated her performance of Bianca or Belvidera but also made them more exciting.

In contrast to Quincy and Sedgwick, English-born Philadelphia shopkeeper Joseph Sill had difficulty looking past Kemble's biography to see her in these characters. Sill was a regular habitué of Philadelphia theater in the 1830s and wrote detailed reviews of the plays and operas he attended, analyzing both the plays themselves and the style and dramatic interpretations of touring stars like the Kembles, Edwin Forrest, and William Charles Macready. Sill's writing also reveals his familiarity with theatrical criticism. For example, he noted his disagreement with critics who preferred Macready's thunder to Charles Kemble's quieter acting style, for Sill felt that Kemble continued to reveal his excellence in tragedy. Sill was much more taken by Charles than Fanny. Though he praised Fanny's conceptions of her roles, he felt she was too young for some of the parts she chose to play. He felt that "Bianca appears unfit for Miss Kemble—it is not sufficiently natural—the horrid idea of betraying her own husband shocks you; and her subsequent anguish & loss of Reason scarcely does away with the impression." Though Sill was moved by Kemble's "anguish" at the death of Bianca's husband, he did not find Kemble convincing in the play as a whole, for the part was not "sufficiently natural" for her.[64]

The character Julia, on the other hand, realized Sill's expectations for the actress. Sill and his companion Sanderson went to see Kemble twice in *The Hunchback*, the second time bringing their wives, who were so delighted that they spoke about going again the next evening. Like Bianca, Julia also struggles with overpowering emotions, but while Bianca satisfies her desire for revenge, Julia takes responsibility for the caprice that leads her into a disastrous engagement. Julia is rewarded for her obedience and ultimately marries the man she realizes she truly loves.[65] Sill thought *The Hunchback* as "perfect [a] piece of acting as I ever saw," such that Kemble as Julia and her father as Sir Thomas (incidentally, Julia's love interest) seemed to be "the actual characters they only represent."[66] Sill needed Kemble to perform a character closest to his conception of her identity in order for her acting to realize the contemporary critical ideal that a theatrical performance should approximate nature.

Quincy and Sedgwick clearly enjoyed an affective experience very different from that of Sill because of their youth and gender. Their excitement over Kemble's celebrity likewise inspired more fraught questions, for Quincy in particular, about the appropriate parameters of ambition and sphere of accomplishment for genteel white women. Twice during Kemble's Boston engagement Anna met her at private parties in the actress's honor and attempted in her journal to parse the relationship between Kemble's social mien and her powers onstage. Quincy scrutinized Kemble the private woman for signs of the actress, seeking to understand how Kemble's experience with the public gaze onstage informed her negotiation of genteel sociability. Quincy assumed that Kemble's public exposure would have some bearing on the actress's private character but was surprised by what she saw: "I could hardly believe that this delicate, gentle, subdued *shadowy* creature, was the Bianca, who had been exhibiting such power, & who had made me feel so much." No doubt this unassuming persona was "one of her fine pieces of *acting*." Quincy vacillated in assessing the relationship between Kemble the actress and Kemble the woman. On the one hand, she recognized in Kemble the social performances expected of and enacted by every "young Lady" at a "private party." However, Kemble's powers as an actress made it impossible for Quincy to imagine Kemble ever being a neutral, nonperformed self: "Still she chose her part well—& plays it with good effect."[67] Kemble's power on the stage called attention to the performativity of gender in private life, which made Quincy uncomfortable, as it likewise highlighted Quincy's own complicity in a gendered social performance.

In spite of the pleasure she took from Kemble's stage performances and meeting her in society, Quincy drew a clear boundary between her own gendered social role and Kemble's. At the conclusion of Kemble's Boston engagement, after witnessing her final performance in *The Hunchback*, Quincy composed verses in honor of Kemble's acting. Though Quincy believed that there was "nothing . . . in the world more beautiful, more striking, than such a gifted, graceful woman," she expressed "regret" that those "powers [were] only employed in *acting*."[68] Acting was a poor medium for female accomplishment. Kemble's social proximity to Quincy intensified the fascination the actress held but clearly exacerbated Quincy's discomfort. Quincy questioned whether theater was the right sphere for female genius. Kemble would have agreed that her powers were best suited elsewhere—the page rather than the stage. Quincy's ambivalence underscores the more subversive implications of Kemble's celebrity, even as she shied away from seeing Kemble's stage career as anything but an aberration from more legitimate spheres of female genius. Kemble's celebrity might well have inspired other girls and women to pursue print or the stage or even begin to question the contours of their lives.

Quincy was unusually perceptive in recognizing how tenuous Kemble's status was, though she may not have realized how much this celebrity object was struggling to fulfill her role offstage. Women who stretched the terms of their gendered sphere were on unstable ground. As an Englishwoman, Kemble failed to understand American social and cultural cues. She also disparaged the contradictory social and cultural expectations she faced, many of them shaped by America's burgeoning celebrity print culture. Kemble's reputation as a model of genteel white womanhood compromised her ability to enjoy being young and unmarried; meanwhile, she was frequently socially ostracized for being an actress. Through ancillary commentary in her published journal, Kemble tried to account for her uneven and disappointing social experiences. On the one hand, she was exhausted by the seemingly endless parade of visitors that began the day after the Kembles arrived in New York. But with the exception of merchant and former New York mayor Philip Hone, a devoted theater patron, Kemble was snubbed by the New York social elite, who may have applauded her from the Park Theatre boxes but did not invite her into their homes. An Episcopal clergyman explained to the Kembles at a private dinner that he could "neither call upon us nor invite us to his house, much less set foot in the theater," though some of his parishioners, including Anna Cora Ogden, undoubtedly did.[69] In England the Kembles had occupied a social status that set them apart from other members of the profession; in America, in spite of her celebrity, Fanny's social position was much less sure. And whereas "newspaper writers and editors have never, I believe, been admitted into good society in England . . . it is otherwise here."[70] Kemble did not like it.

Elite homes slowly opened to Kemble as she toured, but she struggled to reconcile her expectations and desires with the American social worlds she encountered and the contradictory expectations placed upon her. The problem was that Kemble refused to act the part of the celebrated actress. Gradually, she developed satisfying relationships with American writers, including Washington Irving, William Cullen Bryant, and Catharine Maria Sedgwick. The Sedgwicks became her close confidants and later aided her in divorcing Butler. Kemble contrasted the society these intellectuals "formed . . . among themselves" with the "vulgar *fashionables*" she felt pressured to "mingle with" but never failed to disappoint. In Philadelphia Kemble was ostracized by friends of Emily Chapman, who discovered in Kemble a rival for the affections of Pierce Butler. Kemble lashed out in her journal that here, "society is led by chits."[71] When Kemble *was* invited into American society, she failed to live up to the expectations of her hosts, especially the procession of would-be suitors. She was invariably found wanting by "some man or other . . . who was horrified at my taking up a book, and then a newspaper; and, in short, being neither tragical nor comical, at a dinner-party."[72] Quincy also noted Kemble's retiring manners at Boston parties, though Kemble found Boston society the most welcoming and intellectually satisfying. Philadelphia socialite Julia Kean wrote to her mother about the collective disappointment when guests encountered a "dark complexioned, unhappy, diminutive little person" rather than the "graceful and elegant female they had seen on stage."[73] Offstage, Kemble was never quite the woman her publics expected.

After she retired from the stage, Kemble used her writing to defy the restrictive terms of women's engagement with public life. Kemble's foreign celebrity made her more susceptible and perhaps a more astute observer of a shifting culture that placed increasingly contradictory expectations on female public figures. She became a lesson about the boundaries being drawn around women's publicity.

"A Blot . . . upon the Name of Kemble"

In 1833, after a flurry of outrage over an Englishman's satire of a ladies' fair at Faneuil Hall in Boston, a city journalist noted ruefully, "If Charles Kemble and Fanny Kemble do not, on their return to England, repay the civilities and the liberalities of Americans with ridicule, slander, calumny, and lampoon, it must be because Nature will have so changed her laws as that the viper will cease to bite."[74] With the publication of her journal, Kemble became part of the growing cohort of English visitors whose commentary animated nationalist tensions. The outrage over Kemble's journal was proportional (and proportionally gleeful) to the lionization of Kemble as an avatar of female gentility within the theater. The response to the journal inverted the terms of Kemble's celebrity, as reviewers argued that her career had actually compromised her womanhood. In so doing, critics reasserted their ability to shape female celebrity while criticizing Kemble for her refusal to conform to their terms.

Many of Kemble's colorful but unstinting descriptions of urban life in America were common to English travel literature. She wrote about pushy tradespeople, meddlesome journalists, and the uncomfortable barebones accommodations of newly constructed hotels. She delivered opinions about the literature she read, the society and intellect of people she met, and the capacity of audiences who failed to appreciate her and her father's acting. She wrote frankly about unpleasant aspects of her profession, like male costars who pawed at her body and disrupted her artistic vision, the pressure to satisfy the demands of her American publics, and her disillusionment with the stage as artistically fulfilling. The frankness and style of the journal were unusual. Kemble seemed to allow herself a "passionate expressiveness" through her prose that she was forced to constrain in all other aspects of her life, even in her acting.[75] But for Kemble's public, such self-exposure violated the very terms of her celebrity and even transgressed emerging contemporary standards of "literary domesticity." Readers felt that Kemble's voice as a writer disrupted this character rather than confirming her reputation as a genteel literary actress. This revealed her to have been a confidence woman, further evidence that the stage was inherently corrosive of womanhood.

Kemble's youth and femininity were central to the fallout over the journal. Kemble had violated unspoken rules about what women were and were not permitted to say publicly. In his review for the *Southern Literary Messenger*, Edgar Allan Poe noted that "a female, and a young one too, cannot speak with the self-confidence which marks this book, without jarring somewhat upon American notions of the retiring delicacy of the female character." Kemble's observations and opinions were more offensive because she was a young woman. Though most reviewers found Kemble's journal entertaining, even funny, they agreed with Poe that it was impossible to "[separate] the author from the work."[76] It was vulgar because it was written by a young woman. Reviewers pointed to her unstinting and "hasty" opinions, general "shrewishness," and "coarse and vulgar" language and humor.[77] The *Literary Journal* identified an "indelicacy of expression . . . inexcusable in a lady."[78]

In searching for explanations for this character, critics pointed to the stage. Poe was certain that few American women could have developed the character Kemble revealed in this book. Poe, who was the son of an actress, agreed with Kemble's criticisms of the theatrical profession while noting that "she is probably unconscious" of the degree to which her early life on the stage also shaped "her own feelings, and manner of thinking and writing." Rather than elevating the stage, Kemble's brief tenure as an actress had nurtured "a precocious self-dependence and a habit of forming her own opinions" that made her unwomanly.[79] Most reviewers came to a similar conclusion. They thus inverted the logic according to which Kemble had been celebrated as an agent of uplift in the theater. Now Kemble's language and style were evidence that she was unwomanly, and she was deemed unwomanly *because* of her stage career.

Because much of what she said was judged unflattering, her statements also helped undermine Kemble's reliability as a social critic. An "English lady" and longtime resident of America used examples of Kemble's conduct, such as dancing in mixed company, singing on the Sabbath during the Atlantic crossing, allowing herself to be manhandled by her male costars, and using words like "humbug," to question whether any of Kemble's judgments could be taken seriously. The "English lady" sarcastically asked her readers to consider "the singular mind of the intellectual Fanny, and that peculiar delicacy and refinement of sentiment [that] qualif[ied] her to become the censor of the morals and manners of the people among whom she was . . . to sojourn."[80] Kemble was mistaken in her assessment of American society because she was not adequately equipped to judge it.

Joseph Sill, who was among the "thousands" who crowded bookstores to buy a copy, echoed many of these sentiments in his diary. However, he drew a distinction, as did Philip Hone, between the opinions Kemble might hold and those she should express, let alone publish. Sill commended Kemble for passages worthy of poetry, but these moments were overwhelmed by the "fault finding spirit" of the text, made even worse by the "coarse, vulgar, unladylike language." Sill listed all the offending terminology: references to "Hell" and the "devil," as well as "humbug, dauldrumish, gulped, cuddle, fetch'd a walk." Sill concluded that the journal was a "true record" of Kemble's "thoughts and feelings at the time" but as such should have been reserved for "private circulation" or "suppress'd" by her friends.[81] Philip Hone read with embarrassment Kemble's cutting account of his party in her honor, in which she looked vainly for finger bowls and criticized the motley fashions and poor society of his daughters. Hone regretted that while he had seen Kemble's brilliance and wit, the journal instead revealed "childish prejudice [and] the hasty conclusions from erroneous first impressions." It was all in very "bad taste" and seemed "unworthy" of her abilities.[82] When Hone met Kemble Butler at a ball several years later, he took pleasure in their warm reunion. He noted with regret that her "literary reputation" had been "compromised" by the publication of "inconsiderate, girlish remarks."[83] Both of these men, active diarists themselves, were more embarrassed for Kemble than outraged, more willing to permit a certain laxity of manners and expression had those not been placed before the public eye. They felt that Kemble had failed to appreciate her role as a public figure, but it was also clear to them that Kemble was pushing against the terms of this role.

Satirists, on the other hand, relished the opportunity to hurl Kemble from her pedestal. The virulence of these pieces represented a fierce backlash against all that Kemble symbolized as a public figure. Satirists depicted her engaging in behavior that was well outside the boundaries of genteel white womanhood. A cartoon and poem from Philadelphia lithographer James Akin casts Kemble as a desperate fortune hunter making a play for a "rich husband," then promising, "I will be gone." The verses highlight her apparent hypocrisy: "And now a Wife she damns all Stages" while "publishing loose tittle tattle."[84] Satirists also deployed the familiar image of the dissolute, drunk, and deceptive actor—the very one from which the Kembles worked so hard to distinguish themselves. In *My Conscience: Fanny Thimble Cutler's Journal of a Residence in America*, a Philadelphia satirist portrays Kemble as a drunk, self-aggrandizing, and sexually loose woman dogged in her pursuit of "Fierce Cutler." Kemble consumes "julips," wine, and whiskey liberally; goes out in her "negligee," which becomes the fashion by nightfall; and falls into a drunken stupor on Cutler's bosom. She receives visitors in the hall of her hotel, seated on a "throne" of mahogany bedecked in silks while "dressed as Lady Teazle" from *A School for Scandal*.[85] Illustrated satires took delight in reviving stereotypes of the actress as a libertine through visual double entendres. In a plate from *Sketches Supposed to Have Been Intended for*

Figure 6. This plate from *Sketches Supposed to Have Been Intended for Fanny Kemble's Journal* turns passages from the 1835 journal into racist double entendres, evoking contemporary charges of miscegenation leveled at abolitionists in this period. Library Company of Philadelphia.

Fanny Kemble's Journal, Kemble lies prone on the floor surrounded by a gluttonous array of dishes while a black servant kneeling above her pops a cork from a bottle wedged between his knees, a clear suggestion of interracial sex (fig. 6). In another, Kemble's complaints about untrained and physically and sexually aggressive male costars have been refashioned into a fantasy of the actress as an (inept) seducer, with Kemble as Juliet fondling the doublet of the prone actor and asking, "Why, where the devil *is* your dagger, Mr.—?"[86]

Much of this satire, particularly concerning Kemble's observations of race in America, played with the imagery of social inversion, suggesting the consequences when women transgressed gendered boundaries. In *Fanny Thimble,* Kemble's interest in New York's free black population is reworked in the style of the "Bobalition" caricatures that mocked free black political and social life. Fanny Thimble is ousted from her Philadelphia hotel by a meeting of the "Bobalition Society." She fails to understand racial rules governing American society. While traveling on a steamboat she is laughed at by "chambermaids" after berating a "coloured woman" for "coming among whites" when the woman's child vomits on Thimble. Everywhere Thimble goes, she fails to know her place or accurately read the society around her. She navigates a world in which her outsized sense of importance draws her into absurd situations, such as her excursion to the notorious Five Points slums to view "the fashionables." After a social slight, Fanny Thimble rages at "Fierce Cutler" about the "impudent, ignorant, ragtag and bobtail sluts and hussies," calms herself with a "julip," then instructs her father and Cutler to arrange a duel, yet she worries that she "displayed too much of my natural temper to . . . [p]oor Cutler."[87]

These satires relished the disintegration of Kemble's former celebrity while asserting that Kemble was a confidence woman. The journal demonstrated not only that the terms of her celebrity were mistaken but also that Kemble had also consciously manipulated her publics. Kemble's journal revealed her to have been false *off*stage, which was worse than being a mere actress. The "English lady" was shocked that Kemble could have "so powerfully masked [her mind] in communion with the inartificial society into which she had been introduced," concluding, "This indeed was acting, and with something more than machievalian [*sic*] skill."[88] Kemble's inadvertent revelation of her private self recast the tour and Kemble's celebrity as a confidence act committed at the expense of a credulous and eager public. In *Fanny Thimble*, the irritation Kemble felt about her father's solicitation of a poem is recast as a performance of false modesty. After reluctantly agreeing to write a poem, Fanny Thimble selects something from her "bundle of cut and dry prose and poetry; manufactured in Grub Street for the sole purpose of making me a literary character in America."[89] In *Sketches*, Kemble's complaints about mosquitos and journalists come together in a bedroom scene in which the actress lifts the bedclothes to discover swarms of insects along with the titles of newspapers (fig. 7). Kemble's celebrity was not supposed to be an act, even though her celebrity persona had, in fact, been consistently imposed upon her.

Even as such reactions betrayed a deep ambivalence about female celebrity, some of it was clearly backlash from journalists offended by Kemble's outspoken criticism of the press. Reviewers noted Kemble's disparaging comments about journalists, such as her declaration that "next to a *bug*, a newspaper writer is her disgust." These statements were especially galling to the men who felt that they had been made "very great hum*bugs*" for "fawning about her" and "puffing her performances," in turn making her tour successful.[90] The *New York Mirror*, which professed more embarrassment for the writer than outrage, regretted the "bad grace" of Kemble's attacks on the press, given that "all the

Figure 7. Another plate from *Sketches Supposed to Have Been Intended for Fanny Kemble's Journal* satirizes her complaints about insect life and journalists as newspapers literally become bedbugs. Library Company of Philadelphia.

honours of her family have arisen from the notice of the press."[91] The newspapers understood their own role in helping construct the persona that English and American publics found so fascinating. However, in their reaction to Fanny's journal, satirists and reviewers blamed Kemble for these maneuvers. The fawning journalists became dupes of her perfidy, aligned in sympathetic outrage with the theatergoers who had flocked to see her.

In her journal, Kemble showed her publics that acting and celebrity were work, thereby disrupting the myth of her acting as an emanation of her genius. She revealed a complex, conflicted, and ambitious woman. Contrary to the terms of Kemble's celebrity, which called upon her to be the ideal creature of her publics' desires and to show gratitude to her American audiences, Kemble revealed that she was grappling with many of the same questions that animated their interest in her. She questioned the moral and aesthetic qualities of the theater, wondered at the social and cultural differences between America and England, and, finally, was skeptical about whether a woman could labor as an actress and be a public figure while satisfying her own and her publics' conceptions of true womanhood. But in exposing the ambitious woman grappling with contradictory gendered expectations and patriarchal structures, the journal simultaneously revealed and ridiculed the very mechanisms of celebrity that had made Kemble so appealing and given her a rare public platform. Kemble had used that platform to challenge the gendered standards governing it.

The reaction to Fanny Kemble's journal manifested the double edge of stage celebrity in America that Kemble navigated from the start of her American tour. Kemble's 1832–34 US tour served as a watershed in the growth of the American starring system and female celebrity. She joined together the figures of actress and poetess, becoming the unique "literary actress." Her champions imagined her as a vehicle for uplift in the theater because of her genteel upbringing and elevated status within the English theater profession. However, the terms and mechanisms of her celebrity largely remained outside Kemble's control and were swiftly drawn into the social and cultural politics of the moment.

Kemble's American celebrity spoke to intersecting social and nationalist tensions in American cities as clashes between different segments of the American theater public played out around national identity. Tastemakers who sought to elevate dramatic tastes and reshape theater culture looked to Kemble as a vehicle of literary and cultural uplift; meanwhile, her status as an Englishwoman placed her in a more precarious position in light of American sensitivity to English travel writing. Kemble discovered that she neither controlled her image nor was able to create separation between her status as a public figure and her private self. She chafed at this tension and consistently defied expectations that she conform to a narrow gendered persona.

Kemble's female publics celebrated her because she represented a new kind of public woman. Her celebrity dramatized questions about the degree to which genteel white women could challenge gendered boundaries of public life while successfully realizing a narrowing gendered ideal. When Kemble took ownership of celebrity through her literary voice, the male journalistic establishment pushed back—she could only stretch the boundaries of female publicity so far. In trying to enact the promise of her own celebrity, Kemble violated the gendered power dynamics that shaped it.

In spite of this, Kemble's career had been quite successful. It was unusually short-lived but profitable. She acted for five years, two of which she spent touring America, but within a narrower geography than that of other stars. The Kembles never ventured south of Washington, DC, nor left the eastern seaboard to perform, but they managed to earn enough of a fortune to allow Charles to return to England and retire from the stage, while Fanny rushed into a deeply unhappy marriage with Pierce Butler. The fallout from the journal occurred as her marriage was rapidly deteriorating. She withdrew from public life for over a decade, then reemerged amid the scandal of her divorce and rebuilt her career as an elocutionist in England in the late 1840s.

Though the terms of Kemble's celebrity were unique, her success with American audiences continued to reveal the potential of the American market. Over the 1830s and 1840s, growing numbers of women from England and continental Europe sought the profits of an American tour, joined by ambitious stock actresses from American theaters. The American starring system expanded to encompass widening regional circuits in the South and trans-Appalachian West. English-born actresses remained the most popular stars of the 1830s but increasingly presented entertainments that stretched the boundaries of taste, alarming champions of the "legitimate drama." Starring women likewise navigated contradictory pressures governing female celebrity because they were expected to follow rigid standards of genteel femininity even as the structural realities of their lives rarely allowed them to do so. As had been the case for Kemble, starring offered women ways to stretch, but rarely shatter, the patriarchal contours of their lives and careers.

4 Bringing Female Spectacle to the "Western Country," 1835–1840

Actor-manager Sol Smith was furious. Back in April 1838, after actress Ellen Tree had concluded a lucrative two-week engagement in St. Louis, Missouri, she "verbally engaged" to play both Mobile, Alabama, and St. Louis the following year. Smith or his partner, Noah Ludlow, planned to iron out the details during the summer. But now, a year later, Tree was trying to "be off from her St. Louis engagement," apparently concerned that the company would "not be ready to receive" her.[1] Smith was planning to open the St. Louis Theatre early "for the purpose of 'playing the stars' on their way to the North" and make up for the losses in Mobile, where the other theater that he and Ludlow managed lay in smoky ruins.[2] Smith needed what he called a "great card," a star capable of pulling in full houses and sizeable returns to offset slower weeks or unprofitable engagements. He had stopped in New Orleans to see about French pantomime actress Celeste, who had never played St. Louis. Her husband, Henry Elliott, who managed Celeste's business, was ill "on the point of death" and unsure whether they could make the trip.[3] As he traveled up the Mississippi River, Smith "stopped more than an hour at Vicksburgh" to meet with Tree and come to some arrangement. She wanted to play a few more towns in Mississippi rather than travel a week out of her way to St. Louis. Smith "would not listen to it." They agreed that *"if the company"* came through "Vicksburgh," Mississippi, before she left for Natchez, Tennessee, Tree would "come up & play one engagement."[4] This was a risk Smith would take.

Stars were vital to the success of emerging western theater markets, which in turn created new professional opportunities for female entertainers. In April the St. Louis stock company opened the 1839 season to decent houses before it started "raining cats & dogs." Houses dried up. "Nothing less than the *big stars* will draw them—especially *wet nights*," Smith lamented. He tried to keep his sense of humor, joking, "Ellen Tree—Ellen Tree—is all the cry now—& Forrest, Booth & Celeste—they would like to see them *all together!*" Tree arrived midmonth, and, weather notwithstanding, the returns were "immense." Smith's mood improved. If American actor Edwin Forrest was successful, and Celeste followed soon after (apparently, a meeting with Ludlow in Mobile had done the trick), Smith expected to "make a good little season," even though the stars would "take all the profits, pretty much."[5] But attendance dropped so precipitously after Tree that the next star, Charles Mason, forfeited his engagement and took off for the East. Forrest's engagement competed with a concert by an Italian opera singer, which kept audiences away. Celeste arrived in late May to more thunderstorms, but her benefit night realized the "highest receipts on any one night in that theatre," a $1,149.50 windfall, of which Celeste took $574, equivalent to $16,000 today.[6]

Examining the starring system of the 1830s from the vantage of St. Louis, then the western periphery of Anglo-Atlantic theater, looking east to New York and south to New Orleans, reveals the national reach of "big stars" like Ellen Tree and Celeste and how their careers shaped the context in which an expanding cohort of women and girls sought the opportunities of expanding markets with a new female-centered repertoire. Over the 1830s, starring became the foundation of a viable theater, especially in expanding western markets. Business correspondence by partners Solomon Smith and Noah Ludlow affords a rare window into the operation of the starring system from the vantage of their western theater. Managers nationwide recruited stars able to introduce new dramas, opera, and dance to theatergoers eager for novelty and the ability to participate in Anglo-Atlantic entertainment culture. Women took advantage of new opportunities to star in these markets and experiment with new repertoire, though they also faced pressures to conform to aesthetic norms policed by managers and critics. While women achieved unprecedented wealth and prestige through starring, the men in their lives consistently took greater control over women's careers.

In 1838 St. Louis was at the western periphery of expanding entertainment markets, struggling to draw the most prominent star itinerants, who remained vital to the success of the "first theatre west of the

Mississippi."[7] The 1830s saw a new wave of theater construction in the Ohio River Valley and lower Mississippi funded by members of the local business-class elite who associated the viability and institutionalization of English theater with the growth of western and southern frontiers and incorporation into the nation. English theater first arrived in the trans-Appalachian West around 1815, brought by small traveling companies that offered seasons of eight to ten weeks in a regional circuit. Establishing theater as a profitable year-round venture remained difficult. Over the 1820s, a transportation revolution stimulated by steam technology brought new commerce to towns along the Ohio and Mississippi Rivers, a boon for theaters. By the 1830s, theater audiences in river ports like St. Louis included an expanding settler population, seasonal laborers navigating the Mississippi, and commercial travelers. These publics expected to see itinerant stars who had been written about in eastern papers and whose celebrity circulated nationwide. Successful recruitment of stars to play in regional theaters increased patronage, which contributed to theaters' financial viability, and connected audiences in the trans-Appalachian West to a broader Anglo-Atlantic metropolitan culture while making western regions more "American." In St. Louis, managers Sol Smith and Noah Ludlow tried to make their theater profitable while aligning its content and demographics to their ideas of aesthetic and social uplift. However, because of their remote location, they had less control over the stars coming through.

Western managers needed stars for a successful season, while stars looked to western markets to extend the length of their tours and increase profits. The continued influx of foreign entertainers overwhelmed eastern markets, making southern and western tours appealing to the stars of the 1830s. Like other itinerants, Tree and Celeste began in New York, playing the major eastern seaboard markets of Boston, Philadelphia, Baltimore, and Washington, DC. Southern tours took performers to New Orleans by sea, sometimes with stops in Richmond, Virginia, or Charleston, South Carolina, and followed New Orleans with a circuit of the lower Mississippi. As upriver steam travel improved, performers increasingly made their way back to Boston or New York via Cincinnati, Ohio, a rapidly growing city with a more established theatrical market than St. Louis, which was a sharp detour and thus a harder sell. Or performers coming from the East could travel the "Western Country routes" to Cincinnati and then make their way downriver to New Orleans.[8]

The expansion of southern and western markets offered performers a wider field in which to earn a living and shape their careers. Stars of varying caliber strategized these markets differently. During the 1830s, performers from theaters and opera houses in Great Britain and continental Europe looked to American markets to sustain, remake, and grow their reputations and increase their earnings. They were joined by American-born performers like actress Josephine Clifton, who modeled her career on Fanny Kemble and was compared to Ellen Tree. While some ventured south and west to extend their earning power, others developed their careers in these markets, becoming regional favorites. In the 1830s it became more common for performers with no European reputation or even a New York pedigree to develop itinerant careers, either as soloists or in family ensembles.

Women and girls dominated the starring system in the 1830s through the popularization of new repertoire coming from Europe. As purveyors of popular but controversial new repertoire, starring women became the focus of competing ideas about what theater should be. Women were key protagonists of domestic and adventure melodramas, English operas (many adapted from German or French originals), and ballets from royal European opera houses, much of which fell outside what American critics considered "legitimate drama." This repertoire afforded women new expressive possibilities while featuring women's bodies in new ways. Critics nationwide questioned whether women performing outside the "legitimate" drama deserved to be receiving so much money and public acclaim.

In St. Louis, the stakes of these battles were connected to the politics of colonization and incorporation as boosters looked to theater to advance aesthetic and social uplift and counter stereotypes of frontier society, goals that existed uncomfortably with the popularity of stars like Celeste whom they judged indelicate, devoid of art, and overvalued. Efforts at reforming entertainment content through criticism were relatively ineffective. Even as managers actively tried to reform the culture of spectatorship, ideals of dramatic taste rarely won out over calculations about what would draw profitable houses. Managers discovered that new forms of female performance filled theaters, though not always with the white middle-class respectables they sought. This created important openings for female entertainers—and pressures.

While women clearly saw new economic and expressive possibilities in embracing an expanding repertoire, they may have faced pressures to connect professional viability with the deployment of sexuality. Though the archive offers limited insight into female performers' perspectives on this shifting entertainment culture, itinerancy clearly offered women a larger field in which to experiment aesthetically. Women played with gender expectations in an expanding repertoire, offering audiences heroic gender transgression and sexualized display and in turn achieving new levels of wealth and cultural prominence. However, this remained subject to the interests of their families. Men remained the major gatekeepers of the business, and, more often than not, women's careers were directed by the men in their lives. Women found ways to stretch and manipulate, though not reshape, the gendered parameters of their lives and the patriarchal structure of the industry.

Coming to Terms for St. Louis

In reply to Henry Elliott's query about a Mobile engagement for Celeste in 1839, manager Sol Smith pitched St. Louis, where they had a "splendid theatre, large and far superior to that of Mobile." He assured Elliott that both "Miss Tree and the Ravels did as well here as in Mobile."[9] Elliott decided to settle for Mobile, but Celeste did make it out to St. Louis in May, her first and only appearance in that city and an extremely successful one. St. Louis was a hard sell—even for stars traveling the Western Country routes. In response to a circular and query from French dancer Augusta St. James, Smith again tried to arrange for appearances in both Mobile and St. Louis, explaining that each theater featured gas lighting and a "good Stock" of scenery and held a capacity of $1,200 at "present prices."[10] Actually, nightly returns rarely approached this in either city, but Smith wanted to assure prospective attractions coming from the East that the Mobile and St. Louis markets were worth the trip.

Mobile was an easier sell than St. Louis. It was a short detour from New Orleans, which had become a major entertainment center, particularly for dancers and singers, with multiple theaters, two English and a French theater. Stars like Celeste, Augusta St. James, and Ellen Tree earned profits in the tens of thousands. St. Louis had only one theater, a new structure completed in 1837. In July 1837 a correspondent for New York's *Spirit of the Times*, which increasingly functioned as a trade paper for entertainers, praised the "first Temple of the Drama West of the Mississippi" as the "most magnificent Theatre in the whole Mississippi Valley, (the St. Charles [in New Orleans] alone excepted)." The new St. Louis Theatre had been funded by public subscription of $30,000 (an amount later doubled), raised by the projected lessee and manager, Noah Ludlow.[11] It replaced an old converted warehouse that had served theater companies for the last decade. The new theater was built with a capacity of fifteen hundred, still smaller than the barn-like "Drurys" of the East but featuring elaborate decoration and new technologies. The painted interior dome, boxes with "cherry wood" balustrades that "looked like mahogany," and a stage "forty-five feet deep" were lit by gas lamps. Ludlow also commissioned eight scenic panels with corresponding wings for the stage.[12] St. Louis in turn became a more appealing destination for touring entertainers.

The theater was closely connected with efforts by local elites to remake St. Louis in the guise of an eastern city while consolidating their social and cultural leadership. Its managers hoped to rival major eastern theaters in the quality of performances (Smith consistently complained about the costs of their high-caliber stock company) and the culture of spectatorship, shaped to appeal to emerging ideals of genteel respectability. This was particularly important, given that commercial travelers were a key market, for as Smith observed to his partner, "Receipts vary according to the *arrival* and *departure* of the boats."[13] The managers tried to create a theater that countered stereotypes of rough frontier life to appeal to new eastern migrants and commercial travelers. It contained individual chairs rather than benches, which prevented "crowding." The uniform one-dollar admission to the parquet and lower tiers meant that unlike the rowdy pit culture back east, in St. Louis the "parquette is filled (when full) with men of respectability, taste & learning," or so a new migrant from Philadelphia characterized it. The theater still catered to "hard customers" through a separate entrance to the half-price gallery, to which theater managers also restricted black patrons. Management's "scheme of reformation" involved closing the gentlemen's saloon (St. Louis otherwise had a prolific drinking culture, particularly in riverboat gambling dens) and barring prostitutes and unaccompanied women.[14] In the coming decade, managers in eastern theaters also tried to move prostitution out of theaters by eliminating private rooms and enforcing a culture of male chaperones.[15]

Because of the economic risks involved with this reform vision and a public that varied with the river tides, it was extremely important to secure celebrated entertainers. The economic viability of a permanent theater "far, far West" depended upon its ties to national commerce, which brought both entertainers and the audiences to see them. Managers generally conducted negotiations through correspondence. Letters between managers and performers or their de facto agents traveled by post and via steamboat, working out the financial "terms" and "time," which was tied closely to performers' movements east and south of St. Louis. Some stars left engagements with rough details of a return the following season. Out-of-work entertainers occasionally showed up unannounced (especially if they got behind schedule elsewhere and had to forfeit), hoping to find spare nights to play. Managers also went on recruiting trips of their own. In 1837, shortly after the new theater opened, Smith traveled to Cincinnati but was disappointed to learn that there would be "*no Stars* here of any account, (that I can hear of,) except *Augusta*," who was engaged to "play one" engagement before "returning East."[16] Augusta never made a detour to St. Louis, but she did play Mobile following New Orleans. In the spring of 1837, Celeste also followed New Orleans with engagements in Mobile, then proceeded through James M. Scott and James Thorne's theater circuit of Vicksburg, Louisville, and Cincinnati before continuing directly to Boston and New York without playing St. Louis.[17] It would be another two years before Celeste arrived in St. Louis.

The customary starring arrangement of the 1830s was sharing the net proceeds after deducting each night's expenses, which put most of the risk on the manager. Terms varied according to the stature of the performer, with major stars offered more advantageous sharing terms (sharing after a lower gross) that required management to shoulder more of the risk but guaranteed the performer a larger profit margin. Negotiations between managers and stars mobilized competing conceptions of risk and reward: managers weighed engagements within the arc of a season, with its expenses and uncertainties, while stars strategized engagements in relation to the profitability of different markets and the real personal costs of remaining continually on the road. Smith and Ludlow had several strategies for negotiating terms that were representative of the industry as a whole. In response to Thomas Davenport's inquiry for his daughter, Jean Margaret, Smith explained, "Our usual terms to Stars [is] to divide the receipts after a deduction of $300 per night charges," which he and Ludlow calculated as their nightly bottom line, "and half Benefit," meaning a clear division of the gross receipts for the star's benefit night. Smith offered Davenport a discount of sorts, given the child star's success in New York: divide after $250.[18] In comparison, established foreign stars like Tree and Celeste could demand a lower net before splitting receipts, which in St. Louis meant sharing after $150. In such cases, management shouldered more risk, while the star took a larger cut of the gross. The lower the sharing terms, the greater the itinerant's take at the end of the engagement.

It was during the 1830s that managers developed the critique of the "starring system" that came to dominate theater histories, reflecting the uncertain economics of the 1830s and the shifting gender politics of the business. Managers' struggles to sustain solvent, let alone profitable, theaters were exacerbated by the nationwide depression of 1837–43, which saw greater turnover of theater leases, many going dark for periods of time, while stars and sundry paratheatrical entertainments proliferated. Managers were simultaneously more reliant upon stars to make ends meet, but only if stars were willing to come to terms that adequately covered the theater's bottom line. Managers came to see starring as the source of their economic instability rather than the key to their stability. As Ludlow complained in his memoir, stars "march off with the money and leave the managers with the bag to hold, until they find it convenient to come back." He reserved special ire for the "two-penny candles and farthing rush-lights . . . 'lesser luminaries'" who like "a certain fungus on a log . . . [give] just enough light to mislead one," generating a financial loss for management from mediocre returns.[19] In their efforts to satisfy public desire for novelty with a splash of dramatic genius and to fill the season—or simply figure out who and what drew consistent patronage—most managers, particularly in peripheral markets like St. Louis, recruited "lesser luminaries" eager to trade a weekly wage in a fixed market for a shared speculation on the road—and to try out controversial new amusements. Still, managers felt that stars did not share enough of the risk.

Gender was central to discourses around the starring system. Managers' critiques of the system betray a compromised vision of themselves as benevolent capitalist patriarchs supervising the livelihoods of a company while making correct aesthetic choices. This ideal increasingly clashed with their dependence on stars and the popularity of controversial new forms of entertainment dominated by women. Managers' growing frustrations with starring thus reflected the changing gender landscape, in which women were some of the theater's highest earners during the 1830s and purveyors of its most exciting new entertainments, albeit in a patriarchal industry where men continued to exert control as managers and agents.

Women rarely handled their own correspondence; much of managers' business dealings is between men. Theater managers negotiated with husbands and fathers on behalf of wives, children, or family troupes. While this does not indicate that men controlled the terms of women's careers, they could certainly exert significant influence over touring decisions and financial arrangements. Few performers in this period remained unmarried, and even husbands with no connection to the business, like Joel Seaver, newly married to actress Mary Ann Duff, still handled arrangements for wives. In contrast, unmarried women who had the advantage of age and experience, like Ellen Tree, who was in her early thirties, and widow Frances Drake, then around forty, did handle their own business.

Unmarried actress Josephine Clifton chose to rely on a brother, Turner Merritt. Incidentally, Sol Smith was a bit skeptical about this relationship, commenting in one letter, "his *sister*(?)" with a punctuated rise of the eyebrow.[20] Both women and men recognized the capital in developing female talent: after separating from her alcoholic actor husband, retired actress Sophia Brown made a living managing the burgeoning career of child performer Kate Meadows.

Marriage was an important professional decision for female entertainers, especially itinerants. An effective marriage partner could provide escape from overbearing parents and create new professional opportunities, though it is not always clear how much husbands shaped the terms and trajectories of women's careers compared with fathers. Both Charlotte Watson (Bailey) and Annette Nelson (Hodges) were brought to the United States by their parents as teens, married shortly thereafter (Charlotte under a hint of scandal), and went on the road with their spouses. In addition to handling business correspondence, Nelson's husband probably helped her secure the lease of a small New York theater, which she managed in late 1836. In a rare departure from professional naming practices, the actress continued to perform as "Miss Nelson" rather than "Mrs. Hodges," thus retaining a recently established professional identity that was enhanced by the allure of sexual availability. When marriage to Celeste brought Henry Elliott into the theater business, he crossed the language barrier for his French wife and served as her agent, helping her to navigate a foreign entertainment industry. He continued to line up engagements for her even after she decided in 1839–40 that she was ready to return to Europe (as she did, deserting him in June 1840).[21]

Negotiations did not occur within a vacuum. Itinerants tried to figure out exactly what managers offered different performers, which they used to negotiate better terms, and also reported beneficial arrangements made with rival theater managers. Smith reminded Alexander Gibbs of his place in the hierarchy after the singer requested sharing after $100 for his wife and another vocalist: "When we shall become satisfied that Mrs. Gibbs attraction is greater than other stars—Celeste, the Ravel Family, &c &c—We may feel it to be our interest to give her better terms than we give them."[22] When Smith and Ludlow eventually agreed to sharing after $300, Smith reminded Gibbs, "We presume you consider as we do the *terms of all engagements* strictly confidential."[23] Sophia Brown wanted to know whether Smith and Ludlow offered her what they gave other stars. Smith replied, "To some we give better, & to others not so good," and he reminded Brown that "she did tolerably well at the former terms." Still, he wondered "by what method she ascertained the terms we gave *other Stars*."[24] Smith's belief in his influence within his own market was disrupted by the possibility that Brown compared notes with others or expected context before making an arrangement. Stars clearly did not keep their terms confidential.

While Ludlow and Smith complained privately about greedy stars who pushed too hard against the managers' way of doing things, open conflicts with stars or their agents were rare. Instead, correspondence reveals a subtle politics of largess as managers sought to position themselves as benevolent patriarchs engaged in fair and equitable dealings—and, in so doing, assert their influence. They recognized that they could not "dictate terms," as Henry Elliott accused Smith of doing in negotiations for Celeste, but stars also did not want to appear too desperate. In a rare conflict, Smith and Henry Elliott each accused the other of failing to realize masculine standards of goodwill. Smith charged Elliott with appearing to think that he could use *"threats"* to force an arrangement that was not "just and equitable." The manager was careful to keep Celeste out of the conflict, reassuring Elliot that he felt no *"coldness . . .* towards Mrs Elliott" and would not "[treat] any lady in that manner." Ultimately, Smith finalized the arrangement, possibly by agreeing to Elliott's counteroffer, and expressed anxiety to remain "on friendly terms."[25] Smith might have been less conciliatory with a less popular and coveted entertainer. Still, a successfully concluded engagement did not guarantee that a star would make it to St. Louis in time. Steamboats were delayed by weather, low water levels, and the dreaded snags that made upriver travel dangerous. Stars even defaulted on engagements when a better-paying opportunity came along, a problem experienced more acutely in St. Louis, given its relatively remote upriver location.

When women violated the terms of their engagements or challenged managers directly, Smith and Ludlow vacillated between their ideals of how gendered hierarchy should work and the realities of a business in which popular starring women were often able to call the shots. For example, their outrage when women in their stock company negotiated for raises was disproportionate, reflecting a preference that women act as grateful dependents rather than the strategic professionals they actually were.

A conflict with Josephine Clifton over honoring her St. Louis engagement for March 1838 brought these gendered tensions into the open. After the Mississippi River reopened in March 1838, Smith anxiously followed news about the movements of stars, hoping Clifton would come before

Ellen Tree, though he was "confoundedly afraid Miss Tree & the Ravels," a family troupe of acrobats, "will hit on the *same time.*"[26] This would cut into profits. But there had been no correspondence from anyone confirming dates. He worried that the stars had "heard of the bad business" in St. Louis and changed their minds or were "waiting till they hear it has improved." Smith was caught in a vice: business would only pick up with stars, but if these performers waited to come until they heard news of good houses, Smith feared that he would be ruined.[27] Clifton's movements confirmed Smith's fears, while her gender placed him in a predicament about how to respond. Clifton had arrived in New Orleans by way of Charleston in January 1838. In February she played an engagement with Ludlow in Mobile and then returned to New Orleans. Smith expected her in St. Louis in March, but she ventured only as far as Vicksburg, Mississippi, and picked up another engagement, as Smith noted sarcastically, in "the Metropolitan city of *Grand Gulf!*" Clifton returned to New Orleans rather than travel a week upriver by steamboat to St. Louis. Smith heard a report that Clifton had "said she was not coming up here to play *for nothing.*"[28] Fortunately, Tree's arrival in mid-April saved the managers from a ruinous season, though now Clifton was in the unenviable position of following Tree's engagement. Stars paid attention to the performers they preceded and followed, just as managers worried about the arc of a season. When Clifton's impromptu tour of the lower Mississippi delayed her arrival in St. Louis, Clifton simultaneously expected Smith and Ludlow to find a place for her later in the spring lineup and was "in a d—d of a stew for fear she could not get here before Miss Tree." Rightly so: Smith "wouldn't give a sixpence for Miss Clifton after Miss Tree."[29]

Even though Tree saved the season, Smith decided not to let Clifton off from her engagement. He grappled with how to treat her, whether he should call her out for violating her contract or employ benevolent restraint on behalf of her gender. Smith's outrage over Clifton's contract violation won out over her gender. In April he published a biting item in the local paper, reprinted in New Orleans: "'Wonder' if Miss Josephine Clifton has *forgotten* her engagement to perform in the St. Louis Theatre. 'Wonder' if the managers will *remind* her of it?"[30] Clifton had thrown St. Louis over to return to New Orleans but then fell terribly ill and did not play anywhere in April. When she finally arrived in St. Louis in May, Smith made a big show of welcoming the prodigal actress. Even as he sneered privately at the letter of apology from New Orleans manager James Caldwell, Smith's self-conception as a benevolent patriarch and the financial interests of the theater guided his next action. He thought it best, "she being a *woman*," to "hold off for a while, to *forgive her.*" He agreed to start Clifton's engagement in June to open a short summer season.[31]

As touring increased, competition developed among headliners, even cutting across gender. Because actors and actresses were hired for gendered lines of business, they did not vie with each other for positions and only rarely for roles. Stars did compete with each other for space in a season and more advantageous terms. The correspondence of comedian Henry Finn, onetime manager of the Federal Street Theatre in Boston turned itinerant, is suggestive of conversations that may have occurred off the page. Finn's direct communication about his resentments is unusual but exposes the extent to which the professional playing field had changed by the 1830s. A chance conversation between Finn and Clara Fisher Maeder in Charleston prompted an irate letter from Finn to the managers in Mobile, demanding to know "what has . . . our friend Mrs M done . . . [m]ore than your friend Mr F" to secure sharing terms, while Finn was only offered a fixed certainty for his engagement.[32] Even though Smith apparently explained things to Finn when he came to Mobile, the disgruntled comedian continued to raise the matter of his terms. He became defensive, assuring Smith that he would not "arrogate *better terms* to myself than you accord to men of more merit." He considered himself equal to if not above Clara Fisher Maeder, and he "thought it *hard* to fare worse than some one of the *softer* sex."[33] With his decades of experience, Finn resented being passed over for an engagement or given inferior terms, particularly to a much younger woman whom he did not consider legitimate competition.

Stars tried to work out starring engagements to their best financial and professional advantage. But the profitability of a particular engagement was not easy to anticipate. Market dynamics shaped by preceding and succeeding engagements, competing paratheatrical entertainments like lectures or concerts, and poor weather all factored into returns. Upon arrival, stars negotiated with managers over what to perform in what order and with what frequency. Managers sought to balance the market pull of novelty with their own sense of taste and reading of their publics. In emerging entertainment markets like St. Louis, managers and theater boosters grappled with the significance they attached to the "first theatre west of the Mississippi" in relation to the shifting gender and sexual content of commercial entertainments brought by celebrated female performers.

"Classical Actress" and "Danseuse": The Big Stars of the 1830s

Both Ellen Tree and Celeste Elliott, marketed simply as Celeste or Mademoiselle Celeste, amassed fortunes touring the expanding United States, though they followed very different trajectories to stardom. Tree came to the United States as a star in late 1836 following a fifteen-year career on London and provincial stages. She toured the United States for two and a half years, then returned to the English stage and married actor Charles Kean (apparently a lifelong love interest). Celeste's celebrity owed far more to broader American geographies of the 1830s. She first arrived in 1827 as an obscure dancer from the Paris Opera, then used touring to develop a transatlantic reputation, achieving new levels of stardom over the 1830s and then returning to London following her divorce. Both women would resume international touring after another decade following successful managerial careers in London.

Tree and Celeste likewise map the aesthetic poles of transatlantic entertainment culture in the context of its widening markets. Tree represented an older dramatic tradition that American critics were anxious to sustain, while Celeste pushed boundaries of taste, making American markets receptive to new forms of female performance. Tree was a classical English actress in the mold of Fanny Kemble, while Celeste, a dancer who reinvented herself as a pantomime actress, stretched genre categories. Celeste and her husband navigated creatively within a broadening Anglo-Atlantic starring system, experimenting with genre and promotional techniques. She developed new pantomime roles in adventure melodramas that showcased her athletic and expressive abilities, also introducing Romantic ballet to American audiences. While Tree's renown recalled Fanny Kemble, Celeste's celebrity anticipated the Elsslermania of the following decade.

Tree's reputation as a "classical actress" reflected her more mannered acting style, as well as her repertoire, which drew heavily from the "legitimate drama" and favored new dramas emulating this older repertoire.[34] She encouraged comparison with Fanny Kemble, who continued to serve as a model for ideals of dramatic acting after her 1834 retirement, particularly in the United States. Tree usually opened engagements as Julia in James Sheridan Knowles's *The Hunchback*. However, her repertoire also reflected the growth of English melodrama. For example, during her fourteen nights in St. Louis in 1838, Tree performed six English melodramas; four nights of Shakespeare; Hannah Crowley's late eighteenth-century comedy of manners *The Belle's Stratagem;* and her most famous role, the protagonist of T. N. Talfourd's classicizing tragedy *Ion, or the Founding of Argos.* When she adopted Ion, a role intended for an actor and debuted by tragedian William Charles Macready at Covent Garden Theatre in 1836, Tree stretched the dramatic range of the "legitimate" actress.

Tree arrived in St. Louis sixteen months into her American tour, having debuted in New York in December 1836. The demand for return engagements kept her based in the North Atlantic for a full year, playing several engagements in the eastern cities of New York, Philadelphia, and Baltimore, as well as once in Boston in early 1837. Managers of southern and western theaters could rarely expect new stars out their way until late spring, which created a crush of big names coming through in April and May. As manager Smith fretted in May 1839, following Tree's second and last engagement ever in the city, "What is to be our great card in the fall, I should like to know?—There is nothing at the North worth importing—& any how, importations from England will not be through in the Northern Cities in time for us here."[35] After a December 1837 engagement in Baltimore, Tree commenced her first southern tour, probably traveling by sea to Charleston and then to New Orleans. She came up the Mississippi to St. Louis, then returned east by way of Cincinnati, the only reason she considered a St. Louis engagement at all.

Drawing a London star like Ellen Tree to St. Louis was a measure of incorporation, as expanding regions became culturally and economically integrated into the United States and a wider Anglo-Atlantic culture. Stars both stimulated local economies and catalyzed debates about the culture of rapidly developing western cities. When Tree disembarked in St. Louis on April 13, 1838, weeks behind schedule, manager Smith was jubilant, "for the people had about quit coming to the Theatre." He predicted that "she will draw *Tree*-mendously," yet even Smith was surprised by the crowds at the dock trying to "get a squint at her."[36] Accounts from eastern papers that circulated in the port city made residents familiar with the actress "of the Theatre Drury Lane & Covent Garden, London," as playbills nationwide boasted.[37] Smith made sure that Tree's engagement would not be missed, leading an anonymous letter writer to chastise the managers for "gagging the citizens of St. Louis" with the "manner of announcing Miss Tree."[38] The profusion of posted bills used to advertise the engagement seemed an embarrassing, tasteless excess.

Concerns about excessive expressions of enthusiasm reflected boosters' desire to downplay elements of regional culture. As a result, it is often difficult to isolate local reception of transatlantic stars. Papers like the *Missouri Republican*, published in St. Louis, which began to publish sustained drama criticism around 1837, emulated the tone and terms of eastern papers. Critics nationwide agreed that Tree's acting realized ideals of the "legitimate drama." They deployed the adjectives "chaste" and "natural" to commend her interpretations of roles that seemed written for her and through which she epitomized ideals of genteel white femininity. Praise focused on her voice and emotional range, which achieved a middle ground between the "cold, studied declamation of the old school, or the rant of the modern," the latter exemplified by followers of Edmund Kean.[39] In St. Louis, a theatergoer quipped, Tree "does every thing so naturally that it almost seems, that she has not studied [James Sheridan] Knowles, but that he had studied her."[40] Some were surprised to find her acting a bit boring but concluded that the fault lay with the role, because Tree had clearly realized the pinnacle of her art.

In their efforts to imitate eastern discourses and discipline public behavior, boosters connected the viability of theater to the politics of colonization, sometimes quite explicitly. During Tree's 1839 engagement, a local correspondent asked whether "some of the admirers of Miss Tree cannot testify their approval of her acting by demonstrations, a little more refined than such yells and whoops as enliven the wigwams of the Pawnees and Pottawatamies."[41] The analogy here conveyed an established trope in Anglo-American culture that life in a frontier society threatened to turn "civilized" settlers into "savage" Indians. Observers clearly feared that the excessive public enthusiasm for Tree signaled the parochial nature of St. Louis and that local theatergoing publics were not sufficiently disciplined.

While theater boosters in St. Louis worried about audience behavior that did not seem to fit Tree's reputation, critics nationwide grappled with their conceptions of the legitimate drama in light of some of Tree's roles. Like Kemble, Tree introduced new repertoire in America that stretched the category of the classical actress, but unlike Kemble, she also ventured into breeches acting. Tree had performed breeches roles on the London stage, on one occasion acting Romeo to Fanny Kemble's Juliet. As she matured as an actress, Tree sought out opportunities to widen the "legitimate" actress's dramatic range. In America, she played Rosalind in Shakespeare's comedy *As You Like It* and Ion, a role intended for an actor who could model ideals of heroic masculinity (fig. 8). While Ion clearly delighted audiences, critics had a harder time accounting for and assessing the strengths of the performance, given their assumptions about the parts that a classical actress elevating the English drama *should* play. Throughout her US tour, Tree's Ion generated bland encomiums from

Figure 8. This portrait of Ellen Tree as Ion was made
for the *New York Albion*, a literary monthly, by
printmaker Alexander Dick based upon a drawing by
English artist Margaret Gillies. Used by permission of
the Folger Shakespeare Library.

American critics compared with her other roles. The muted responses
to Tree's Ion mapped the boundaries of female performance within the
"legitimate" drama, limits actresses with less established pedigrees were
better able to challenge.[42] St. Louis audiences shared with theatergoers
nationwide enthusiasm for a range of female performances of gender. But
whereas Tree's Ion filled the theater with a conspicuously elite crowd,
according to Sol Smith's report of carriages lining up at the close of the
rainy evening, neither newspaper reviewed the performance. Even as critics worked to discipline tastes, in St. Louis they clearly preferred silence
to censure when facing an English star of Tree's stature in a breeches role
that disrupted their expectations of female performance.

Tree was celebrated within recognizable categories that conformed to ideals of tastemakers and theater boosters, which made some of her roles challenging for critics. Celeste, in contrast, stretched and combined categories of entertainment. She opened up more subversive and sexualized avenues for female stage celebrity. This created the context in which less established players experimented artistically and professionally. Crucially, Celeste embraced the opportunities of an expanding transatlantic entertainment marketplace with her innovative repertoire.

Celeste built her career through transatlantic itinerancy, moving strategically up the hierarchy of metropolitan theaters in New York and then London and launching herself as an itinerant star in an expanding American geography. The seventeen-year-old dancer came to New York from Paris in 1827 with her mother after she was engaged by manager Charles Gilfert for the new Bowery Theatre. He hired her on a two-year contract at $37.50 per week, at the high end of a stock performer's salary and equivalent to $974 today.[43] There she worked with other dancers engaged from Parisian theaters, including her sister, a constant presence in Celeste's rising career. In early 1828 Celeste married Henry Elliott, who helped her navigate a foreign entertainment industry, though conflicts over her commitment to touring dogged their marriage. After the Bowery Theatre burned down in June 1828, the sisters secured an engagement at the Park Theatre and then toured eastern theaters. In 1830 they departed for England, where Celeste gave birth to a daughter. She began developing a new repertoire while moving up the hierarchy of London theaters, securing coveted engagements at the Drury Lane and Covent Garden Theatres in 1833.[44] In late 1834 Celeste returned to the New York as a star with an original repertoire, now billed as the "celebrated melo dramatic Actress, from the theatres Druy [sic] Lane and Covent Garden, London, and the Grand Opera, Paris."[45]

Celeste toured American theaters from late 1834 until July 1837, when she returned to England, and again from September 1838 until June 1840. She circulated within an expanding geography that increased the profits of an American tour and could sustain an itinerant performer for consecutive seasons, particularly with the strategic introduction of new pieces at return engagements. She began in New York in November 1834 and over the following year played engagements in Philadelphia, Boston, Albany, New York, and Montreal, Quebec. She traveled south for the winter to New Orleans and Mobile. In early 1836 Celeste traveled back to Washington by land, then moved up the Atlantic coast, repeating the circuit of the previous year. During the winter of 1837 she returned to the Deep South via the Western Country routes. She played Louisville,

Kentucky, on both sides of the journey to New Orleans (and Mobile), also adding engagements in Vicksburg and Cincinnati.[46] Her 1838 tour began in New York in September. She reached New Orleans in early 1839 and eventually made her way to St. Louis in May 1839. Celeste planned to return to England at the end of the yearlong tour, but though she booked a transatlantic passage for October 1839, her husband continued to line up engagements for her.[47]

Celeste's stylistic promiscuity and inventiveness contributed to her popularity and professional longevity. During the height of her American celebrity, in the late 1830s, Celeste featured her pantomime skills in protean or multirole melodramas that were set in exotic locales with plots built around disguise and adventure. Pantomime was a form of theatrical dance that developed in Parisian boulevard theaters in the eighteenth century using "gestural action to tell a story" rather than song or dialogue.[48] The form was adopted by English acting troupes and by the nineteenth century was being used to showcase women in elaborate adventure melodramas or fantasy spectacles. Protean melodramas adapted and popularized by Celeste allowed the actress to play multiple "characters," often remaining almost entirely in transvestite disguise while performing various athletic feats. The nautical drama *The Wizard Skiff; or, The Tongueless Pirate Boy* included the "Greek Sailor Dance" and the "Grand War Dance," a stage combat. In *The French Spy*, a "grand Military, and historical, Dramatic Spectacle, founded on the late conquest of Algiers," Celeste played a woman who, in order to rescue her captive lover, takes on the disguise of a soldier and then that of a "wild Arab boy," in turn performing the "Wild Arab Dance."[49] These plots contained conceits such that the actress never spoke, her muteness facilitating the character's gender transgressions (fig. 9). Celeste also developed a repertoire of pieces founded on American frontier mythology. An adaptation of a James Fenimore Cooper novel, *The Wept of Wish-ton-Wish*, followed the adventures of Puritan Hope Gough as she becomes Narramatta, the wife of a Narragansett man, and gets caught up in King Philip's War.

Plot descriptions or surviving scripts are a poor substitute for the different registers on which these pieces operated and the subversive possibilities contained in them. On the one hand, "actress-as-boy" roles in protean melodramas that manifested the "ubiquitous association between childishness and femininity" rendered transvestism in these dramas less problematic than tragic male roles involving the performance of adult masculinity (Tree's Ion was often read within the "actress-as-boy" framework as well).[50] Yet with their myriad "transgressions of gender, race and sexuality [and] lots of athleticism," these pieces clearly also functioned

Figure 9. Engraving of Celeste in *The Wizard Skiff*, the
figure's face and body conveying the "actress-as-boy"
aesthetic of protean breeches roles. Harvard Theatre
Collection, Houghton Library, Harvard University.

as "free-ranging fantas[ies]" of female "heroism and sexual display."[51] A
straightforward example of the sexual fantasies attached to dance pantomime is an erotic print of unknown provenance titled *Madlle Celeste
as the Wild Arab Boy*, which depicts her transvestite character from *The
French Spy* with the addition of wings associated with the fairy ballet
La Sylphide (see figs. 15 and 16 in chapter 5). The skirt lifts away to reveal bare legs and a detailed drawing of female genitalia, a novel peek-
a-boo feature tied to the erotic possibility of a dancer's twirls and leg
extensions. The transgressive power of her performances, on the other
hand, is suggested by a remarkable commercial lithograph also of Celeste's "wild Arab boy," which undoubtedly circulated well beyond the
touring circuit of a big star like Celeste (fig. 10). In this image, the artist
struggles to capture the transvestite performance against conventions

Figure 10. This remarkable portrait of Celeste as the
"wild Arab boy" in *The French Spy* hints at the transgressive possibilities of Celeste's male roles in protean
adventure melodrama. Harvard Theatre Collection,
Houghton Library, Harvard University.

for illustrating the female body, especially of dancers, while suggesting
elements of Celeste's performance that excited audiences. The extreme
musculature of the figure, which both marked the transvestite character and may have been a more accurate representation of Celeste's tall,
athletic build, strains against the common elements of sentimental fe-
tishization common in dancer imagery. A pantaloon costume drapes a
tiny waist, and a high full bosom curves beneath a one-shouldered costume. A bare breast is obscured by the figure's arm, suggesting the kind
of exposure that may have been an erotic fantasy for some. The delicate
facial features (though dressed in a moustache) and small feet clad in a
dancer's slippers conform to conventions for representing the female

form. Yet the overall effect of the image retains a gendered ambiguity both arresting and erotically charged.

Though Celeste was one of the biggest stars of the 1830s, serious criticism of her remained sparse compared with the earnest analysis reserved for thespians like Tree. Celeste's "extraordinary success," noted the editor of *Godey's Lady's Book* in 1836, prompted "great indignation" from the "gentlemen of the press," hence the relative critical silence.[52] Another women's literary monthly, the *Ladies' Companion*, correctly (if derisively) attributed Celeste's popularity to her stylistic inventiveness, "vitiating the public taste by extravagance [and] by Gladiatorial attitudes as unfeminine as they are unnatural."[53] For these critics, Celeste's extreme popularity should not have been. She defied a hierarchical logic according to which genteel publics, particularly the readership of these periodicals, should prefer legitimate drama to the exciting displays of transvestite athleticism in Celeste's adventure melodramas.

Critics struggled to position these entertainments within existing frameworks while grappling with their universal popularity. A New Orleans newspaper surveying the rival performances of *The French Spy* by Celeste and English actress Bertha Lewis asked whether it was "*leg*-iti-mate" drama, conveying anxieties about the taste level and erotic appeal of breeches performance with a pointed play on words. The humorist noted that "*legs* draw" when "nothing else" can, for "no man who ever goes . . . is satisfied until he sees them again." Built into the pun on legitimate drama was a question about whether these performances could be called legitimate, concern with the draw of sex appeal, and fear these entertainments might erode public taste for legitimate drama. According to the New Orleans satirist, "When he sees them for the second time, [he] is worse off than he was before."[54] Though the imagined spectator in this scenario was a man, women were prominent in Celeste's audience. In St. Louis, where Celeste opened on May 22, 1839, in *The French Spy*, critics assured "the most fastidious" that they "might look upon her exhibitions without a blush," an aside that may have managed discomfort about an excited female public.[55]

Celeste also introduced American audiences to Romantic ballets from the royal Paris Opera, performing *La Sylphide* and the temple dance from Daniel Auber's opera *Le dieu et la bayadère*, though she quickly dropped *La Sylphide*, the least successful in her repertoire. The ballet was more popular with Americans when performed by dancers who remained firmly within the royal ballet tradition, like Augusta St. James and, ultimately, Fanny Elssler.[56] Elssler's unprecedented celebrity tour in 1840–42 built upon the familiarity of American audiences with Parisian dance forms introduced by Celeste and Augusta. Unlike other European dancers touring the United States in the 1830s who came out of the Paris Opera, especially her immediate rival, Augusta, Celeste developed an original repertoire that combined elements of the royal Paris Opera ballet and the "melodramatic ballet-pantomimes" of Parisian boulevard theaters.[57] Still, she innovated from these traditions as she developed new adventure melodramas for her Anglophone audience. In billing herself as a "melo dramatic actress" who performed mute pantomime roles, Celeste carved out a rare niche for herself in a shifting Atlantic entertainment culture interested in sentimental storytelling, acrobatic and expressive movement, and erotic display. She inspired imitators like Bertha Lewis while encouraging further innovation.

Celeste further defied American expectations about the earning threshold for a star performer. This was more remarkable because she was not a legitimate dramatic actress like Fanny Kemble or Ellen Tree. In March 1836 a correspondent of the *Spirit of the Times* reported that Celeste had earned $84,530 in fifteen months, equivalent to $2.3 million today, and by December 1836 there were rumors she had "already cleared over *One Hundred Thousand Dollars*," or $2.7 million. The paper marveled at a "theatrical person realizing such a large competency at the age of twenty-five," much of it *"without speaking a solitary word on the stage."*[58] Legitimate actresses had not made such fortunes. These numbers were probably not an exaggeration: in August 1835, writing to Sol Smith about an engagement for Mobile, Henry Elliott boasted that in her first eight months, Celeste "received . . . thirty five thousand dollars," in today's value, her first million. The *Spirit of the Times* later reported that her twelve nights "in the comparatively small town of Mobile . . . cleared upwards of $4000," and she cleared $18,000 from two New Orleans engagements.[59]

But with Celeste and, later, Fanny Elssler, the mania for public figures was treated as a dangerous irrational excess that could threaten the republic. A New Orleans paper referred to this excitement as a "species of mania—*Celeste mania*," applying a term generally associated with public fads that had earlier been used to describe excitement over Edmund Kean and Clara Fisher.[60] In 1836, a contentious election year, a political cartoon titled *The Celeste-al Cabinet* deployed discomfort with Celeste's popularity to attack President Andrew Jackson and his government. In the cartoon Celeste performs before Jackson and his cabinet, portrayed as old lechers and ineffectual leaders. They are distracted from the "weighty matters" of state by a woman with "grace enough to dance all the surplus Revenue out of the Treasury," an allusion both to Jackson's disastrous financial policy and Celeste's reputed earnings.[61]

Celeste and Henry Elliott were savvy promoters. As Philadelphia dancer and theater chronicler Charles Durang recalled, Elliott used his (waning) fortune and then Celeste's growing wealth to "inaugurat[e] a new system of newspaper puffery and expletive play-bill display."[62] Playbills in this period highlighted the name of the star and the title of the main drama and afterpiece, usually accompanied by a cast listing and some of the features that would interest audiences. Bills might also broadcast how many times a play had been performed (upward of four hundred nights!) and where. Celeste's billing emphasized her protean transformations. Her name on playbills appeared in the largest type, followed by an "expletive" listing of her roles:

Celeste in two Grand Dramas! Celeste as the Wild Arab Boy !
Celeste in two Grand Dramas! Celeste as the Gipsy Boy ! !
Celeste and the Pirate Boy! ! ! Celeste as the Greek Girl ! ! !
Celeste as the French Lancer ! ! ! ! Celeste as the Algerian
                 Girl ! ! ! !

CELESTE IN TWO GRAND
   COMBATS ! ! ! ![63]

Theaters pasted massive advertisements on their exteriors and throughout the city. It is reasonable to imagine this kind of "expletive play-bill display" plastering walls, fences, carts, and placards.

Celeste's reputation also played with the question of her identity as a Frenchwoman married to an American. This was accomplished through Celeste's savvy use of the curtain speech. Though Celeste did not deliver dialogue in her dramatic performances, she did speak to her audiences after the performance, adapting the curtain speech popularized in the United States by Edmund Kean during his tours of the 1820s, particularly during her two farewell tours, in 1837 and then 1839 (the farewell that was not). When published in newspapers, these speeches extended the reach of Celeste's celebrity. They spoke back to some of the skeptical, dismissive, or critical commentary then circulating about her. In a farewell address delivered in New Orleans in March 1837, Celeste spoke of her "unexampled success" and "gratitude" for the "brilliant expressions of your favor." She both highlighted her achievements and attributed them to her publics, who gave a "welcome and a home" to a "wanderer" and "stranger." Though "about to visit Europe," Celeste insisted that America was the "home of my heart." "I proudly boast myself an American," she declared, no doubt eliciting a cheer from the crowd.[64] Later that summer in Baltimore, she pledged to make the city her home, gushing, "Would you know how a French girl loves America with all her heart."[65] Certainly, her decision to adapt American frontier fantasies into staged pantomime melodramas enhanced this notion that Celeste was fascinated with her adopted homeland.

Celeste's marriage to an American early in her career made it easier for her to navigate a foreign entertainment industry dominated by male powerbrokers. The marriage also made it possible for Celeste to maintain an imprimatur of respectability in her private life. While Celeste crossed boundaries of gender and race onstage, she appeared to conform to the roles of wife and mother in her private life. This protected her professionally during a crisis in her marriage that culminated in her husband's (unsuccessful) divorce suit in early 1841. By 1839 conditions within her marriage had deteriorated significantly. Henry was seriously ill and anxious to keep Celeste on American stages. He refused to return to Europe with her in October 1839. In June 1840 she sailed for France without his knowledge just as he had concluded an engagement for her in Philadelphia. A week later, a Philadelphia paper published a rumor that Celeste had eloped with the Brazilian consul to Le Havre. This story was swiftly and successfully countered by reports from friends correcting the details of her destination (France), company (alone and under the "protection" of the captain of the vessel), and reasons for leaving (a dying mother).[66]

While Celeste's husband may have had an interest in making alleged adultery public, the press latched on to a more appealing image of Celeste as a model of duty and forbearance. The expected scandal of an adulterous dancer instead became a melodrama about the limits of wifely sacrifice and the relative weight of a woman's duty to obey and nurse her "invalid" husband or bid farewell to a dying parent. Because Celeste had "hitherto maintained an unsullied reputation" and had cultivated friends whose testimony was believed by the press, the more appealing sentimental narrative of a devoted but suffering wife won out.[67] This characterization actually fit quite well with the roles Celeste played onstage, in which she entered frays to rescue a lover or a parent, a transgressive means to a worthy, emotionally satisfying end. Even the Philadelphia paper that broke the scandal referenced rumors that Celeste suffered "ill usage," though it clarified that this was no "justification of adultery" when "legal remedies" were available, "provided his treatment . . . was harsh and unbecoming."[68]

Celeste's defenders also appealed to a boundary between her private life and public celebrity that they urged journalists to honor even while strategically deploying details to generate sympathy. A "Friend of the Family" reminded readers to respect the "sacred" domestic sphere. If there "be any domestic differences . . . the world has no right to trouble itself."[69] Another referenced the worthy sentiments in the letter Celeste had left for her husband, then reminded readers that "nothing *ought* to be said on the subject, as it is a private, and not a matter of public concern."[70] Celeste's allies did not so much keep her private life from disrupting her celebrity as strategically deploy her private life when it threatened to disrupt both her career and her celebrity.

In spite of her unprecedented success as a star entertainer, Celeste actually had little to show financially for the last decade of her career. Henry Elliott controlled much of her fortune and had lost sizeable amounts in bad investments. Money troubles were probably a major factor in his divorce suit, along with disagreements over Celeste's desire to return to Europe. In January 1841, while Celeste was still overseas, Henry sued for a legislative divorce in the state of Maryland. If the suit was successful, a Baltimore paper reported, Celeste "would lose all right of dower to the property she earned."[71] It is not clear from surviving records whether Henry filed on the basis of desertion or adultery, both grounds for divorce in Maryland. During the proceedings he tried to "blast [Celeste's] reputation . . . by endeavoring to prove that she had been faithless to the marriage vows."[72] Elliott was probably behind the rumors of adultery that followed Celeste's departure for Europe. The divorce was an attempt to seize control of the remainder of his wife's fortune in her absence. Henry was seriously ill but clearly dependent upon Celeste's earnings. Or maybe he merely hoped the divorce suit would compel Celeste to return to him.

In February the Maryland legislature rejected Elliott's suit, yet he continued to control his wife's fortune even after his death in July 1842. He left Celeste's sister $7,000, though executors found that the estate was ultimately worth only $10,781.68, or $343,000 today.[73] Celeste, meanwhile, left America and her squandered fortune behind. Henry may have been a skilled promoter, but he was a disastrous financial partner, and maybe worse. Her success navigating a shifting transatlantic entertainment culture had not survived the property laws governing marriage.

Experimenting with "Novelty" in the Field: The "Lesser Luminaries"

Celeste must have been surprised to arrive in New Orleans in March 1837 and encounter competition at a rival theater from Bertha Lewis's interpretation of *The French Spy*. Celeste's artistic inventiveness and celebrity created the context for Lewis's career. In fact, by the time Celeste and

Ellen Tree, the big stars of the late 1830s, played "Far West" St. Louis, many of their most popular pieces had been performed by lesser luminaries or the stock company. Itinerant performers like Bertha Lewis, who debuted *The French Spy* in the river city in March 1838, a year before Celeste arrived there, formed crucial cultural bridges across the expanding nation.

Western markets allowed a new cohort of stars with obscure origins to emerge over the 1830s, touring regionally and nationally and introducing exciting but controversial forms of female performance. They were vital to regional theaters, particularly in the South and West, where managers had to wait until the big stars had made a circuit of northern theaters. Managers spaced performers like Lewis, Frances Denny Drake, Frances Pritchard, and Annette Nelson (Hodges) between the big stars and stock novelties. Though managers like Ludlow complained that these "two-penny candles and farthing rush-lights" were economically unreliable, actually they were vital to the shifting economics of managing a viable theater in a growing commercial city like St. Louis.

A peripheral market like St. Louis offered performers the opportunity to experiment with new repertoire and play with the diverse tastes and demand for novelty across regional markets. Both Frances Drake and Frances Pritchard developed starring careers in the trans-Appalachian West and South in the 1830s but positioned themselves very differently in relation to new repertoire as they each sought to compete in an expanding starring market. Drake began her career as a teenager in 1817 as part of a strolling (itinerant) company along with Noah Ludlow. In the intervening decades, she married a fellow actor with whom she managed a circuit of theaters in Kentucky. After his death in 1830, she focused on her itinerant starring career. Pritchard's popularity as a star actress came a good decade after she arrived in the United States from the British West Indies in 1822 as part of an equestrian troupe, then performing as "Mrs. Tatnall." Shortly after, she left the circus, refashioning a career as a stock actress and later as a star under her maiden name (her fourth husband preferred that she not connect his family name with the theater).[74]

During the 1830s both Drake and Pritchard appealed to western audiences by refreshing familiar repertoire with new melodramas. For Drake's 1837 engagement, Smith asked her to "play in as many new pieces as possible" to keep attendance steady. While much of the two actresses' repertoire overlapped, Drake remained firmly within the tragic "line of business," while Pritchard drew on her experience as an equestrian to perform a series of adventure roles with great success.[75] Both actresses appeared as the tragic title character of Matthew Lewis's *Adelgitha; or, The Fruits of a Single Error*, an English play at this point three decades old. Drake had been playing it her entire career. In such roles, actresses aspired to move their audiences through a cathartic sympathetic experience that rested upon audience familiarity with the play. However, during her 1837 St. Louis engagement, Drake, who was nearing forty, seemed too distant from the character to "impart . . . the deep interest and admiration which it once commanded." The local critic preferred her in a more mature fallen woman character, Madame Clermont in Walter Diamond's melodrama *Adrian and Orilla; or, A Mother's Vengeance*, in which Drake "exert[ed] her wonted sway over the feelings of her audience," inspiring "decided, though not rude applause, and the tears of the female, aye, and several of the male portion of the audience."[76] Both actresses also included the new French melodrama *La tour de Nesle*, about the adulterous murderer Margaret of Burgundy, in their 1837 engagements. Unlike Drake, Pritchard interspersed these with breeches parts, in some cases inciting controversy.

In contrast to Drake, who was critically celebrated, Pritchard was popular with audiences but controversial. Managers tried to discipline her daring breeches repertoire, though it was clearly popular with audiences and economically beneficial to theaters. In addition to *Adelgitha* and *La tour de Nesle*, Pritchard's 1837 engagement featured her in breeches as the title character of the adventure melodrama *Alberti Contarini; or, The Bandit of the Abruzzi*. She followed this with a "Melo Drama of *Wallace, or the Scottish Chiefs*," in which Pritchard as Marian (but not Wallace) donned a male disguise. A clear divide emerged between enthusiastic St. Louis audiences and a local critic who satirized the entertainments. The critic subtitled *Alberti Contarini* "the Comedy of Blunders" and speculated that the historic William Wallace "tremble[d] in his urn" over "the brave *Marian* as the Knight of the Golden Plume."[77]

Some of Pritchard's explorations of male repertoire pushed too far. In an 1836 engagement, she played the male hero of *Pizarro*, a well-known and popular German melodrama from the late eighteenth century written by August von Kotzebue (and translated by Richard Sheridan) about the Spanish conquest of the Americas. Her performance as the hero, Rolla, produced a scandal not only because she chose a heroic role formerly played only by men but also because of her costuming. Manager Ludlow considered the hero of *Pizarro* "*most* unfit for a lady," especially when, as she tumbled, the actress's "white Peruvian shirt" was "carried nearly over her head," exposing the "flesh-colored 'tights'" beneath and "exhibit[ing] a *stern* reality that caused the men to laugh and the ladies to hide their blushes." For Ludlow, indecent exposure exacerbated inappropriate casting. For her 1837 engagement, Pritchard may have agreed to "appear in petticoats" as Rolla's love interest, Elvira, because of pressure from Ludlow, a decision possibly at odds with their mutual financial interests.[78]

Ludlow and Smith featured women in breeches roles but remained conflicted, especially when women tried to play roles intended for actors, like Rolla and even Richard III. Smith was relieved when the Lewis family of English actors, consisting of Bertha, Henry, and their daughter, "Petite Bertha," arrived in St. Louis in March 1838 at the end of a cold, cash-poor winter. Smith felt conflicted about whether to feature "Mrs. Lewis" in "her men's parts"—"monstrosities" he called them in his memoir. Smith relented and "put up *Richard*," starring Bertha Lewis as Richard III. Smith's dread of public taste was realized, "for altho' it was a very disagreeable night, it produced the best receipts of any night of the season" thus far.[79] The *Missouri Republican* was less appalled but felt the performance "lacked—just what a *lady's* personification might be expected to lack—masculine energy." It was "passable" strictly as a "novelty."[80] St. Louis press and management preferred Lewis in *The French Spy*. Though the actress actually spent much of the piece in breeches costume, the paper noted approvingly that compared with Richard III, "Mrs. Lewis looks 'herself again'—a splendid woman," though "a little more regard to delicacy of costume" would be ideal.[81] Later that season the *Commercial Bulletin* and *Missouri Republican* diverged in their assessment of Lewis's performance of masculinity in different roles. While the *Bulletin* hoped Lewis would play Romeo to Ellen Tree's Juliet, noting that Lewis's "step" and the "deep tones of her voice" suited the role, the *Republican* disagreed.[82] Ludlow ignored this, and Lewis delivered a "chaste and beautiful" performance as Romeo—according to the *Bulletin*, at least.[83]

Actresses had more opportunities to experiment with new repertoire in regional markets and, in the rare case of Charlotte Barnes, used touring to star in original dramas. While women like Mary Clarke and Louisa Medina, in-house playwright for Thomas Hamblin, tried with varying degrees of success to sell original dramas, Barnes starred in her own dramas. Given the absence of dramatic copyright law, playwrights did not possess the same legal rights to their compositions as other authors; thus, their profits came exclusively from the sale of a manuscript to a manager or star performer. Most managers preferred to produce new plays that had been successful in England, which cost them no more to produce. Even after passage of dramatic copyright law in the United

States in 1856, profits continued to be controlled by managers and per-formers.[84] Barnes's unique combination of actress and playwright helped her to sell her plays and compete as a star. Her parents, Mary and John Barnes, arrived in 1816 from England and developed reputations as reliable stock actors based out of New York's Park Theatre. Eventually, they prepared their daughter, Charlotte, born in 1818, for a stage career. Except for a two-year sojourn in England, the Barnes family remained in the United States. By 1836 they had left stock work and were touring the eastern seaboard as far south as Charleston.[85] Ludlow had a low opinion of their talents, recalling how they "wandered out . . . depending upon such chances as they could get to play" in order to "give their daughter . . . as much practice as possible before mak[ing] a grand attempt in the cities of the East."[86] They toured to augment their professional stature and earning potential but also to support Charlotte's burgeoning play-writing career.

Itinerancy allowed Charlotte to try new leading business and stage her own dramatic works. During engagements, Charlotte often used her benefit night to put on one of her own compositions. Managers were rarely willing to present an untried piece during regular nights, but on benefit night, performers shouldered more risk—and reward. For an 1837 Mobile engagement, manager Smith made a different calculation and de-cided to bill Charlotte's drama *Lafitte, the Pirate of the Gulf* during the regular engagement. *Lafitte* was based on a popular new novel of the same name about a notorious local pirate. Although Smith was extremely dis-missive of the "trashy piece," it drew the biggest receipts of the family's ten nights.[87] In his memoir, Ludlow dismissed Charlotte's playwriting, which extended beyond the acceptable sphere of labor for women in the business, but dwelt at length on her failing as an actress due to her poor "stage face," "unmusical and weak . . . voice," and "near-sighted[ness]." For Ludlow, Charlotte failed where he expected a woman in theater to succeed; her lackluster abilities as a lead actress made it impossible for him to take her seriously as a playwright. Still, one manager's reluctance to countenance Charlotte's dramatic authorship did not matter in the scheme of her career. Itinerancy made it possible for Charlotte to produce her compositions and develop a renown that did not require conforming to standards of beauty expected of actresses. Over the 1840s, Charlotte actually achieved more renown for her playwriting than for her acting. In 1841 she traveled with her widowed mother to London, where she successfully produced several of her plays.[88]

Even as star actresses embraced new forms of female spectacle fea-tured in English and American melodramas and European operas, this expanding repertoire circumscribed women's careers in new ways. With the popularization of pantomime spectacles, expectations that female stars conform to narrower standards of youth, beauty, and sexual desirability intensified. When Annette Nelson first played in St. Louis as a star in 1836, she was en route from New Orleans to New York with a company of vocalists. She began acting in London around 1830 and came to New Orleans in 1833 with her father to join the Camp Street Theatre company. She married English tenor Charles Coppleton Hodges a year later.[89] Marriage may have been an avenue to professional autonomy. The couple joined a small touring company in 1836, its members seeking out both ensemble and solo engagements. Only Nelson played St. Louis, the management having no "wish, or intention to do any important Operas."[90] Unfortunately, the engagement "amounted to nothing—*for her.*"[91] None of Nelson's houses reached the threshold for sharing terms except her benefit. After division of profits, Nelson took only $35 for two weeks, a mere $974 today.[92] By comparison, the highest-paid actress in the St. Louis company, Eliza Petrie, made $30 per week. St. Louis may have seemed a wasted detour for Nelson; however, she was earning more on the road than at the Camp Street Theatre and building her reputation. She had also secured an engagement at the Bowery Theatre in New York, which would enhance her reputation and grow her earning potential.

Annette and Charles arrived in New York in September 1836 only to watch the Bowery burn to the ground in another devastating fire. Nelson did not have the stature for an engagement at the Park Theatre. She might have tried to find a stock position at another theater or go back on the road, but it was late in the season for both options. Instead, she made a remarkable professional move, opening a small uptown theater, Richmond Hill, as "Miss Nelson's Theatre" for a two-month season, featuring spectacle melodramas and light opera. The highlight of the season was her debut of a new opera from London's Lyceum Theatre, *The Mountain Sylph* (an adaptation of *La Sylphide*). By the new year, she was back on the road as a star, supported by her husband, a shadowy figure who was probably instrumental in his wife's professional moves.[93]

Though she performed in operas, Nelson's reputation became tied to her roles as a "pantomime actress" and her ability to perform dangerous aerial work on a wire (fig. 11). Nelson's celebrated adaptation of *The Mountain Sylph* used stage machinery that created the illusion of flight while "display[ing] . . . her form of 'purest mould' . . . to great advantage."[94] Nelson might have remained a relatively obscure stock actress, but instead she adapted new repertoire from England to carve out a niche as a star performing pantomime spectacles. Her second year of touring

Figure 11. This 1836 engraving of Annette Nelson in *The Mountain Sylph* exemplifies the genteel eroticism of dancer portraits, the dancer as both an otherworldly creature and sexualized object. Library of Congress Prints and Photographs Division Washington, D.C., http://hdl.loc.gov/loc.pnp/cph.3b36369.

brought her to national notice with a widely reprinted account of her performance in *The Mountain Sylph* in Washington, DC, before a Native American delegation. The article deployed the familiar white trope of the credulous Indian, suggesting that the "untutored men" misunderstood Nelson's aerial work as "a more than human exertion of power." This account dramatized the very feature of Nelson's performance that made it exciting nationwide but through the eyes of an exoticized, colonized subject. The excerpt that reached readers in St. Louis, however, drew dismissive commentary from a local editor for owing more to "imagination" than "facts."[95] St. Louis was not so credulous as readers in other metropoles, though it would have to wait six more months for its chance to see the sylph's daring ascent.

A repertoire that privileged beauty and sexual desirability just as readily trapped female performers in narrowing expectations about the qualities of a compelling star. Audiences brought new expectations even to old favorites, like the opera *Cinderella*, which was mounted with increasingly elaborate scenery, machinery, and female spectacle. The relative importance of svelte virginal beauty even overrode a singer's voice. English opera singer Charlotte Watson Bailey wanted to perform *Cinderella* during her October 1837 St. Louis engagement with fellow English singer Charles Plumer, but at seven months pregnant, the newly married twenty-year-old singer did not conform to manager Smith's conception of the piece. There were other calculations in play. Management preferred to use the opera as a stock piece, which kept all profits in-house and featured the company's young, unmarried, and popular lead actress, Eliza Petrie, in the title role. When Smith refused Bailey, the stars "tried hard (thro' the Press &c) to *force*" the piece, but as Smith boasted in private correspondence, "L[udlow] & S[mith] are the hardest 'colts' to *force* into harness." Smith was probably behind some of the articles defending management, including a bald allusion to Bailey's "condition" asserting that she could not "hold the mirror up to nature."[96] Smith was less circumspect in his private correspondence: Bailey was "big as a small hogshead! It was no go." Instead, Smith offered Bailey the role of Fairy Queen, but she insisted on "Cinderella or nothing."[97] Bailey expected to be able to choose the roles she played for her starring engagement. The singer must have been furious. But by taking recourse through allies in the press, Bailey avoided a direct appeal, making herself invisible as an interested party in the matter of casting. Unfortunately, the strategy backfired. As an itinerant, Bailey did not have enough pull in the local market to generate support for her Cinderella, but neither was she beholden to the aesthetic vision and company dynamics of the St. Louis theater. She left.

At the opening of her Bowery Theatre engagement in September 1842, Celeste delivered a curtain speech. She did not express gratitude or praise her audience, as in the past. Rather, she reminded them of the context and longevity of her career. "I was here longer than Elssler," she declared, referring to the Austrian dancer, who had recently returned to Europe. "I drew more money. Everywhere the houses were crowded to overflowing. Elssler could do no more." Nor could Celeste resist an additional dig at her competition: "I am younger than Miss Elssler, and flatter myself . . . that I am rather prettier!"[98] In contrast to Elssler, who toured for two (remarkable) years in the United States, Celeste had shaped her career by an almost continual transatlantic circuit. Celeste clearly worried that she would not be viable if she could not distinguish herself from other European entertainers who would follow. Celeste ultimately spent the next decade in England, becoming manager of London's Lyceum Theatre, where she developed new repertoire, even branching into speaking roles. In the mid-1850s she returned yet again to the United States to tour.

Celeste was part of a cohort of European women who developed their professional reputations and earning potential within rapidly expanding American theater markets. At key moments over the 1820s and 1830s, foreign women explored the capacity of the American starring system to grow and transform their careers, and they would continue to do so through midcentury. The 1832 debut of English actress Fanny Kemble represented a watershed for English stage celebrity in the American market. But most starring women coming from England and continental Europe over the next decade toured more widely than Kemble had and with a more diverse repertoire. Nor would the transatlantic starring system of the 1830s be dominated by stars of legitimate drama. Most of the major stars had more in common with Lydia Kelly and Clara Fisher than Fanny Kemble. They played to American audiences eager for new European melodramas and operas that featured female spectacle.

The expansion of residential theater into the South and West over the late 1810s and 1820s created new potential markets for itinerants. Likewise, these theaters came to depend on stars to satisfy the tastes of new settlers and commercial migrants. While foreign starring women of the 1830s continued to debut in New York and make a northeastern circuit, most continued south or west, touring for at least two years. Theaters in growing western cities like St. Louis simultaneously sought appearances by big stars like Celeste and Ellen Tree and relied on a roster of second-tier star entertainers. Some of these performers, like Frances Denny Drake, had built careers as stock performers in the United States. Increasingly, new immigrants, like Annette Nelson, used regional itinerancy to shift rapidly out of stock work, increasing their earning potential. Itinerancy also gave them the ability to experiment with new repertoire, though women faced more pressure to deploy their sexual desirability as part of their appeal.

Increased professional mobility and earning power did not automatically translate into professional autonomy for these women. Men remained the gatekeepers within the business as managers of theaters, local critics, and, crucially, agents for starring women. Fathers and husbands handled business for daughters and wives, which meant that marriage remained a crucial professional decision. While some women, mostly unmarried women and widows, achieved real autonomy on the road, for the majority, family continued to form a key context for their starring careers. Men could be professional allies and strategists, but gender-based hierarchies in the business and the legal and ideological frameworks governing the family meant that women could lose their earnings and professional autonomy quite easily.

As Viennese dancer Fanny Elssler discovered when she came to the United States with amateur theatrical agent Henry Wickoff in 1840, transformations in American celebrity culture intensified public scrutiny of female stage celebrities. Their enhanced earning potential, meanwhile, made them vulnerable to male gatekeepers competing for a cut of their profits. Many of Elssler's experiences mirrored Kemble's, but whereas Kemble had arrived as the avatar of an established entertainment form, Elssler arrived in a country with a mere decade of exposure to European theatrical dance forms. The starring women of the 1830s were a bridge for a new transatlantic celebrity mania.

5 Danger, Desire, and Celebrity Mania

Fanny Elssler in America, 1840–1842

Fanny Elssler had no idea her donation to the Bunker Hill Monument Association would create such a fuss. She was merely inspired by the "expressions of *national* feeling, so widely called forth for the completion" of the memorial obelisk overlooking Boston that commemorated one of the first skirmishes of the American War for Independence. As Elssler explained in her letter to Joseph T. Buckingham, the president of the Bunker Hill Monument Association, a donation, in the form of either a gift of money or a benefit performance at the theater, would allow her to "manifest her deep sense of obligation to the Americans for their unparalleled generosity to her."[1] Americans, or rather Bostonians, flatly disagreed. The monument, which remained unfinished fifteen years after the cornerstone had been laid, "should be built by American citizens, or it should not be built at all," the *Boston Morning Post* declared. It was "not proper."[2] Nonetheless, Buckingham accepted the offer on behalf of the association. Buckingham's newspaper, the *Boston Courier*, became Elssler's lone defender in the uproar that followed.

Elssler decided to perform a benefit rather than donate directly, perhaps hoping to mollify some of the critics. On October 1, 1840, Boston's Tremont Theatre opened its doors for a performance of the Romantic ballet *La Sylphide*, Elssler's second to last performance in the city. Boston's partisan mercantile dailies, meanwhile, joined the religious press in condemning Elssler's gesture as inappropriate and insulting. Papers

throughout the country followed and chimed in. The controversy manifested some of the troubling implications of Elssler's celebrity that had
been building over the first six months of her tour about the relationship between Americans and European culture and the susceptibility of
Americans to foreign celebrity. In the Bunker Hill donation controversy,
Elssler's popularity with American audiences and the financial windfall
of her tour threatened to corrupt a civic institution of public memory. As
critics swiftly recast the "divine Fanny" as a "dancing girl" and French
prostitute, they responded to what they regarded as the dangerous excess of her celebrity. The controversy captured anxieties around the outsized popularity of a European opera star and the changing boundaries of
American entertainment and culture.

The Viennese dancer, lately the star dancer of the Paris Opera, had
arrived in the United States in the spring of 1840 at the height of her career. Elssler was not the first European ballerina to appear in American
theaters. Since the 1790s dancers trained in Europe had not only toured
American theaters but also established themselves with stock companies and trained subsequent generations of American-born dancers. One
dance scholar has characterized Elssler's 1840–42 American tour as the
"culmination" of a half century of dancers from France in the United
States.[3] Elssler's celebrity built upon the familiarity of many theatergoers
with the conventions of French dance, though she remained one of the
most accomplished ballerinas to perform in the United States. Americans in turn drew on established critical frameworks used to assess her
predecessors and concluded that Elssler surpassed them with her "poetry
of motion."[4]

Elssler and her sister Therese had trained for the ballet in Vienna
in the 1820s and gone on to perform in the royal theaters of Europe. In
London in 1833, critics made comparisons between Elssler and Marie
Taglioni, one of the most celebrated dancers of the Romantic ballet. The
Elssler sisters' London success produced an invitation from the Paris
Opera, where Fanny and Therese established themselves in 1834. Fanny
rose to prominence as a counterpoint to Taglioni, excelling in Romantic
ballets while introducing a new exotic repertoire of national character
dances. These soon rivaled the Romantic ballet as the most popular vehicles for her kinesthetic and expressive abilities.

Agents for New York manager Stephen Price first attempted to get
Elssler to tour America in 1838. Price hoped Elssler's star appeal would
help rescue the finances of his theater, which, like many others, struggled in the depressed economy after the Panic of 1837. But Elssler worried about the conditions she would face in America and the financial

and professional risk of the venture, for she would have to break her contract with the Paris Opera. Elssler rebuffed Price's offers until Henry Wikoff, a wealthy young American touring Europe who turned theatrical agent at Price's behest, succeeded in convincing her that the financial prospects of the venture outweighed the professional risks. Nor was America the cultural backwater that Elssler, having danced in the royal theaters of Vienna, Berlin, London, and Paris, feared. Wikoff assured Elssler that even in hard times, American publics would fill theaters to see her dance, making her a fortune. And they did. By varying estimates, Elssler earned at least $140,000 from 208 appearances. Even when accounting for $40,000 in expenses, $5,000 in charitable donations, and sundry losses due to bad management, she stood to return to Europe with a small fortune, the relative value of which would be worth over $3 million today.[5]

In the first six months of her American tour, the phenomenon that critics called alternately "Elssler fever," "Elsslermania," and even "Elsslermaniaphobia" skirted the bounds of seemingly appropriate behavior from American audiences who were receiving a foreign dancer during an economic depression. Much of this public excitement, which manifested in ticket sales, the profusion of Elssler-themed material culture, and crowd behavior, was covered and thus shaped by an expanding print culture, especially the penny press. These cheap daily papers, which rolled out on steam-powered presses and sold for as little as a penny, kept Elssler's image continually before the public. This press culture encouraged readers to see everyday life in their communities as newsworthy while also seeing themselves as participants in shared national experiences like Elsslermania.[6]

Elsslermania in turn revealed the possibilities of new forms of mass media and marketing, contributing to the development of a key feature of modern celebrity, what one scholar calls the "illusion of intimacy."[7] Editors, publishers, and sundry petty producers discovered that there was a market in stories and objects associated with Elssler, ranging from hagiographic to salacious. She was both an idealized object at a remove and an individual whose taste and style might be imitated and whose biography offered valuable lessons, warnings, or other prurient delights. The broad circulation of new editorial material generated from the tour, along with Elssler imagery and biography, rapidly outpaced any managerial or editorial control. This profusion of Elssler ephemera worked against a stable image of the dancer or narrative about the tour; instead, it fueled a series of competing narratives about dance as an art form, Elssler as an artist and figure of interest, and the implications of her celebrity for her

American publics. These competing narratives increased public interest in the dancer, inspiring new adulation and alarm.

The discourses around Elssler's celebrity both heightened and worked to manage questions about the legitimacy of her celebrity. Assessment of her worthiness as an artist and public figure involved scrutiny of the composition and behavior of her publics. Constructions of Elssler as a "divine" avatar of dance superior to her predecessors existed uneasily alongside salacious accounts of her love affairs in Europe. When reviewers cast Elssler within an idealized sentimental framework and celebrated her dancing as "poetry of motion," others countered that such views made her dancing more dangerous. Elssler's middle-class, mixed-gender publics figured prominently in panics about the implications of her celebrity. Across a spectrum of coverage, assessment of Elssler's dancing and celebrity remained tied to readings of her publics.[8]

Two sets of conversations developed that cast Elssler as a dangerous influence on American society. The first fixated on excess in both the public excitement over Elssler and her resulting profits. This excess was explained by the differences between European and American culture and taken as a sign that some forms of European culture were dangerous for virtuous republicans, both men and women. Republican society could not metabolize the product of decadent European court society. This coverage cast Elssler as a dissolute prostitute and profiteer who had humbugged credulous Americans, though the focus here was largely on susceptible republican men.

The second conversation fixated on Elssler's popularity with middle-class white women, part of a larger shift in middle-class leisure culture. Some pointed to this as an indication that French dance was beyond reproach, while others warned that such views made Elssler *more* dangerous to respectable women. Such alarm not only came from antitheatrical reformers but also sounded the dissatisfaction of male theatergoers who considered female publics a threat to men's scopic pleasures and dominance of theater culture. Ultimately, this voluminous discourse actually revealed the inability of self-anointed tastemakers to shape, define, and contain who saw Elssler and how they responded. Observers discovered the limits of their ability to control the terms and parameters of a growing culture of celebrity in which Americans maintained a ravenous appetite for new forms and avatars of European culture, especially in an economic depression.

Elsslermania is an underappreciated watershed in the history of celebrity in America that stands out in contrast to a more heavily scrutinized moment, the 1850 tour of Swedish opera singer Jenny Lind, or

"Lindomania." As scholars have shown, Lindomania helped consolidate white middle-class dominance of expanding mass entertainment culture. While many features of Elsslermania anticipated Lindomania, it differs in this crucial way: in Elsslermania an increasingly prominent, feminized middle-class public remained suspect rather than celebrated, their proximity with an older mixed-class masculine theater culture cause for alarm. Both Lindomania and Elsslermania experienced forms of male working-class backlash, but a significant component of panic around Elsslermania involved elites' inability to control working-class male enthusiasm. They warned that Elsslermania compromised elements of moral and social order. The distinctness of this earlier moment reflected both the unstable status of dance as a legitimate art and also changes in theatergoing culture as theater increasingly hailed a genteel feminized market.

The Elssler who appeared in various guises in American media was a character participating in a drama of national moment. Elssler's tour catalyzed a conversation about American tastes, moral standards, and public behavior, reflecting back a version of America that surprised many. For while Americans may have shown France they could appreciate the best of European culture, some asked whether this was worth celebrating or patronizing. These stakes extended beyond the moment of Elssler's tour as observers debated the long-term implications of the transatlantic starring system for American culture. Perhaps America was becoming too much like Europe, and not for the better.

Manufacturing Elsslermania

Hours after the transatlantic steamer *Great Western* landed in New York harbor on Sunday, May 3, 1840, the *New York Herald* printed a double sheet extra filled with European intelligence. The headline promised "Correspondence of the Herald. By the Great Western. State of Affairs in Europe—Arrival of Fanny Elssler." Elssler was an object of interest, and her arrival was an event in the history of the city. Having "enraptured London, Paris, and all Europe for five years," the *Herald* reported, the dancer had finally "arrived in New York" and was scheduled to debut the following week. Readers could follow the London response to Elssler's April appearance and imagine her twirling before Queen Victoria, then turn the page to read about the "sensation" at the New York Custom House when the dancer's portmanteau was unloaded, as men and women "jumped to catch a look of every petticoat as it came ashore."[9]

The term "sensation" recurred in press coverage and private correspondence about Elssler's tour. That evening, retired businessman and avid theatergoer Philip Hone mentioned Elssler in his diary. "She has been anxiously looked for" and, he predicted, "will create a sensation like that which marked the advent of George Frederick Cooke."[10] Hone's reference to the 1811 tour of the tragedian implied that public reception of the dancer would be greater than that of stars who preceded her and maybe as great as Cooke's. Katti Prinster, Elssler's cousin and traveling companion, also marveled at the "unbelievable sensation" created by Elssler's arrival. In letters to her father in Germany, she repeatedly found herself at a loss for words. It was "impossible to capture the Sensation that Fanny Elssler's appearance in New York has aroused."[11]

Press coverage of Elssler's movements reported but also shaped this surprising public phenomenon. Prinster's letters home illustrate the connection between press coverage and public interest in Elssler. News spread quickly once the passenger list of the *Great Western* was publicized, and "within a few hours, the theater seats for four of her performances were completely exhausted." Perhaps Prinster and Elssler watched the crowds forming outside the Park Theatre from their rooms at the American Hotel. Did they dare risk discovery to walk out together around the square? Prinster likened the feeling of coming ashore to the "health and happiness of goldfish after their water has been changed." The metaphor was prescient for other reasons. When Elssler and Prinster returned to the Custom House to collect their luggage, the crowd surrounding their carriage was so thick that they "feared that an accident had occurred." In the following weeks, "a flock of busybodies and art enthusiasts followed [Elssler's] every step"—even into the theater when Elssler was not performing.[12] As the *Herald* put it, Elssler was "the observed of all observers."[13]

The press coverage surrounding Elssler's tour was unprecedented, made possible by a revolution in print involving new technologies, distribution mechanisms, and changes in content. Steam presses introduced in 1835 made it possible to produce "five-thousand impressions an hour," which transformed the economics of print. The "penny papers" (in New York the *Herald*, the *Sun*, and the *Evening Transcript*) sold cheaply to an expanding readership. While mercantile papers were mainly sold by subscription, penny papers were hawked on the street to passersby, which significantly increased their circulation. Expanded use of advertising also broke the financial reliance on political parties and elite subscribers. The penny press thus reached a wider, more democratized readership.[14]

These innovations in form were joined by a major redefinition of the very nature of news itself. News expanded from politics and commerce to include the facets of daily life in American cities, encompassing crime and commercial entertainment. Editors sent journalists to report on daily affairs in the city, while letters from paid correspondents informed readers about goings-on in other major cities. Line items about the movements and misadventures of public figures also appeared in columns of on-dits, or gossip. Penny papers continued the practice of reprinting, even while expanding local coverage.[15] Readers from all social backgrounds could participate in a shared collection of experiences at the local, regional, and national levels. As elements of daily life became newsworthy commodities, penny papers became vehicles for celebrity. They were joined by pamphlets and books, which proliferated as printing became cheaper. Together, new forms of print culture drew readers into imagined relationships with public figures like Elssler, creating the "illusion of intimacy" so crucial to modern celebrity.[16]

The *Herald*'s declaration, two days after the steamer's arrival, that "Fanny Elssler is all the word—all the rage—all the mania—all the talk of New York" invoked the paper's own influence.[17] Such press coverage drove, shaped, and signified public response to Elssler. In that first week, the *Herald* used various narrative devices to keep Elssler's image before readers and impress them with the significance of her arrival, which was framed in gendered nationalistic terms. A piece ghost-written for the *Herald* by Elssler's manager, Henry Wikoff, dramatized Elssler's excitement about coming to America while evoking founding myths. "Arrival of Fanny Elssler" recounted how, as the boat approached shore, Elssler "kissed" the "American earth" on the ship's lead line—used to measure the ocean's depth—"with all the *empressement* that Columbus first kissed the shore, when he first set his foot on the continent." This narrative of rediscovery had transparent appeal for American readers but also assured them that *America* was the point of Elssler's visit, not simply American dollars. Elssler was a curious visitor more than a greedy opportunist. She traveled overseas, even though the "fashionable *salons*" in London and Paris "remonstrated against [her] wild desire . . . to visit America." While the "Parisians talked of declaring war against America" for coaxing Elssler out of her contract with the Paris Opera, still Elssler followed her "passion to see the land of democracy."[18]

The *Herald* kept Elssler's image before readers, helping drive demand for both theater tickets and newspapers. One of Bennett's more innovative pieces, praised by Wikoff as a "glorious illustration of a *double l'entendre*," connected the dancer's aesthetic and erotic appeal with the paper's novel journalistic practices.[19] In order to beat competing papers to foreign news, the *Herald* kept a fleet of boats that sailed out to meet transatlantic steamers like the *Great Western*. The week after the debut,

Bennett featured a short story about the new skiff "Fanny Elssler." As a British steamer approached, the *Herald*'s men "were in the Fanny Elssler . . . and dashing over the bright waves," cheering "skim along, Fanny— skim along." The piece concluded, "The Fanny Elssler is a beauty of a skiff. If you want to see her, go to Whitehall at sunrise any morning, or to the Park this evening."[20] People did—by the thousands.

Tickets for Elssler's first week of performances were hard to come by. The morning after her steamer docked, the Park Theatre ticket office was "thronged with applicants" for tickets to the lower tiers. A week before her debut, theater boxes were sold out for Elssler's first three or four nights (accounts varied). A brisk speculation followed, with box tickets resold at an average of three times their usual price of one dollar. Some papers claimed that individual tickets were going for five dollars, which was equivalent to the regular price of a private box.[21] There was no advance sale of pit tickets, however. The morning of Elssler's debut, the theater office opened at ten o'clock. It closed a half hour later. Pity the would-be theatergoer who stumbled into the square at midday and was greeted by placards announcing "Pit full" and "Boxes all taken."[22]

These crowds "astonished" the Park Theatre manager, Edmund Simpson, who had been reluctant to go ahead with the Elssler tour after his partner, Stephen Price, died.[23] The engagement was risky. Wikoff's terms for Elssler were steep and unprecedented: half the receipts, with a $500-per-night certainty. In addition to covering the regular upkeep of the theater, Simpson also needed profits to cover the salaries of the ballet company hired in New York and Elssler's dance partner, John Sylvain, who traveled with her from London.[24] Months later, when Wikoff negotiated an $800-per-night certainty for New Orleans, St. Charles Theatre manager James Caldwell called it an "absurd sum" and shot back that he feared the "Drama" could not "prosper" if "exorbitant terms are to be extracted by a momentary popular excitement."[25] Wikoff refused Caldwell's counteroffer, so the manager agreed to $800. Managers of smaller theaters in less populous markets had to weigh public demand against the prospect of loss incurred from covering both Elssler's certainty and their own expenses. If profitable, the Elssler engagement could help a theater recover from the losses that many were suffering in the depressed economy. Fortunately, Elssler's debut Park Theatre engagement more than exceeded Simpson's hopes. The *Evening Post* described a house "filled . . . from the pit to the Shakspeare gallery," while the *Star* called it "crammed."[26] The *Herald* reported that the sixteen nights brought in $20,000, close to $600,000 today. The returns from her summer engagements at theaters in major northeastern cities were comparable.[27]

During her two years touring, higher ticket prices and ticket auctions indicate the prominence of socioeconomic elites. Elssler's "Great Début" was likewise an affluent affair. However, continuing demand for tickets and full houses, which persisted during several weeks of performances in most cities, indicates a much broader, economically diverse public. Fawning press coverage, on the other hand, emphasized the high end of the social spectrum. The *Spirit of the Times* was "pleased to add that the audience was composed of the *élite* of the beauty and fashion of the town."[28] Though the unflagging enthusiasm of genteel women later fed critical backlash and handwringing over the implications of Elssler's American celebrity, in May 1840 the narrative surrounding Elssler's debut celebrated rather than censured Elssler's popularity with a feminized public. This also confirmed American taste levels, countering European stereotypes of uncouth, greedy Americans that had appeared in the French press prior to Elssler's departure (and were reprinted in some American papers).

Accounts of Elssler's tour concerning incidents within and outside the theater reached beyond New York. On May 23, 1840, a single line item appeared in the *New Orleans Daily Picayune* at the bottom of the center column on the second page, the heart of the paper. It read, "Elssler is the *mania* in New York." The following day, another line item appeared: "The charming dancing lion of the Park theatre is said to be receiving from Simpson *seven hundred and fifty dollars a night*."[29] Familiarity with the "dancing lion" was expected. In this period, packet ships and steamboats carried newspapers, as well as commercial freight and migrants, up and down the Atlantic seaboard and inland via natural waterways and canals. In New Orleans, the largest port city of the South, the *Daily Picayune* editors followed the New York coverage closely and kept up a daily stream of items, usually on a one-week lag from events in New York. Over 1840–41, items related to the dancer and her travels appeared about twice a week, allowing readers who wondered if they would ever see "The Greatest Danseuse Yet" to still keep abreast of her tour.[30]

Brief, humorous line items culled from other urban dailies not only served as filler but also helped newspaper sales, priming readers to pick up the next day's issue to look for more extensive coverage, such as a review of Elssler's debut in her next city. While the *Picayune* reprinted some of its Elssler material, much of its copy was original, often from its own network of paid correspondents and delivered in the paper's chatty, jocular style. Thus it participated in and shaped Elssler's celebrity, regionally and nationally, well before she disembarked in the Crescent City. The profusion of coverage could also be disorienting. There were "so many stories afloat" that the *Picayune* editors did not know "what to believe."[31] Still, they printed them.

This material also connected a geographically expanding nation. Through varying levels of coverage, readers in New Orleans could follow Elssler from New York to Philadelphia, Washington, DC, and Baltimore. She returned for a second New York engagement August 1840, then played Boston, Philadelphia, and New York before venturing south to Charleston, South Carolina, by way of Richmond, Virginia. Caldwell, the New Orleans manager, encouraged Wikoff to negotiate an engagement in Havana, Cuba, which made a sea voyage into the Gulf of Mexico worthwhile. Elssler finally played New Orleans in May 1841, exactly one year after her New York debut.[32]

During Elssler's first year, male power brokers competed with each other over their ability to shape Elssler's image. Wikoff tried to control the narrative of the tour and her character. He cultivated a relationship with the *Herald*, sending Bennett puffs and correspondence from the road. But the relationship deteriorated as Bennett began to hold back some of Wikoff's letters from publication and then in 1841 began to publish unflattering, even salacious commentary. Wikoff was appalled when a week before Elssler was to commence a fourth New York engagement in 1841, the *Herald* referred to her as a "sylphide of 34, with a son of 18," which suggested that she was too old and morally compromised to be a "sylphide." Bennett also attacked Elssler for the excessive profits made on her southern tour and even recounted a violent incident in New Orleans during a public serenade outside Elssler's hotel.[33] Wikoff was vested in controlling Elssler's public image, Bennett in a saleable paper. This conflict reflected their divergent interests in the tour. It also hints at the hidden politics and financing of such coverage.

Wikoff may have provided financial incentives for publication of his missives. In 1844, after Elssler was reestablished in Paris and Wikoff was trying to clear himself from rumors that he had an affair with Elssler, he published correspondence that suggested that Bennett had bribed and blackmailed Elssler and her agent for preferential coverage. Money or gifts clearly had changed hands. While forms of paid puffing and other business arrangements between newspaper editors and theater managers were well established and an open if unsavory secret of the business, Wikoff's effort to guarantee preferential coverage—or Bennett's to extract bribes for the same—was a new iteration of this dynamic. Generally, theater managers granted newspaper editors free admission and access to the green room in exchange for favorable puff pieces on new stars or plays. As detailed newspaper coverage of commercial entertainment increased over the 1830s, editors tried to appear disinterested and assured readers that they did not lower themselves to these tactics, which nonetheless persisted. Accusation of puffing was frequently the first charge thrown in a newspaper battle over coverage of stars. In fact, early in Elssler's engagement, the *Herald* got into a public tiff with the rival *Evening Signal* over the integrity of the *Herald*'s coverage. Bennett countered that the "miserable penny critics" had conspired to "write her down unless they received a bonus from the manager."[34] Bennett outflanked a bribery scandal by suggesting that his competitors were the ones trying to exchange favorable coverage for money. He was probably doing it too.

Wikoff and Bennett's joint efforts to keep Elssler before the reading public established a pattern that sustained public interest even after Wikoff lost control over the terms. The larger matrix of celebrity into which press coverage fit metabolized *all* modes and manner of coverage into an abiding fascination with Elssler's person, from the hagiographic to the salacious. During Elssler's first year touring, the *Herald* continued to follow her daily life in the city, turning her movements into newsworthy events and fostering an imagined intimacy between Elssler and the *Herald*'s readership. These pieces were also a vehicle for social commentary. For example, Elssler's visit to Wall Street occasioned light comedy at the expense of the money men, who were overcome by the "charming creature then flitting around them." They "stopped counting the specie . . . made a double entry . . . checks were dishonored, and marked on the back 'Fanny Elssler.'" Even the "stock gamblers forgot to cheat."[35] Elssler appeared in the society columns, a new feature of the penny press that played with the notion of a rising American aristocracy and satisfied curiosity about the habits of visiting European elites and nobility. Accounts of Elssler being entertained by Knickerbocker society simultaneously mocked the pretensions of the elite and gave readers a glimpse of their world. Elssler's celebrity inverted the rules of social order: "All the fashionable people of New York—the Costars, the Astors, the Kings, the Livingstons, the Hones are running over each other's heads, and calling upon Fanny."[36]

These fragments created a portrait of Elssler in private life, helping readers imagine what the French opera dancer was like outside the theater world. They also built upon conventions of evaluating a female entertainer's merits in terms of her conduct in private life, which now encompassed details from Elssler's daily interactions while touring. The Elssler character who emerged in these early *Herald* pieces defied stereotypes of the worldly, dissolute European and instead epitomized an American sentimental feminine ideal. Elssler's worthiness was demonstrated by her "lady-like and modest" character and "simplicity."[37] Her foreignness manifested as juvenile innocence rather than arch knowingness. She was more child than woman, more joyful ingenue than worldly European star. These characterizations were also a preemptive public relations strategy designed to head off revelations about Elssler's private life, including affairs with nobility and her (second) illegitimate child, who had remained in London. These were sure to appear in print at some point in her American tour—as they did.

Biographical pamphlets featured both the virtuous, sentimental Elssler character and salacious tales of her immoral progress through the courts of Europe, offering readers a deeper dive into various news stories. The sentimental figure appeared in the biographical pamphlet, *Memoir of Fanny Elssler: With Anecdotes of Her Public and Private Life!*, which was probably written by Wikoff. The twenty-four-page *Memoir* moves abruptly from Elssler's discovery of ballet and her starring debut into a series of didactic anecdotes illustrating her character of "moral courage and genuine benevolence."[38] In this telling, Elssler exemplifies ideals of sentimental womanhood. Rival exposés of Elssler's history and character began appearing in the fall of 1840, many of them generated by comic singer turned sensation journalist George Washington Dixon, who was probably the author of the thirty-two-page pamphlet by "A Lady of This City" titled *Life of the Beautiful and Accomplished Danseuse, Mademoiselle Fanny Elssler, of Vienna*. A condensed eight-page version by Peter Pindar followed; it sold for six cents.[39] The *Accomplished Danseuse* chronicled the dancer's cold ambition, her weak father's failures to keep her from sexual ruin, and the life of prostitution that accompanied Elssler's professional rise.

Dixon also regularly attacked and mocked Elssler in his scandal sheet the *Polyanthos*. The *Polyanthos*, which began publication in 1838, was one of the first "flash papers," another form of cheap urban print culture that participated in the commodification of news. Over the 1840s, these weekly papers offered exposés of urban vice and sporting culture. The *Polyanthos* aped the tone and style of the moral reform press, which also emerged in the late 1830s, albeit with flagrant delight in the "vice and wickedness" it purported to "chastise."[40] The paper offered its readers a different framework through which to consume Elssler's celebrity.

These pamphlets and penny press coverage were part of a broader world of material culture that trafficked in Elssler imagery and dance iconography generally. Bennett reported, with minimal exaggeration, that "ten minutes after [Elssler's] arrival was known . . . a lithographer was at work on her likeness."[41] American painter Henry Inman's scene of Elssler in her dressing room was reproduced as an engraving. However, most of the portraits and scenes sold by stationery stores both alone and as sheet music covers were reproductions of European originals. Thus the same images circulating in Paris, Leipzig, and London now appeared in the American market. Idealized depictions of Elssler's most popular dances adorned pianos in middle-class homes, their melodies played as part of domestic leisure. Today it is nearly impossible to tease out the provenance of archival dance ephemera, much of which uses identical iconography to illustrate different star dancers.

This print media expanded Elssler's publics beyond habitual theatergoers while also mediating exposure to the celebrated dancer, especially significant for those who might never see Elssler perform.[42] The *New York Mirror*, a literary weekly, notified readers that "busts of the great danseuse," which were "in great demand," could be purchased from Mr. Colman's book shop on Broadway. The portraits were a lure for customers. As the *Mirror* noted, "Those who cannot see the first dancer in the world, at the theatre," or who would not go could still satisfy their "curiosity to see how so celebrated a woman *looks*."[43] The boost in business for booksellers like Colman was an obvious perk. In 1841 phrenologist L. N. Fowler published twin phrenological assessments and biographical sketches of Elssler and sculptor James Varick Stout, who was then at work on a statuette of Elssler. Fowler's sketch featured the sentimental, virtuous Elssler and paired nicely with the "well balanced . . . character" revealed by her physiognomy. While her "amativeness," or propensity for love and sexual desire, was "full and active," it had less "influence" than some of her other "faculties," like "cautiousness" and her "*very* large" and "active . . . benevolence"—Elssler's sizable donations to charities had been reported in the news. While Elssler "prefer[red] the society of gentlemen," this was merely "to gratify her intellect" and not to take them as "lovers."[44]

An expanding consumer marketplace capitalized on Elssler imagery in creative ways. Her biographer Ivor Guest offers the most extensive—and entertaining—list of objects sold with her name: "boots, stocking, garters, corsets, shawls, parasols, fans, even Fanny Elssler cigars, boot polish, and shaving soap."[45] When Katti Prinster informed her father that "the applause in America is the popping of foamy Champagne," was she aware of the Fanny Elssler Champagne advertised by F. Sal Manson of Water Street in New York?[46] Elssler-themed marketing strategies were easy targets for humorists. Was the *New Orleans Daily Picayune* jesting when it listed "Elssler coal, Elssler whitewash, Elssler sarsaparilla syrup," and then "Elssler roast beef, Elssler catfish, Elssler vegetables"?[47] In the wake of this consumer frenzy, the *Picayune* editors introduced the term "Fannyelsslermaniaphobia" to describe the disease that left the city of New York "convalescent, but horribly pockmarked" with Elssler fashions and Elssler-themed goods.[48]

Use of Elssler's name by others demonstrated and enhanced her popularity and potentially buoyed the profits of American retailers struggling in a depressed economy. In the next century, multi-million-dollar deals involving the licensing and marketing of celebrity names became a feature of consumer society and celebrity culture. In 1840 "no one . . . believed her name was a kind of property, much less that it belonged to Elssler."[49] Advertisements in the *Baltimore Sun* show how retailers adjusted their marketing and stock to capitalize on Elssler's popularity. In September, druggist Seth Hance featured a special ad in the *Sun*, replacing his usual description of how his cream benefits the complexion with special copy that read, "FANNY ELSSLER USING HANCE'S LILLY WHITE—*nuf sed.* Walk in, Ladies. A deduction of one hundred per cent. made to Shopkeepers. O K.—Hance, is the word. For sale by SETH S. HANCE. Corner Charles and Pratt streets." Hance included a woodcut of a lady holding up a looking glass. Perhaps Elssler's implicit endorsement would improve sales.[50] The *Daily Picayune* reprinted the advertisement and joked that New Orleans "trades people" ought to "take the hint and be ready . . . if Fanny should come here. . . . Nothing will sell that is not Elssler."[51]

Entrepreneurs across the spectrum of print and consumer culture capitalized on the public's presumed familiarity with and interest in all things Elssler. They used her image to drum up sales and increase profits, which potentially came back to Elssler and the theater at the box office and certainly helped Wikoff secure engagements in other cities. Tellingly, salacious coverage became more prominent as Elssler's tour progressed. It signaled the salability of her image and appealed to the pornographic fantasies of some publics, but it also fed into the backlash, diminishing Elssler's accomplishments as a celebrated dancer by suggesting that they were illegitimate. As press criticism worked to fix the meaning of Elssler's dancing firmly within the framework of the divine, sexualized exposés served as a reminder of the permeable divine/depraved, virgin/whore binaries that had long shaped reception of foreign dancers.

Defining Elssler's Dancing

Elssler came to the United States at the height of her career, the most accomplished and successful dancer to have crossed the Atlantic. She was preceded by dancers who had also trained in European opera ballets, such as Celeste and Augusta. When Philip Hone called Elssler "by far the best dancer we have ever seen in the country," he was evaluating her in relation to the itinerants of the 1830s who had familiarized Americans with the conventions of French dance.[52] American critics drew on a virgin/ whore dichotomy for understanding dance that constructed the dancer as either divine, transcending corporeality through dance, or resolutely embodied, her physicality and expressiveness affirming her corporeality. Through this language, critics talked about sex appeal and grappled with the athleticism and facial expressiveness of these dancers. This framework was also paralleled by biographical treatments of Elssler.

In London and Paris, Elssler had served as a foil for Marie Taglioni, who developed the most iconic roles in the Romantic ballet, including in *La Sylphide*. According to French writer Théophile Gautier's famous formulation, Taglioni was the "Christian dancer" and Elssler the "pagan dancer."[53] As American critics struggled to define the particular qualities, merits, defects, and effect of Elssler's dancing, they drew on this binary but recentered it, either looking to Elssler as the epitome of Romantic ballet or debating whether she fell short. The qualities critics identified in Elssler usually depended upon their view of dancing generally. Many still grappled with aspects of Elssler's repertoire and style that fell outside their ideal of dance as divine. This circled back to questions about whether Elssler was a worthy object and dance a legitimate art form. Either Elssler was more divine than those who came before, or all dance was "licentiousness, indelicacy and immorality."[54]

Elssler's repertoire combined the classicizing Romantic ballet epitomized by the ballet *La Sylphide* with nationalistic character dances that she had developed in Paris in 1834 to distinguish herself from Taglioni. *La Sylphide* epitomized the Romantic ballet of the 1830s. It had been Taglioni's most celebrated vehicle. In *La Sylphide*, both the athleticism of ballet and its unmistakable eroticism were conveyed by a protagonist who was not a flesh-and-blood human woman but a divine other. The title character of *La Sylphide* is a wandering sylph or forest sprite in love with a farmer. Their mutual desire is thwarted by witchcraft at the behest of the farmer's jealous and very human bride. As the sylph, Taglioni originated the iconic costume of the Romantic ballerina, the diaphanous white dress with sash. She also introduced the new athletic accomplishment of achieving a spin on the edge of her toes, described as "a pirouette on tip-toe" or a high half-pointe. (Only later in the century would dancers insert blocks in their shoes to achieve a full pointe.)[55] In America, Elssler's performance of *La Sylphide* became the touchstone for assessing her abilities as a dancer and defining the aesthetic and moral value of Romantic ballet.

Elssler's character dances, while extremely popular, fit uneasily with these ideals. They were part of full ballets but could also be offered as stand-alone acts during a comparatively bare-bones foreign tour. The most popular of Elssler's character dances was the cachucha, a Spanish dance based on the bolero in which the dancer accompanied herself with castanets. It also became one of the most prolific representations of the dancer, appearing in the newspapers as a woodcut, on sheet music covers, and as a commercial lithographic portrait sold by vendors like Atwill's Music Salon.[56] The exoticism of this and other character dances, which built on the aesthetics of ballet but were received as the aesthetic essence of foreign cultures, carried over well with American audiences. However, these dances failed to excite critics as much as her performances of *La Sylphide*, which epitomized their idea of the aesthetics and affective power of French dance.

During her first year in America, Elssler debuted with either the ballet *La tarentule* or *La Sylphide* (managers often insisted on the latter) and one of her most popular character dances, the cracovienne or the cachucha. She repeated *La Sylphide* for multiple nights before introducing another ballet on the third or fourth evening. The only engagement to break this formula was her first: in New York, Elssler held back *La Sylphide* until June 1, 1840, near the end of her engagement, because she needed that first month to rehearse her American corps of eight dancers.[57] Critics were divided in those first weeks, though public enthusiasm was unflagging. Elssler's *La Sylphide* transformed the tenor of criticism. Whereas in London and Paris she was deemed inferior to Taglioni as the sylph, in the United States, her performance as the sylph set her apart from her predecessors *and* made the ballet a success.[58] Through this role, critics constructed Elssler's dancing as fairy-like and even divine and managed discomfort with aspects of her repertoire and style that seemed to deviate from these ideals.

Struggles to define Elssler's dancing in her first weeks reveal the expectations critics brought to the theater. For her Park Theatre debut on May 14, 1840, Elssler appeared in the cracovienne, a Polish mazurka or folk dance (known as the krakowiak), followed by *La tarentule*, a "comic ballet" set in Sicily in which the deadly bite of a tarantula threatens true love. Descriptions of the debut capture the heightened expectations. Elssler "came bounding upon the stage" for the cracovienne but could not start for the "peals of applause." She curtseyed, then commenced. Critics did not know what to make of the dance, and some disparaged the "heavy and awkward" costume. All noted her powerful charisma, particularly her "dark flashing eyes" and smile, which "took the house by storm" as she closed the dance in a "military salute." (Despite the costume's awkwardness onstage, its military-style jacket, trimmed with brass buttons and gold braid, and tall red boots with metal taps quickly inspired fashion trends.)[59]

Elssler's next piece, the ballet *La tarentule*, "fully realized" audience "anticipations." Her mimicry of the death throes suffered by the victim of a tarantula were hailed by the *Evening Post* as a "masterpiece of pantomimic acting."[60] Efforts to capture Elssler's distinct qualities as a dancer indicate that she possessed superior technique. The *Post* marveled that the "movement[s] of her feet are as swift as a flash," while the *Spirit of the Times* praised the "rapidity and strength of her execution" and "her wonderful transitions from a brilliant and animated movement to a sudden and statue-like repose." Because it could not find the language for a "peculiar . . . characteristic" of Elssler's dancing, her musicality, the paper inserted an (unattributed) excerpt by American writer Nathanial Parker Willis that was actually about Marie Taglioni, whom Willis had seen in London several years earlier: "Whether the motion seems born of the music, or the music floats out of her dreamy motion, the enchanted gazer might be almost embarrassed to know."[61]

Descriptive language also contained moral narratives. The consistent emphasis on Elssler's "grace and ease," what the *Star* described as a "thing born with and incident to her . . . as if a moral were gifted with a new quality of motion," distinguished her from her predecessors and marked Elssler's dancing as a higher form of art. According to the *Post*, Elssler's dancing was not to be conflated with the "extraordinary leaps, whirlings and frightful distortions of the body and limbs which usually mark stage dancers." Elssler whirled and Elssler leaped, but she did so differently. She achieved "great celerity of movement" with "perfect grace and ease." The performance was "extremely chaste and at the same time full of spirit and force."[62] Allusions to mythical creatures like the "zephyr" did similar work.[63] All of this made Elssler's dancing less morally suspect.

For the handful of New York critics who remained skeptical during her first two weeks, Elssler's performance of *La Sylphide* on June 1 was a revelation. The critical about-face was enthusiastic and highly self-reflexive. Initially, the literary monthly *Ladies' Companion* felt Elssler was overrated. Her "poetry of motion" was rather "anapoetic." Elssler was a fine dancer, but "not so immeasurably superior to other performers in her line, either, to justify any very extraordinary excitement."

After *La Sylphide*, the *Companion* discovered that the problem had been the pieces chosen, not the dancer herself. In *this* ballet, Elssler finally achieved that "complete personification of all that is lovely, graceful, and fascinating."[64] In *La Sylphide*, Elssler *was* poetry of motion. Editor Park Benjamin issued an effusive retraction in his *Evening Signal* on June 2, declaring, "We have sinned; in other words, less elegant, we 'back out.'" In his May 15 review, he had characterized Elssler's dancing as "mere exertions of physical strength and endurance" and judged it "far inferior" to Augusta and Celeste. But on June 2 he wrote, "Her performance of *La Sylphide* was grace combined with an expression that we thought speech only was capable of." He concluded, "Mademoiselle Elssler is without question the most perfect dancer seen on the American stage in our day and generation."[65]

These critical discourses, which continued to shape reception of Elssler over her tour, mobilized sentimental ideals to support claims that Elssler elevated dance as an art form and that dance was a legitimate form of amusement. Description of dance as "poetry of motion" captured the relationship between movement and music achieved in the Romantic ballet, which rendered French dance acceptable for American publics. It also contained a moral judgment: poetry of motion was dance in its most elevated and least suspect form. For a culture that celebrated poetry as achieving the height of human feeling and placed great value on the cultivation of feeling, or sentiment, poetry of motion was dance that produced an elevated sentimental affect among the audience. This in turn suggested that Elssler merited the popular excitement and unprecedented ticket sales.

Biographical accounts offered a supporting framework in which to read Elssler's dancing; conversely, they insisted that the true meaning of dance was always rooted in an immoral sensuality. Wikoff's *Memoir of Fanny Elssler* establishes Elssler's fundamental respectability through her origin story, clarifying that her parents "had no connexion with the opera." Her first visit to the opera shaped Elssler's "destiny," and she discovered a "passion" for dance that "fixed [her] lot in life." Hers was no passion for a dissolute art form; rather, Elssler experienced the ballet as a divine art, as a "heaven, *illuminated in honor of God's victory over Satan!*"[66] This of course echoed the terms of ballet criticism in the press. For readers less comfortable with dance, the *Memoir* testified to Elssler's character, arguing that she was a figure of interest beyond the theater. In these anecdotes, Elssler transforms those around her through her goodness and "holy love," for example, by saving an invalid from a violent "Rum-Fiend" husband.[67] Such accounts helped shape readings of her dancing. If Elssler was pure and virtuous, surely there could be nothing illicit in her twirls.

Conversely, Dixon's *Life of the Beautiful and Accomplished Danseuse* uses famous scandals from Elssler's Paris Opera career, including the rumor of an affair with the duke of Reichstadt, son of Napoleon Bonaparte, to underscore the strong association between ballet and sexual immorality, onstage and off. Elssler's dancing is not innocent; instead, her "bewitching charms" and "beauty embellished" by her costume enflame "Count Rheemsted's" desire. The "passion that glowed in her breast" during her performance compels "the Count" to arrange an assignation, sealing Elssler's fate as a fallen woman.[68] Her father disowns her. Her mother and sister (not yet a dancer) spurn her. Elssler then enjoys a succession of lovers in the capitals of Europe before finally reuniting in secret with her mother and Therese. Dixon recasts her professional successes as the wanderings of an exile, until the reunion, when Elssler pledges to train her sister properly and protect her from moral danger. Elssler is (somewhat) redeemed. The appeal of this narrative was unmistakably pornographic for the time, offering readers a rather different kind of fantasy in which to frame Elssler's performance.

These rival versions of Elssler's history further demonstrate that however much sentimental discourses tried to fix the meaning of her performance and celebrity, this meaning remained highly unstable. Competing discourses offered various frameworks for capturing the sensual delights of dance. The questions that concerned biographers, about the relationship between a woman's sphere of labor and her sexual purity and moral character, overlapped questions about the implications of this new art form. Dance scholars have emphasized the anxiety that attended Elssler's performances and interpreted representations of her dancing, particularly the displacement of the corporeal woman with the otherworldly sylph, as a strategy to manage eroticism in her dancing and her ties to the decadent and immoral world of European aristocracy. Contradictory reactions suggest that Elssler functioned as a "lightning rod" for processing the shifting relationship between ideals of refinement and levels of public sensuality in American society.[69] These discourses also served as a genteel language of erotic delight similar to renderings of women's bodies on sheet music covers. These new forms of genteel eroticism were part of a larger cultural shift that generated alarm from reformers and ridicule from male libertines.

Sheet music covers offer a complementary illustration of the sentimental ideals attached to dance that, far from disavowing the erotic, functioned as a form of genteel eroticism. These images followed idealized conventions for depicting the female body, even and especially the body of a dancer. The cover images *Madlle. Fanny Elssler in La Tarentule*, published by Atwill's Music Salon in New York (fig. 12), and *The New Smolenska / As danced by Madlle Fanny Elssler*, printed by a sheet music publisher out of Philadelphia (fig. 13), are representative. Both depict a dancer in costume and posed as if in performance, indicated by an extended leg and pointed foot. In the first image, the figure's back is to the viewer. She looks over her left shoulder, castanets raised in her hands. The figure in the second image faces the viewer and extends hand and foot as if inviting a partner—not pictured—to join her. Her expression is decidedly flirtatious, chin tucked back and to the side while she looks at her invisible partner from the corner of her large, expressive eyes.

Figure 12. Sheet music cover, *Madlle. Fanny Elssler in La Tarentule*, 1840. Series III, Sheet Music, box 15, folder 204—People, Portraits, Elssler, Fanny, Bella C. Landauer Collection, New York Historical Society.

Figure 13. Sheet music cover, *The New Smolenska /
As Danced by Madlle Fanny Elssler*, 1840. Series III,
Sheet Music, box 15, Folder 204—People, Portraits,
Elssler, Fanny, Bella C. Landauer Collection, New
York Historical Society.

In each image, representation of the dancer's body followed aesthetic
conventions that dominated commercial illustration, with particular
"female body parts," especially the eyes, waist, and feet, "adoringly fe-
tishized."[70] It is impossible to imagine the "new Smolenska" figure, with
her elongated neck and extreme sloping shoulders, full bosom atop tiny
waist, and slender calves curving into miniature feet, carrying out the
feats of athleticism described in reviews of Elssler. Rather, these images
captured highly eroticized feminine ideals that could operate on different registers, not unlike airbrushed images in commercial advertising
that today sell a range of products by mobilizing contemporary ideals of
female desirability.

Critical and visual languages worked to shape how American publics experienced and interpreted dance and may have served as a form of genteel eroticism. Still other experiences and meanings were possible, if difficult to locate. They also remained highly mediated by critical frameworks. In 1841 Bostonian Caroline Dall, an otherwise reluctant theatergoer, overcame her scruples and went to see Elssler during a return engagement. Dall was not impressed. In contrast to the sylph she expected, Dall discovered a performer with "the largest foot and ancle [sic] I ever saw—on a woman." Dall admired Elssler's slender arms but criticized her large hands and felt that the costume made Elssler's "bosom [seem] deficient and the bones of her neck far too prominent." Nor did Dall consider Elssler pretty; instead, Dall complained, she "laughs too much—with a broad ugly mouth[,] an expanded forehead—and quick roguish eyes." Though Elssler's "naive childish manner . . . charms," Dall concluded, "she did not realize my conception."[71] Dall's diary entry illustrates the dissonance between critical discourses that established viewer expectations, framing how performers were to be read and what viewers may actually have seen. The "real" Elssler probably existed somewhere between the idealized sentimental portrait in the press and Dall's rather cutting scrutiny of Elssler's body and manner. If we attempt to separate the values Dall assigned to Elssler's body and physiognomy, we can begin to imagine what Dall may have seen: a muscular dancer and charismatic performer whose physicality threatened to destabilize the sentimental characters she portrayed in the ballet La Sylphide.

Dall's attendance in the Tremont Theatre is also indicative of the expanding publics who came to see Elssler. Dall's reticence about theater was becoming less common among white women of her social class. But even while Elssler drew a more genteel feminized public into theaters, she continued to inspire enthusiasm from socially diverse male theatergoers. Ambivalent readings of Elssler's publics became part of the conversation about Elsslermania. Discussions of what theatergoers saw and what it meant and of the pleasures involved in Elssler's dancing could never be separated from readings of her publics. Observers read Elsslermania as a threat simultaneously to white republican manhood and to genteel white womanhood.

Elsslermania as Democratic Excess

The dangers of Elsslermania revealed themselves in an incident in Baltimore in late July 1840. The evening of her benefit, excited (and by many accounts drunk) men unhorsed Elssler's carriage and pulled it through the streets from theater to hotel, then commenced a public serenade. Elssler and her companion, Prinster, played along with what must have been a terrifying end to the evening (Prinster commented only on their exhaustion). Urban dailies throughout the country reported the incident. The *Herald* rendered the scene with a comedic lightness (probably from Wikoff's pen). "Startled" guests "in their nightcaps" watched as the "smiling, the bewitching Fanny, descended from her car triumphal" and "skipped up the steps of the hotel." She "curtsied" to the "brazen-voiced crowd" and delivered a brief speech of gratitude in "trembling tones." She "withdrew" with a kiss of her hand, "but not to rest," for the serenade continued into the night.[72] In Baltimore, this prompted inquiry into the larger implications of the tour, while mass-produced lithographs of the incident firmly linked Elsslermania with a threat to male republican virtue.

Voices both earnest and satirical pointed to this and similar incidents as evidence that Elssler's popularity threatened American republicanism. Such displays disrupted the idea that Elssler's popularity was a sign of Americans' elevated taste. Elsslermania exposed the continued threat that dissolute aristocratic European culture posed to American values and institutions, particularly by threatening the virtue or self-control of American men. Images of Elssler as a debauchee and prostitute formed a subtext for critiques that blamed Elssler for exciting male excess and destabilizing American society. Having awakened male lust, Elssler reduced (potentially) virtuous citizens to slavish beasts. She coaxed hard-won earnings out of the hands of laborers, men and women, and threatened to bankrupt both individuals and institutions to satisfy her own greed. Acknowledgment of Elssler's merit as a dancer usually accompanied these critiques. Their authors did not want to appear opponents of theatrical amusements. They insisted that the problem was with the excessive public response to Elssler, which they interpreted as a sign of the dangers European culture posed for a republican society.

Many of the rituals of audience adulation Elssler experienced had emerged in the 1820s around English thespians, manifesting America's active audience culture. Theatergoers cultivated a direct relationship with celebrated performers through both the floral tribute and the curtain speech, which Elssler adopted during her tour.[73] Her fans also paid tribute to Elssler with public serenades by local musicians. Prinster was astonished by some of these rituals. When Elssler took the stage at her New York debut, "the entire assembly arose . . . waved with handkerchiefs, swung their hats and caps and burst into a convulsive welcoming cheer [that] lasted five minutes" while Elssler, "struggling with delight and anxiety, bowed her thanks." This and the "three-part hurrah" at the evening's close was all "very new for us, a hurrah from a few thousand people," Prinster explained to her father.[74]

Initially, coverage of enthusiastic American audiences folded into a narrative about the nation's democratic culture. Whereas in Paris and London elites were "drilled to act like automatons," according to the *Herald*, in America the "free children of nature . . . applaud whenever they are pleased, and that is all the time, without reference to the ridiculous rules . . . of the aristocracy in Europe."[75] Theatergoers who cheered and showered Elssler with "spring flowers" and "wreaths" revealed the best features of their democratic culture.[76] But once such reception was no longer firmly tied to elite publics and occurred outside the theater, the association shifted. Observers questioned whether this was in fact a dangerous form of idolatry unbecoming of true republicans, particularly when directed at a European opera dancer.

While the serenades of Elssler in Philadelphia and New York (the latter broken up by gang violence) were carefully planned events that also drew elite spectators, the social composition of the Baltimore parade was ambiguous and usually cast as low. Humorists played on the putative transformation of Baltimoreans into beasts of burden. As the *Baltimore Sun* put it, the city's "republican freemen" now included a "team of . . . 'two legged mules.'"[77] A New York paper suggested the "biped donkeys . . . be stabled, rubbed down with brickbats, and fed on straw for six weeks," while the *New Orleans Daily Picayune* notified readers of "a saddler in Baltimore" who had invented "*the Elssler harness!*" The *Baltimore Clipper* claimed to have seen a corn "huckster" at the local market advertising "the longest Elssler *ears* . . . seen in Baltimore since the grand display."[78] Lithographer J. Childs turned the image into a commercial print that depicts men with donkey heads shouting "Echow! Echow!" as they pull a costumed Elssler standing in dancer pose, leg extended, in an open carriage (fig. 14).[79]

The threat of men turned into "jackasses" was also the subtext for a series of angry editorials in the *Baltimore Sun* on the dangers to republican virtue unleashed by foreign stars. The writer placed Elssler in the context of expanding foreign tourists and entertainers, arguing that these visitors promoted models that ran counter to the "republican plainness" of "our young men" and "common sense" of the country's "fair ladies." The writer invoked the patriots of the American Revolution and the veterans of the War of 1812 as counterpoint to men who had "dishonored the character of an American citizen" by dragging Elssler's carriage through the city streets.[80] This prompted a larger debate about the realms of acceptable

FANNY ELSSLER AND THE BALTIMOREANS

Figure 14. *Fanny Elssler and the Baltimoreans*, published in New York by lithographer J. Childs, 1840. Library of Congress Prints and Photographs Division Washington, D.C., http://hdl.loc.gov/loc.pnp/cph.3b17907.

behavior by American citizens. Some of the paper's readership was outraged by such characterizations and wrote in, calling the paper "destitute of taste, insolent towards the public," and guilty of "hypocrisy." The *Sun* refused to back down; instead, it built on its initial critique by making explicit the moral nature of this threat. The crowd of "two-legged cattle" had succumbed to a "double intoxication—the influence of woman and of wine"—and thus was brought to the "condition of brutes."[81]

The race and class politics of the critique were fully visible in the J. Childs cartoon (fig. 14). In this image, a black coachman calmly puffs his cigar while surveying the inverted spectacle of white men turned into donkeys in service of a European dancer. He declares, "I tink the New Yorkers cant beat dis unless dey gib Miss Fanny de freedom ob the City in gold snuff box"—seemingly a more ridiculous gesture.[82] A figure positioned at the bottom of the racial and social hierarchy marvels at the foolishness of white men who disregard hierarchy and order. A different cartoon by an unknown artist makes the coachman's commentary even more explicit: "I shall never get ober de disgrace ob driving such a team ob asses."[83]

An extensive discourse titled "Manliness," which was published in the *Sun* a week later, helped readers connect the response to a European dancer with the history and survival of the republic, which depended upon the fitness of its white men. It provided a history of American exceptionalism that rooted the "civilization of this continent," US independence, and the "astonishing process of our country" to the "manly virtues" of those "early settlers." However, this "trait in our character" was currently being threatened by foreign values introduced by foreign imports. These were the terms of a broader confrontation over the expanding culture of gentility among the middle classes, marked by the consumption of manufactured goods and new leisure practices.[84] The Baltimore writer asserted that this "undue preference" for things foreign would cost Americans their "pride of independence." Independence required self-mastery over the allure of foreign "manners[,] . . . fashions [and] amusements." In short, "young men" prostrating themselves at the "feet of a dancing girl" or drawing her carriage through the street proved "*their* effeminacy" and risked the decline of the nation.[85] This commentary clearly looked toward the upcoming 1840 presidential election. Partisan politics was rife with "gendered slurs" used to undermine the fitness of each party to effectively govern. In Boston during the election, Democrats cast their Whig opponents simultaneously as unmanly brutes and as effeminate and infantile and "thus not fit to vote."[86]

Nativism exacerbated social tensions in the August 1840 riot that took place in New York over a public serenade. A group of German musicians serenading Elssler outside the American Hotel were violently attacked by a city youth gang, described derisively in the *Herald* as "soaplocks," working-class youth from the Bowery.[87] In a speech delivered at the scene, George Washington Dixon connected Elsslermania with national decline but in an unusual move emphasized her Germanness, which he used to highlight the threat of New York's growing German population, redrawing the boundaries of Americanness. His speech mobilized working-class constructions of virtue and nativist politics, censuring those who compromised American honor by worshiping an unchaste woman and "second rate figurante." In contrast, the "plain people" refused to participate in this "degradation." Dixon then asserted that those responsible for the Baltimore incident had actually been German. He went on to attack Germans and "other aliens" for depriving "native citizens . . . the means of obtaining a livelihood."[88] In this speech, Dixon drew on discourses that connected republican values and institutions with repudiation of European culture and mobilized them against immigrants. In the New York context, Elssler's Germanness and affinity with a growing German population recast the nature of the foreign threat to encompass the city's growing German population.

Backlash against Elsslermania also fixated on the unprecedented sums Americans spent to see Elssler—and that the dancer earned. Initially, there was some excitement about the boost to theater generally. In New York, the collateral effect of her debut "revived the fortunes of every theatre in town." Celeste's rival engagement continued profitable at the Chatham Theatre, while comedian William Mitchell drew patrons to the reopened Olympic Theatre with a drag burlesque of Elssler's ballets, including the "Crack-a-vein."[89] Over her first fifteen weeks of engagements in New York, Philadelphia, Washington, Baltimore, and again New York, the *Herald* reported, Elssler's performances had drawn the "unprecedented sum" of "$4000 a week" (at least $120,000 today) for "theatrical treasuries."[90]

A year later, estimates of her gross earnings—the *Herald* put the number at $75,000 for her first year, about $2.2 million today—became evidence of Elssler's greed. She was a "mountebank." Elssler had crossed an invisible boundary being redrawn by the men who created the news. Of course, press support was not disinterested. It is possible that editor Bennett began attacking Elssler as retaliation when Wikoff stopped offering gifts. But in redrawing the boundaries of acceptable public enthusiasm, men like Bennett were also making a gendered argument about the worthiness of different art forms and entertainers. Previously, Elssler's earnings were a testament to American taste, but now Americans were the "laughing stocks of the *dillitanti* [sic] of Europe." Elssler's dancing may have been a revelation for Americans, but for Bennett she remained a "simple *danseuse*" and should not be "set up" above her station as a "patriot, philosopher, leader of the fashion." The year before, the *Herald* breathlessly followed her movements through elite society, but now it warned Elssler to "confine herself to her own position and to her own society," other entertainers. In this context, Bennett reframed Elssler's dancing as something less than art, "$15,000 for a month's hops," making "as much money as her legs can bring her," a crude double entendre.[91]

Elssler's popularity during an economic depression gave new life to old arguments that theatrical amusements were morally compromising *and* a waste of money. Those chary of theatrical amusements castigated Elssler's patrons for their wastefulness. At the start of Elssler's tour, Horace Greeley, editor of the (short-lived and unprofitable) literary weekly the *New-Yorker*, lamented the readiness with which "two thousand of our vast and motley population" were "able to throw away a dollar on the caperings of a dancer" during an economic depression.[92] Greeley would have agreed with the *Baltimore Sun*, which pointed to the "thousands of virtuous and industrious females" who were "starving over the needle" while Baltimore paid Elssler more "in one evening, for whirling a few minutes on the point of her toe" than would support the more deserving seamstresses "for a month."[93] This imagery drew on established tropes in antebellum fiction, both didactic and pornographic, about virtuous working women and girls, often in the needle trades, who succumbed to the sex trade. Across this literature, pecuniary ambition and aspirations to gentility were associated with illicit sexuality. Covetousness made women vulnerable to seduction or awakened desires that led them irrevocably down an immoral path.[94] Given this context, presenting virtuous needlewomen as a foil cast Elssler as a prostitute. One did not have to countenance rumors of Elssler's debaucheries in Europe to recognize that in America she was a seducer of thousands, taking their hard-earned dollars.

This imagery shaped the response to Elssler's donation to the Bunker Hill Monument Association. In contrast to the Bunker Hill Monument Fair, which drew $30,035.53 after expenses (over two-thirds the total amount needed to complete the monument and a full ten times the amount expected from these fairs, worth at least $900,000 today), Elssler's benefit donation was a mere $569 after expenses, or $17,000 today.[95] Yet for opponents who insisted that the money be returned, the donation symbolically compromised the entire project. Even though Elssler's donation came from the pockets of many of the same men and women who had strolled the aisles of the fair (something her defenders in the press were quick to point out), the opponents of the donation constructed the money as ill-gotten gains. Opponents imagined that the Bunker Hill Monument was to be "finished with a pirouette by Fanny Elssler."[96] The *New World*, literary periodical of longtime New York theater patron Park Benjamin, followed the tenor of papers in casting Elssler as a "modern Phryne" and called upon the "ladies of Boston" to "vindicate the honor of your sex" by opposing a donation that would be a "stain and tarnish" on the "clear surface of your achievement." Phryne was a courtesan of ancient Greece who had offered her wealth to rebuild the walls of Thebes, if Thebes would "inscribe on the wall, 'Alexander destroyed this wall, but Phryne the courtesan restored it.'"[97] Like Thebes, Boston should refuse Elssler's offer, or "let the inscription tell the truth [and] proclaim the liberality with which a courtesan gave to the public the lucrative wages of her *trade*!"[98] Outside Boston, editors warned that it would be a deep source of shame and embarrassment for future generations to point out a monument to *"national* glory" that was completed with a donation from "the *foreign danseuse.*"[99]

Elssler's donation defied the implicit desire of those "ardent worshippers" that her labors remain on the far side of the footlights and never mingle with proceeds from the sale of feminine handicrafts at a fair. The latter occupied an imagined and idealized space removed from the commercial market. While genteel Bostonians might flock to the theater to see Elssler dance, opposition to her donation reflected a symbolic need to keep the theater from contaminating other institutions. That risk of contamination seemed greater because of Elssler's celebrity. When Elssler proffered a check to the Bunker Hill Monument Association, discursive frameworks that managed the more dangerous implications of her celebrity—such as the image of "divine Fanny"—broke down.

These attacks had little material impact on the financial success of the tour, Elssler's popularity, or the popularity of ballet. They may have generated more interest. Certainly, they did little to drive away the genteel publics who prompted handwringing from evangelical antitheatrical reformers and theater reformers alike. The outcry over the Bunker Hill Monument donation was a function of Elssler's visible popularity with genteel men and women, which manifested broader changes to entertainment culture that had hitherto gone unnoticed or unremarked except by the most vigilant of evangelicals. Elssler's dancing was not regarded as low or illicit, even while some wondered whether it should be. Instead, publics who had recently spurned foreign dancers and even theatrical amusements were clamoring for tickets to Elssler's performances. Elssler's celebrity was a bellwether of change.

Fanny Elssler's Female Publics

Philip Hone could not understand why the "good newspapers" of New York kept haranguing the "bad people" going to see Elssler. She was in New York for her fourth engagement in June 1841. Hone predicted correctly that "the more [the newspapers] rail the more the people won't mind them."[100] He had probably been reading the *New-York Daily Tribune*, a new penny paper founded by Horace Greeley as a "cheap but moral" alternative to the low sensationalism of the *Herald.*[101] Greeley refused to be silent on an issue in which matters of economy, the morals of American society, and the special role of genteel white women as models of correct behavior came together. He appealed to the "reputable and virtuous WOMAN of New-York" to reconsider the "propriety and rightness of their countenancing" a dancer who was notorious for "leading a life of infamy." Greeley was appalled that women continued to attend Elssler's performances and thus to "countenance" her career.[102]

Greeley deployed ideals of Christian femininity that assigned white women the responsibility for upholding moral order. Respectable women had the authority and responsibility to mark that which was "virtuous, proper, commendable." When women "countenanced" Elssler, they degraded their sex and defaulted on their social responsibility. Greeley shuddered at the idea of the "masculine thousands" watching the "revealings of the pirouette and the cachucha" alongside the "ardent, admiring gaze of intelligent and reputable Women."[103] Greeley was mobilizing ideas about virtuous womanhood that were at the heart of contemporary battles over women's access to sexual knowledge and exposure to various forms of sexual culture. Greeley's construction of genteel white womanhood aligned woman's virtue with her lack of sexual knowledge or expression. While elements of this framework were being challenged by a female-led moral reform movement, Christian reformers agreed that theater remained a threat to a virtuous society. Theater's expanded appeal with middle-class female publics, particularly new entertainments like dance, created a problem for evangelical reformers and also for the men targeted by their reforms.

The female-led Christian moral reform movement that by 1840 had taken hold across the Northeast challenged both the "false delicacy" that kept girls ignorant about sex, and thus vulnerable, and the male sexual license embraced in urban male sporting culture. While moral reformers sought to rein in male sexual libertinage to protect young women, both groups still shared a commitment to female sexual purity.[104] From opposite sides of the aisle, for antagonistic reasons, moral reformers and male libertines grappled with a growing female public for theater. Women's prominence in Elssler's audiences disrupted male dominance of theater and its place in public sexual culture. Debates over the legitimacy of new forms of entertainment as middle-class amusement mobilized unlikely agreement between men who sought to protect their exclusive sexualized enjoyment of this entertainment culture and men and women who sought to protect "virtuous WOMAN" from it.[105]

Elssler's popularity both marked and facilitated a shift in the status of theater as a legitimate form of amusement, particularly with white middle-class women. Theatergoers like Philip Hone typified a long-standing theatergoing public, the New York merchant elite. However, theater remained problematic for an expanding middle class, particularly those responsive to Christian reform culture. Beginning in the late 1830s, managers nationwide began instituting reforms to reshape the culture of theatergoing by eliminating lobby bars and removing the third tier while marketing theater as family amusement. They did so in the context of campaigns led by Christian reformers, for example, in Boston, where groups petitioned city aldermen to withhold licenses for theater bars and then pushed for reform of theater licensing laws.[106] Theater also faced competition from proprietors of new entertainment venues like museums and pleasure gardens, which claimed to be free of public vices. Tellingly, these new venues began appearing during the depression years. They required less overhead than theater and charged less for admission. As efforts to reform theater progressed in the 1840s, managers appealed to white middle-class women as a public whose presence created the imprimatur of respectability. Reformers, on the other hand, viewed this growing embrace with alarm. Elssler's draw with white middle-class women both signaled the economic power of this market and accelerated a larger shift under way.

Women's desire to see Elssler in 1840 was so apparent that Park Theatre manager Edmund Simpson decided to convert sections of the pit into additional "boxes for ladies" for her debut. Regular pit tickets would still be sold to men the day of the performance. This was unprecedented. A "lady correspondent" reporting on the debut for the local French newspaper was shocked by the "plebeian" concession of New York's "feminine aristocracy" as the "part of the theatre most called 'the hell' . . . [was] transformed into an Eden" that "sparkled."[107] In Philadelphia, Baltimore, and Washington, Wikoff reported, not only were theaters "crammed almost to suffocation," but "the usual rules" were again thrown over to allow women into the pit.[108] Though dancers prior to Elssler drew women, Elssler's feminized audience received greater interest from the press. Elsslermania made Elssler's female public more newsworthy.

Women had been a stable public for star dancers who preceded Elssler, but critics and managers lagged behind in embracing these European exports to the same degree. In 1837 the *Ladies' Companion* considered it "singular" that "*females* flock to the theaters" to see Augusta and Celeste, enjoying "sights which they would not tolerate in a private drawing room."[109] Three years later, especially after Elssler's performance of *La Sylphide*, the *Ladies' Companion* reconsidered the merits of ballet and singled out with approval the "larger portion. . . . of elegantly-dressed ladies."[110] In Philadelphia in January 1840, mere months before Elssler's arrival, the Chestnut Street Theatre in Philadelphia added a warning to its bills for Celeste's return engagement specifying that "NO FEMALES will be admitted in the Pit of the Theatre."[111] Elsslermania would change that—temporarily. Those who had been squeamish about the performances of Celeste or Augusta or rarely attended theater, like Caroline Dall, went to see Elssler as much to participate in a major celebrity phenomenon as enjoy a new aesthetic experience. In so doing, the social status of theater shifted.

The cursory mention of these star performers in the diary of Bostonian John Warren Williams underscores the connection between Elssler's celebrity, shifts in theatergoing, and shifts in the status of dance. The flour merchant was an active member of the Whig Party, involved with temperance. He rarely mentioned entertainers in his diary, which otherwise chronicled the movement of ships and sales of stock. In January 1839 he noted the crowds at Celeste's benefit night, which he also attended, but concluded, "It shows a *depraved taste.*" Williams was similarly fascinated by the Elssler excitement in the fall of 1840. He commented on the auction prices for boxes, which he calculated reached a 300 percent markup, and further noted, "Ladies admitted into the Pit ! ! ! For the 2d time."[112] Williams also attended Elssler's benefit for the Bunker Hill Monument and expressed pride in the amount raised. The theatergoing habits of the reform-minded business class were changing, the "ladies" in the pit signs of a corresponding feminization of theatergoing connected with Elsslermania.

But even those who approvingly distinguished Elssler from her predecessors still struggled to make sense of her popularity with women and to respond to the cultural shift under way. Though "delighted" by Elssler, Baltimore's "Omega" felt her popularity with women was indication that the "moral sensibility . . . of our ladies is . . . somewhat blunted." By his recollection, women were appalled at Celeste's Baltimore debut in the early 1830s. "Almost every lady left the house . . . and the few who remained seemed *ashamed* of their presence," whereas "*now* . . . our ladies . . . flock to these exhibitions." "Omega" could not reconcile his enjoyment of Elssler's performance with the enjoyment had by white women of his own social class. He considered it unfortunate that women could "look without a blush" and would "put themselves in a situation" to overhear "offensive remarks which are made by the pit."[113]

The authors of such critiques were clearly uncomfortable sharing the erotic pleasures of seeing dancers with women of their own class. While some forms of material culture, like sheet music covers and the effusive poetry dedicated to Elssler by male admirers and sent to newspapers, explored the erotic qualities of dance within genteel frameworks, dancers were also the subject of more explicit erotica, part of a flourishing pornographic trade among New York booksellers and printmakers. Two rare examples survive. The first, a drawing by artist E. W. Clay that was printed by Henry Robinson, depicts Madame Lecompte, another French dancer who toured the United States in the late 1830s, posed as if in performance but bare-breasted and wearing only a diaphanous skirt, her hair loose about her shoulders and between her breasts.[114] More mysterious is a pair of prints of Celeste as the wild Arab boy and of another dancer referred to as "Miss E. Moore" that contain a novel peek-a-boo feature (figs. 15 and 16). Celeste is costumed as her transvestite character from *The French Spy* with the unusual addition of sylph wings, while Moore is in the cachucha dress popularized by Elssler. The skirt of each dancer, however, lifts away to reveal bare legs beneath and a detailed drawing of female genitalia. Men who consumed dancers within this pornographic framework clearly worried that women's exposure to French dancers might dampen male scopic pleasures or expose women to aspects of this broader sexual culture.

Others argued that there was nothing intrinsically objectionable about dance but instead emphasized the cultural and social context in which it was enjoyed. Elite white male tastemakers worked to make space for their own enjoyment, privileging the interests and habits of their social class. Literary editor Evert Augustus Duyckinck delivered a gratifying assessment for his elite readership. "The coarse and vulgar prefer coarse and vulgar dancing," he explained, so "if the common prejudices against the ballet were verified . . . the most successful dancers" would be the "grossest." Because Elssler's popularity owed much to the "intelligent and cultivated," this indicated that ballet was a worthy art. Duyckinck even contended that appreciation of Elssler was a mark of taste. Her dancing satisfied an "innate desire for cultivation of beauty" that Duyckinck identified with her elite publics and his elite readership.[115] Nathaniel Parker Willis was less sure. He read the "consciousness and alarm" Americans expressed about dance as a sign of its danger. He felt that America was too morally scrupulous to treat ballet as an art rather than an illicit amusement. In Italy and France, the ubiquity of nude sculpture meant that Europeans did not develop "improper association" with the naked form. In the United States, on the other hand, dance would only become an "innocent amusement" when it failed to excite comment. Until then, Willis argued, it remained a "demoralizing spectacle."[116]

Figures 15 and 16. These engravings of Celeste and dancer "Miss E. Moore," costumed in the cachucha dress popularized by Fanny Elssler, have all the features of standard commercial portrait, but a nearly invisible tissue skirt lifts away to reveal bare legs and genitalia. Date and provenance unknown. Binney Collection, Houghton Library, Harvard University.

Transcendentalist philosopher Ralph Waldo Emerson probably read and considered these competing perspectives when he ruminated in his journals on the implications of ballet for young women and men. Emerson saw Elssler in Boston in October 1841. He was delighted and concluded that the merit or danger of ballet "lies wholly with the spectator." The "immorality the immoral will see," but "the pure will not heed it." So long as women remained "pure" and without sexual knowledge, their exposure to the broad sexual culture limited, ballet could not endanger them. The right environment was also key. Emerson ruminated, "I should not think of danger to young women stepping with their father or brother out of happily guarded parlors into this theatre to return in a few hours to the same; but I can easily suppose that it is not the safest resort for college boys who have left Metaphysics, Conic Sections, or Tacitus to see these tripping satin slippers."[117] Harvard students were more at risk because the theater took them away from adult supervision, and they might interact with the more libertine world of theater. No "respectable" young woman would venture to the theater without suitable (male) guardianship. He would ensure that she understood ballet as poetry—nothing prurient.

Unsurprisingly, opponents of theatrical amusements regarded such claims with alarm, while satirists mocked them. A correspondent of the *New York Mercury* charged that it was precisely the "opportunity of seeing forbidden sights under an inoffensive name and in a fashionable way" that drew men and women to see Elssler, whereas "if indecency had been advertised by its proper name," they "would have been ashamed to go near it." In a rare move, this writer called out the metaphorical frameworks of "grace" and "poetry of motion" as a false cover for something else entirely. "Who believes they have any 'Platonic love' [for the dancer]?," the writer asked. Elssler's popularity was due to her erotic appeal. Women were only there to gratify the base desires of their husbands, which put their modesty at risk.[118] Satirists like *Burton's Gentleman's Magazine* turned such objections into humor for their readership while underscoring the reformer's point: a "fastidious damsel" who would not use the word "leg" when describing her piano now sat "spell-bound by the voluptuous movements and elegant contour of a fashionable dancer's well-moulded limbs."[119] White middle-class women should not enjoy ballet as much as they did. In so doing, they risked turning into hypocrites or worse.

Conversations about the nature and implications of women's enthusiasm for Elssler was a reckoning with changes under way in the gendered culture of theater. While some argued that ballet could not be illicit if elite and middle-class women patronized it, others suggested that women were endangering their moral rectitude based on a false premise or to gratify the prurient interests of men and keep up with a popular excitement. This was the argument laid out in a didactic novel by Timothy Shay Arthur from 1845, *The Maiden: A Story for My Young Countrywomen.* The Maiden contrasts the virtuous Anna Lee and her friend Florence Armitage as they navigate courtship in a world of callow and profligate young men. Anna's character and instincts are unimpeachable. Consequently, she disapproves of "stage dancing" and after seeing Celeste comes away convinced that a woman should not be able to "look upon such an exposure without a feeling of deep shame and humiliation."[120]

Conversely, Anna's friend Florence is susceptible to the allures of urban life. She walks out and flirts with young men and even "hatche[s] up a plot . . . [to] make some of our gentleman acquaintances take us" to see Elssler—against her parents' wishes. Later in the novel, Florence discovers that the man she plans to marry (and her theatergoing beau) had seduced and deserted another girl. Speaking from her deathbed, the "polluted" victim, Grace, begs Florence to reconsider her engagement. Arthur's novel spoke of a cultural shift well under way. It advised girls about the implications of new leisure pursuits for their social standing and domestic felicity, with theater implicated in a bad marriage if not also sexual ruin.[121] But with these very efforts to draw the line around gendered middle-class behavior, Arthur's novel suggested the line had already been crossed, if not erased. Perhaps America *was* becoming more like Europe, as Americans imagined it.

Elsslermania was recognized by observers as a watershed in American celebrity and entertainment culture, a new type of celebrity event that revealed some surprising shifts in American culture. Elssler's tour picked up a long-standing conversation about national identity in the context of enduring European cultural influence; however, Elssler's popularity did not fall neatly along a social divide. Elsslermania posed different problems with respect to different publics, which was also a function of her unstable reputation. She was both a sentimental paragon and a decadent European debauchee who undermined republican manhood and compromised genteel white womanhood. When public enthusiasm for Elssler spread into city streets, critics pointed to a dangerous excess they argued was caused by Elssler's Europeanness. The biggest surprise was Elssler's genteel female publics, who represented a growing challenge to theater's culture of white male sovereignty. Elsslermania thus demonstrated the economic viability of an expanding white middle-class market eager to patronize entertainments that a decade earlier had been highly controversial, particularly for genteel white women. Reformers from myriad positions tried to push back, but they did not succeed in chilling Elsslermania. Their tirades marked but failed to discipline diverse theatergoing publics who shared an omnivorous delight in foreign amusements. Over the next decade, managers reshaped theater to appeal more to genteel audiences.

Elsslermania also offered managers and entertainers a series of instructive lessons about the ambivalent power of an expanding mass media. Many of the commercial mechanisms that helped drive Elsslermania remained outside Elssler or her manager, Henry Wikoff's control, in spite of his (or possibly their) efforts. Female entertainers were valuable capital for the men who sought to control and shape their careers, both directly as fathers, husbands, and managers and indirectly through the expanding world of commercial print media.[122] With Elssler, as with earlier celebrities, the less control a star had over her image, the greater its reach and potential to generate new forms of interest—and profit, as a final series of Elssler scandals in 1844 reveal.

Elssler embarked from New York to London in July 1842. She never returned to the United States. Her thirty-year career was made and sustained in the court theaters of Europe, only briefly expanding across the Atlantic. Wikoff, on the other hand, continued to seek out profit from the Elssler tour and began publishing materials that he claimed came from Elssler's journals, though the style was his own. The complete *Letters and Journal of Fanny Elssler* appeared in pamphlet form in 1845 and undoubtedly was written and financed by Wikoff, who was desperate for income. The *Herald* called him out. Wikoff shot back through his own (short-lived) newspaper. Bennett retaliated by publishing correspondence from 1840 revealing Wikoff's dealings with the paper. Wikoff then claimed to have lost $10,000 (or close to $320,000 today) on his management of the tour. Bennett countered with a rumor that after Elssler rebuffed Wikoff's romantic overtures in London in 1842, Wikoff tried to retain funds he had invested for her in US securities, costing her $20,000. Elssler disputed this version of events in a letter to a German paper.[123]

It is impossible to tease out the truth of what happened. Elssler was no doubt being strategic in trying to put the transnational scandal to rest. Wikoff's financial desperation may have been a factor in either an aggressive proposal of marriage or a fraud scheme.[124] But even after his relationship with the dancer ended, Wikoff was inventing new ways of profiting from Elsslermania—Bennett, too. Future impresarios, like P.

T. Barnum, who brought Swedish opera singer Jenny Lind to the United States in 1850, continued to innovate, dreaming up new ways of shaping, disseminating, and expanding the profits for and from celebrity women entertainers.

The implications of Elssler's American tour for performers were far-reaching. During the 1830s and 1840s, European artists continued to seek the profits of American markets. But in a new development, during the intensifying nationalism of the late 1830s through 1840s, a cohort of American artists positioned themselves as the answer to foreign dominance of entertainment. With the conversation about national cultural identity at a new pitch, American actresses innovated upon a playbook developed by foreign stars and their agents, which these women used to shape unprecedented starring careers.

6 The American Actress's Starring Playbook, 1831–1857

In 1856 a printer in Cincinnati published *A Biographical Sketch of Miss Matilda Heron*, probably ghostwritten by the actress herself. The four-inch booklet offered a history of the actress from her childhood in Philadelphia, where she grew up a complete stranger to the theater, through her early dramatic triumphs. It described her discovery of drama and determined pursuit of a stage career over her family's objections. Clearly designed to illustrate Heron's credentials as an actress, the *Sketch* was framed as a lesson in the struggles and "triumph" of a "child of Genius." It drew on long-standing rhetorical strategies surrounding women's stage careers, using the claim of "genius" to frame Heron's single-minded pursuit of professional success while asserting that Heron's "principles were pure, and all her desires on the side of right."[1] The *Sketch* also codified a professional playbook that several generations of women in America had used to grow their careers and celebrity while carefully sidestepping some of the real barriers Heron faced.

Many of the strategies Heron used to maneuver in the American market as a woman with no family ties to the theater replicated Josephine Clifton's strategies two decades earlier. Those same strategies had also proved influential to Charlotte Cushman, who became one of the most famous American actresses of the century. These three women have rarely been placed in the same frame, but together, their stories reveal the intersecting politics of gender, region, nation, and class through which a new generation of American women pursued stage celebrity. Clifton's success as an American actress in the United States rested on strategic deployment of her American nationality, her English acting style, and her pursuit of original dramas by English and American authors, though she struggled with the respectability politics that had become so important to stage celebrity. Clifton rose from obscurity to become one of Thomas Hamblin's Bowery Theatre stars in 1831, then broke with Hamblin and traveled to England to act on the London stage, returning to the United States in 1836 to launch herself as a star tragedian. At the time of Clifton's return, Cushman was attempting to shift from stock to star within the New York market, but with little success. In 1844 Cushman followed Clifton's example and traveled to England, where she enjoyed an unprecedented and transformative London stage debut. She returned to the United States in 1849 a transatlantic celebrity. In the 1856 *Biographical Sketch*, Heron attempted to link herself to Cushman, by then an eminently respectable stage celebrity, by claiming to have played Juliet to Cushman's Romeo and earned Cushman's "praise" and encouragement.[2] This was part of Heron's bid for legitimacy, for, like Clifton, Heron struggled to successfully align herself with the respectability politics governing female stage celebrity.

While family remained a crucial factor shaping starring women's professional decisions, all three of these women were the first in their family to seek a stage career, and they did so in America. Hitherto, most celebrity actresses in America came from English acting families or married into them and began their careers on English stages. Both Clifton and Cushman pursued stage careers as avenues out of family poverty and had to work to achieve respectability. Professional mobility depended upon cultivating alliances with male power brokers, especially theater managers, editors, and theatrical agents, a new class of intermediaries crucial to Heron's midcentury career. While family ties shaped the theater industry well into the century, the changing structure of theater companies facilitated the entry of women without family training or connections, though it increased their vulnerability. The shift from a paternalistic family-based artisan model of theater to a business model exclusively based on contracts did not necessarily emancipate women from the double edge of patriarchal authority that governed women's starring careers early in the century. As Clifton, Cushman, and Heron tried to move out or maneuver around the stock system, each woman's relative success depended upon her ties to male gatekeepers, her geographic mobility, and her cultivation of a viable celebrity persona. Both Clifton and Heron discovered the risks of relying on male power brokers, while Cushman dared to compete directly with men by moving into theater management.

The strategies each woman used to garner public notice and opportunities outside stock work reveal the key elements of theatrical celebrity culture at midcentury—a would-be starring woman's playbook. Geographic mobility was a crucial component of each women's rise, manifesting the reach and density of American theater, as well as the continued cultural importance of England. All connected an English debut with reinvention in the American market, understanding the transatlantic terms of stage celebrity. But ability to maneuver within regional American markets also proved critical to reinvention. Cushman had the most difficulty because she tried to move up through the stock system in the eastern entertainment market, counting on the status of the New York market. But because she supported her mother, siblings, and nephew on her income, she may have been more risk averse—initially. Though starring viability in the East continued to serve as the measure of professional success in the United States, the expansion of western markets made it possible for women like Clifton and Heron to reinvent and support themselves. Heron, like Clifton, was nimbler geographically, which facilitated her starring ambitions as she remade herself on the road.

Choice of dramatic roles and the cultivation of a viable public persona were mutually constitutive of a star's celebrity and central to her strategies of reinvention. Clifton, Cushman, and Heron sought new dramatic compositions and roles to distinguish themselves in a competitive field, with Heron at the vanguard in pursuit of dramatic copyright. They also engaged with an expanding commercial print culture, using rhetorical strategies to align themselves with genteel white womanhood and hail the sought-after middle-class public. But while the expansion of commercial print provided new avenues for the deployment of "public intimacy," each woman struggled for control over the terms of her public persona. Clifton failed to control her public image, while both Cushman and Heron recognized early in their careers the potential of aligning themselves with literary culture, Cushman through her own literary activity.

Especially because these actresses emulated and competed with English thespians, they were very conscious of their identity as Americans, though the meaning and implications of that nationality were unstable. Each struggled to navigate what it meant to be an American actress in an industry in which intensifying nationalist politics were more often associated with theater's plebeian publics, which threatened to work against gendered respectability politics. Both Clifton and Cushman simultaneously emulated and sought to differentiate themselves from Edwin Forrest, the leading American star of the 1830s and 1840s, whose bombastic acting style and repertoire aligned with ideals of rugged white American masculinity and appealed especially to working-class publics. Forrest was a model and cautionary tale for these women. At key moments, Clifton and Cushman linked their careers with Forrest even as they sought to align themselves with the "legitimate drama," emulate English styles of acting, and present themselves as American counterpoints of English actresses. Cushman and Heron similarly struggled to innovate on prevailing dramatic style while cultivating respectability.

Respectability was a central theme in each woman's career, given the larger shift starting in the 1830s in the marketing and class address of theatrical amusements. During the 1830s and especially during the depression of 1837 to 1843, theater competed for audiences with a more diverse array of amusements, particularly lectures and concerts, that also appealed more to the moral concerns of an expanding Christian middle class. Theater managers recognized that they could not survive on the basis of elite patronage alone while worrying about the rowdy pit culture. They increasingly devised a range of strategies to market theatrical amusements to the widest audiences through appeals to respectability. This included reforming theater interiors to eliminate alcohol and prostitution and rearranging seating to break up the rowdy pit culture. By midcentury, when Heron debuted her shocking interpretation of *Camille*, a French play about a courtesan, dramatic theater was highly segmented by class and increasingly marketed around the values of a feminized middle-class public, which is precisely what made *Camille* viable. The American starring woman's playbook involved successful appeals to the tastes and values of this public.

Josephine Clifton's Acts of Reinvention

The rationale behind Josephine Clifton's choice of a play from literary celebrity Nathaniel Parker Willis was clear to avid theatergoer and diarist Philip Hone. After its 1837 debut, he noted that the actress had paid "Willis a thousand dollars . . . in order to have the éclat of a new part, original and American, to enable her to start fair with a Park audience."[3] Clifton hoped to create distance from her morally and aesthetically compromising beginnings at Thomas Hamblin's Bowery Theatre, where she began acting in 1831. She had since traveled to England to act and was launching herself as an American star tragedian at New York's most elite theater with the added arsenal of a new play by a literary celebrity who was himself a champion of national literature. However, Clifton's Bowery history and family ties to prostitution continued to disrupt her professional aspirations, which ironically originated in her mother's efforts to educate her daughters out of her own life in the sex trade.

Clifton's professional rise was part of Hamblin's efforts to rebrand his Bowery Theatre as a democratic, nationalist alternative to Edmund Simpson's Park Theatre and repudiate the Anglo-centric starring system dominated by the Park. In the wake of the 1831 Anderson riots, which broke out at the Park in reaction to English singer Joshua Anderson's alleged anti-American insults, Hamblin briefly renamed the Bowery the American Theatre. Some accused the actor-manager, whom Simpson had actually brought to the United States from England as a star, of inciting the rioters in an elaborate scheme to damage the Park and shore up new business for his own playhouse.[4] Over the next decade, Hamblin's Bowery developed a reputation for its antielite culture, in which melodramatic spectacles predominated. Hamblin capitalized on melodrama while featuring in-house debutantes, whom he promoted in nationalistic terms as "NATIVE TALENT." Training his own star talent helped Hamblin get around the expenses of the starring system.[5] According to an exposé by sensation journalist Mary Clarke, training his own talent also made it possible for Hamblin to push his wife, actress Elizabeth Blanchard Hamblin, into retirement to make way for more marketable, easily controlled, and less expensive debutantes. While Elizabeth was en route to England in 1831 to engage new actors for the American Theatre, Thomas trained and debuted Josephine Clifton, followed by Naomi Vincent two years later and, briefly in 1838, Clifton's sister Louisa Missouri Miller. Hamblin also cultivated an in-house dramatist, Louisa Medina, who penned at least thirty-four melodramas for the theater between 1833 and her death in 1838. Her compositions, which often contained spectacular scenes and adventures, served as successful vehicles for these actresses.[6]

However, a rapid rise from obscurity to starring in a leading New York playhouse did not translate into wealth or professional autonomy for Clifton or her fellow Bowery actresses. For Clifton, a stage career was an avenue out of poverty, an alternative to her mother's work in the thriving urban sex trade. Clifton's mother was reputed to be the Philadelphia madam Mrs. Fermor, later Adelaide Miller. While Hamblin successfully turned untried young women into leading players, he exerted tight control over their careers, with draconian three-year contracts and a meager salary.[7] Clifton later warned her sister about the risks of choosing Hamblin as a mentor.[8] These women—actually girls in their teens at the time of their debuts—remained vulnerable to both sexual and financial exploitation. Vincent became Hamblin's mistress in 1834 and died in childbirth the following year at the age of twenty-one. Hamblin later married Louisa Medina. Both would be implicated in the 1838 death of Missouri Miller, who died several months after her auspicious (though possibly overhyped) debut from an "inflammation of the brain."[9] Medina passed away from apoplexy six months later at the age of twenty-five.[10] The scandals surrounding these young women's deaths brought out angry crowds, mobilized in part by sensationalized press coverage. Meanwhile, Hamblin struggled to finance and rebuild the Bowery Theatre, which burned in 1836 and would burn again before the new structure was completed. Still, these scandals undermined neither his viability as a manager nor his ability to acquire financiers and ultimately rebuild.[11]

Clifton successfully broke away from Hamblin in 1834 and immediately set sail for England, a sure way to remove herself from Hamblin's influence and her Bowery associations. She hoped to develop the dramatic abilities of a leading tragedian. However, the "new aspirant to histrionic fame from the shores of America" failed to make much of a stir when she first appeared on the London stage in October. London critics felt there was "nothing . . . to redeem the character of her voice" and superficial acting, for "the actress appeared in every line."[12] The American press published a very different account of Clifton's London reception. One correspondent even claimed (incorrectly) that Clifton "led the tragedy business of Drury Lane and Covert Garden an entire season, supported by" leading London tragedians "Macready, Kemble, Vandenhoff and Young."[13] Actually, Clifton played supporting roles. But her two seasons acting on English stages reshaped Clifton's reputation and helped her career after she returned to the United States.

Clifton was part of a larger cohort of American performers who traveled to England between the 1820s and 1840s to perform, though she was the first American-born actress to do so. These entertainers were attempting either to reinvent or to pivot stagnant careers, or they had achieved celebrity in the United States and now reached for more global markets and London acclaim. The first American thespian to play England left because there was no market for him in America. African American actor Ira Aldridge began his career in the short-lived African Grove Theatre in New York but found American theaters closed to him. He left for England in 1824 and built a career in England, Ireland, and later continental Europe over the next three decades.[14] During the 1830s, blackface performer Thomas D. Rice and actor Edwin Forrest traveled to Europe from the pinnacle of popularity on American stages, touring to varying degrees of critical acclaim. Clifton and her contemporaries Mary Ann Duff, who returned to England briefly in 1827, Frances Drake, whose plans to travel overseas in the early 1830s never materialized, and later

Charlotte Cushman looked to the English stage when they were frustrated by the capacity of American markets, which were saturated by English stars, to accommodate their ambitions. In contrast to Duff and Drake, who calculated the prospects of entering the high-stakes London market relative to the responsibilities of caring for large families, Clifton was nimbler (if also more vulnerable) because she remained unmarried and had no family in the business.

When she returned from England, Clifton deftly navigated cues concerning national identity and taste. She simultaneously marketed her success in England while emphasizing her Americanness, billing herself as the "celebrated native tragic actress" returned from "her successful tour to Europe."[15] A commercial lithograph, *The Distinguished American Tragic Actress*, probably from this period, depicts "Miss Clifton" (fig. 17). Clifton also worked to distance herself from prevailing associations of American drama with the heightened melodramatic repertoire and style of the Bowery Theatre and her peer Edwin Forrest. While Forrest played to a fantasy of rugged American frontier masculinity through his performance as the title character in John Augustus Stone's *Metamora; or, The Last of the Wompanoags*, Clifton's Americanness was emphatically not visible in either her dramatic characters or her acting style. Instead, Clifton was praised for having learned to "subdue within bounds the exuberance of emotion" associated with her Bowery training and instead channel her "great native powers" in a more temperate, cerebral way. Her acting generated a coveted comparison to the "matchless Siddons."[16] Crucially, Clifton's celebrity remained tied to English standards of acting and dramatic repertoire, even and especially as she forged ties with American writers from whom she solicited original dramatic works.

As Clifton's starring career took off, her reputation as a "native tragic actress" and "American actress" continued to rest on her ability to match English actresses, particularly Fanny Kemble, whose celebrity cast a long shadow following her retirement in 1834. For Clifton's first-ever Boston appearance in October 1836, she opened in *Fazio*. The press understood the significance of her choice, the same "character . . . in which Miss Kemble made her first appearance in this city." Clifton did the part justice: her "conception" was "natural," said one paper, her "tremendous power" and "effect . . . we never saw equaled except by Miss Kemble."[17] If Clifton's acting reminded some of the "Kemble school"—both its "failing and many of the good points"—this was because Charles Kemble had actually coached Clifton in New York in October 1832. Charles found Clifton to be a "very pretty . . . tall woman," yet "her effect is nought."[18] Five years later, Clifton had learned to use her height (and beauty) more

Figure 17. *The Distinguished American Tragic Actress,* an undated lithograph that marketed Josephine Clifton. Rare Book and Manuscript Library, University of Illinois at Urbana-Champaign.

effectively. Due to her early instruction and time in England, her delivery style remained recognizable as a trait of the Kemble school.[19]

While performing repertoire popularized by Kemble, Clifton also sought original dramatic works, emerging as a champion of national dramatic writing aligned with the cause of literary uplift. In 1836 Clifton announced a play contest, offering a $1,000 prize, worth almost $28,000 today, for an original tragedy.[20] Forrest had inaugurated the play contest in 1828, which resulted in John Augustus Stone's celebrated vehicle *Metamora; or, The Last of the Wompanoags.* Forrest continued to patronize American playwrights who wrote heroic and often tragic melodramas that showcased his dramatic style. Though Clifton clearly wanted to cultivate her reputation as a tragedian, patronizing American playwriting was less about showcasing a distinct dramatic style than constituting her place in an emerging nationalist literary movement.

In the 1830s and 1840s, calls for national drama were part of efforts by journalists to foster a national literature, as English authors continued to dominate literary publishing and drama. Literary nationalists disagreed about whether a national literature should repudiate English models and even English approval. In his 1837 address titled "The American Scholar," lecturer and essayist Ralph Waldo Emerson famously argued that fostering native genius depended on the rejection of foreign literary influences.[21] In New York, rival literary camps coalesced around the question of foreign influence, with John O'Sullivan's *United States Magazine and Democratic Review* calling for a "radical exorcising of all British influence from American letters," while the literati who supported the rival *Knickerbocker, or New-York Monthly Magazine* espoused more elite and Anglophilic leanings.[22] Members of this literary and social world, who dominated dramatic criticism and connected ideals of social uplift to literary and dramatic taste, complained that American theater lacked a distinctive national identity because of its "dependence on a foreign market" but then looked askance at dramas by American authors.[23] The sensation melodramas adopted by Forrest or written by Louisa Medina for Hamblin's Bowery were the antithesis of what these aspiring cultural authorities wanted to see as national drama.

Clifton's choice of plays and playwrights suggests that she was well versed in these debates and determined to align herself with elite literary nationalism through dramatic patronage, as one paper put it, "employing her . . . talent to give encouragement and lustre to the dramatic efforts of her countrymen."[24] In 1837 she debuted two new historical dramas by American authors, *Bianca Visconti; or, The Heart Overtasked*, by Nathaniel Parker Willis, and *The Genoese; or, The Bride of Genoa*, by Epes Sargent of Boston. Willis was a prolific writer with an established reputation as a poet and magazine editor. He had recently returned from an extended tour of Europe, where he served as correspondent for the *New York Mirror*, a literary weekly. Back in New York, he continued to position himself as a man of letters at the center of a cosmopolitan social and literary scene, crafting a new role identifiable today as a celebrity journalist. Willis hoped to use his pen to fashion a "new republican aristocracy from the ranks of celebrity" in society, letters, arts, and theater. Playwriting both increased his income and helped cultivate his cosmopolitan bona fides and status as a tastemaker.[25] Theirs was a mutually beneficial relationship of aspiring "native" celebrities: when Clifton played *Bianca Visconti* in Boston in October 1837, a newspaper anticipated a large audience "attracted by the celebrity of the author and the fame of the actress."[26]

Boston journalist Epes Sargent clearly emulated Willis and hoped to escape from his exhausting and uncelebrated work for the *Boston Atlas*.[27] But in the absence of dramatic copyright, it remained difficult for playwrights to make money. Managers and stars generally controlled profits from a new drama: having paid the author a lump sum, they took a cut of receipts from their performances while restricting access to the manuscript. Still, attaching one's literary ambitions to a star patron was the best mechanism for earning money at playwriting and developing a wider literary reputation. Between 1836 and 1837 Sargent wrote *The Genoese* for Clifton and *Velasco; or, A Tragedy in Five Acts* for Ellen Tree, who had arrived in the United States in 1836 just as Clifton was establishing her credentials as an English-style tragedian.

Both Willis's and Sargent's dramas for Clifton were based on historical figures, each tragedy mobilizing sentimental and republican ideals in gendered ways. Willis's verse drama *Bianca Visconti* emulated Elizabethan tragedy and described the rise to power of a fifteenth-century Milanese nobleman named Francesco Sforza and his wife, Bianca Visconti, whose efforts to win her husband's love by securing his political rise form the dramatic arc of the play. Willis was inspired by the historic Bianca Visconti, an ambitious ruler, warrior, and diplomat, but instead he delivered a sentimental cautionary tale of womanly love fixated on an undeserving object. After the spurned bride, Bianca, allows the assassination of her brother to facilitate her husband's ambitions, she promptly goes mad and commits suicide, her "heart overtasked." Francesco takes his crown but learns too late of Bianca's genuine love for him. The play showcased Clifton's emotional range in the tragic heroine's progression from loving innocence to grief and madness. It drew enthusiastic accolades from literati for elevating dramatic tastes, though most agreed that the play's "poetic merit" could not compensate for a lack of dramatic interest.[28] Clifton toured with the piece, which remained an effective vehicle for her "beautiful acting."[29]

Sargent's plays for Clifton and Ellen Tree cast each star actress as a male hero and explored an internal conflict between love and duty to family. Tree's celebrated performance as Ion, the heroic Greek youth in the Thomas Talfourd drama of the same name, created the context in which Clifton decided to play Anthony Montaldo in *The Genoese*. Tree's success portraying a male protagonist in a classicizing drama briefly realigned breeches acting with legitimate drama, allowing ambitious actresses access to more interesting and distinctive roles. Both Clifton and later Cushman emulated Tree in trying to align with dramatic uplift, though adopting male roles remained risky, given the prevailing association of breeches acting with low, melodramatic spectacle. In *The Genoese*, Sargent reimagined the historic Montaldo, who became doge (chief magistrate) of Genoa in the late fourteenth century, as a plebeian freedom fighter torn between love for the patrician's daughter, Laura, who is pledged to the tyrannical doge, Fiesco, and duty to avenge his father's death at the hands of Fiesco and liberate the people of Genoa.[30] Clifton was able to personify heroic ambition through a male protagonist in a breeches role. This play inspired Cushman, who played Laura in Clifton's debut of Montaldo and then went on to adopt Montaldo as part of her early explorations of breeches acting. Unfortunately, Clifton's Montaldo never received the same degree of critical attention as her Bianca Visconti, a disparity probably due to Willis's stature.

Both dramas written for Clifton were played because of their star actresses and in spite of each playwright's effort to produce something of lasting literary and dramatic value. *Bianca Visconti* and *The Genoese* succeeded because of the growing reputation of the actresses for whom they were written. Neither Willis nor Sargent found lasting fame or success as a playwright. Sargent eventually gave up playwriting and, much like Willis, cobbled together a multifaceted literary career, publishing poetry and novels and working as a journalist and magazine editor. Later, Sargent encouraged another aspiring author, Anna Ogden Mowatt, to write for the stage.[31] Still, writing plays for preeminent American and English tragic actresses and cultivating ties with the theatrical world enhanced these men's literary reputations and cultural capital.

Even as Clifton's patronage of American dramatic authors facilitated her reinvention, she struggled to maneuver within the narrow respectability politics around female stage celebrity. During the period of her professional comeback, Clifton and her allies crafted a redemption story about a virtuous, self-made striver who had escaped from the world of vice unscathed and chosen a better path. This echoed the discourse of moral reformers and tropes in antebellum fiction, which fixated on economic and social injustices against women while drawing a stark distinction between "immoral" behavior and women's response to poverty. After Clifton's sudden death in 1847, Willis lamented that the actress spent much of her life having to "contend" with "universal prejudice against her" and "injurious estimate of her character," though he testified that her "virtue and goodness [were] never yet heard doubted . . . by one who knew her well."[32] Though Clifton managed to reinvent herself in 1836, her background and early association with Hamblin always threatened her. In 1838 Clifton's career was rocked by a personal tragedy, the death of her sister Louisa Missouri Miller, that had real professional ramifications, reviving scandals from early in Clifton's career. At this pivotal moment, Clifton used print to speak directly to her public about female virtue in the theater profession. Her continued success as a star depended upon her ability to maneuver within the intensifying respectability politics governing theater, both onstage and off.

Three months after her auspicious stage debut, in June 1838, sixteen-year-old Louisa Missouri Miller collapsed in the arms of Louisa Medina, who was then married to Thomas Hamblin. By all accounts, the girl "died *almost a maniac,*" her extreme psychological distress exacerbated by the *"publication of an abusive article"* about Hamblin's sordid history in the *Polyanthos*, a gossip rag.[33] Missouri Miller had been at the center of a custody struggle between her mother, Adelaide Miller, a notorious prostitute, and Thomas Hamblin, whom Adelaide had paid to prepare her daughter for the stage. The coroner's inquest read like a Bowery melodrama: Louisa's brother testified that he intervened on behalf of their mother after Thomas tried to travel alone with Louisa, to which Thomas countered that Adelaide was trying to break the contract for Louisa's instruction and control all the profits from Louisa's career herself.[34] The question of whether and how a girl might earn a viable living while protecting her sexual virtue, or the appearance thereof, was central to the conflict over Louisa. Adelaide apparently wanted to return her daughter to boarding school, but Louisa was determined to become an actress. The girl was caught between the competing financial interests of her mentor and her family. Missouri Miller's professional prospects were vulnerable to exposure of her mother's profession and to gossip about Hamblin's proclivity for seducing actresses—and patronizing brothels. Clifton's resurgent career was vulnerable as well.

Missouri Miller's death was devastating news for Clifton both professionally and personally. She canceled an engagement in Lexington, Kentucky, and rushed back to New York, where she faced rumors that she had tried to convince Missouri Miller to quit out of jealousy. According to these reports, the strain of the family conflict, instigated by Clifton, led to the girl's flight, ensuing emotional collapse, and death. The penny press had a field day with the scandal, which outlasted initial attacks on Hamblin. In the early days after Louisa's death, angry crowds hounded the theater manager, threatening riot and destruction of his property. Rumors circulated that Medina had poisoned Missouri Miller out of jealousy. But the inquest ultimately exonerated both Medina and Hamblin of any suspicion of wrongdoing—and indicated that Missouri Miller had died a virgin, "demonstratum intactum esse."[35] The theater of public opinion in the street receded before a contest of print as editors entertained a readership eager for sensationalism with descriptions of Louisa's deranged, dissolute mother and jealous sister.

Clifton responded by publishing a "Card—To the Public" in the papers. It offered a counternarrative that deployed middle-class frameworks of virtuous labor to explain the sisters' chosen career while challenging the theater's association with sexual immorality. Clifton's mode of address made a claim to respectability. She was reluctant, suffering "sorrow and humiliation" in thus "present[ing] herself before the public," but she was driven to defend her "honor as a woman" and sisterly "affection."[36] Clifton then worked to position the stage as a legitimate path to self-sufficiency, in contrast to the sex trade. "Children of misfortune from our very birth," she explained, "it was due to our characters that we should by our own efforts protect and maintain ourselves." This narrative would have resonated with the burgeoning white middle-class moral reform movement then active in New York, which labored to protect girls from seducers and entrapment in the sex trade. Clifton asserted that girls from humble or morally ambiguous origins could pursue a virtuous path aligned with middle-class standards. Clifton further clarified that, contrary to rumor, she had actually encouraged Louisa to pursue a stage career. Though Clifton avoided accusing Hamblin of wrongdoing, she explained that she had delivered a "warning (alas unheeded) as to the . . . instruction which [Louisa] should *avoid*."[37] This admission was risky, as it acknowledged the harassment women in the theater faced while still asserting that actresses could nonetheless preserve their character and virtue.

The scandal surrounding Missouri Miller's death revisited the ongoing question whether the theater as a place of labor could protect and preserve the virtue of female performers. This had direct implications for the patrons it could draw. Theaters in the late 1830s faced intense competition with paratheatrical entertainments, especially lectures and concerts, that also appealed to the moral concerns of an expanding Christian middle class, a crucial market. Managers in turn devised a range of strategies to market theatrical amusements to the broadest possible audience by appealing to respectability. Thus in 1836 and 1837, Bowery Theatre playwright Louisa Medina also wrote for the *Ladies' Companion*, which portrayed the Bowery as a fashionable and respectable venue.[38] Rumors surrounding Missouri Miller's death briefly threatened Hamblin's bid to finance and complete the new Bowery, but the risk to Clifton, who needed managers nationwide to engage her, was much greater. When sensation journalist and frustrated playwright Mary Clarke used the Missouri Miller scandal to expose Hamblin's sexual crimes (and revive her own stagnating literary career), Clifton became collateral damage, cast as a fallen woman and a threat to the virtuous American publics sought by managers and stars.

Clarke's *Concise History of the Life and Amours of Thomas S. Hamblin, Late Manager of the Bowery Theatre* corroborated some of Clifton's narrative while leveling scandalous accusations of sexual impropriety at Hamblin. Clarke presented herself as an advocate and confidante of Hamblin's first wife, Elizabeth Blanchard, a position that allowed her to deliver a "public recitation of the rumors and scandals" that had attached to Hamblin over the years.[39] Much like moral reformers, Clarke asserted her respectability through her efforts to expose a dangerous man and the immoral confidence women around him, including Clifton, who Clarke argued posed a wider social threat. Clarke reported that Hamblin had "extracted" Clifton from the "dens of infamy" run by her mother, expecting to "become proprietor" of Clifton's "personal beauty [and] dormant talent." He merely appeared to rescue Clifton only to prey upon her and turn her into his "public mistress." Clarke thus reified an old association between actresses and prostitutes. Women like Josephine Clifton threatened the "young and virtuous girls" of "the green-room" and insulted respectable theater patrons. Clarke even insinuated that Clifton became pregnant by Hamblin, which "sent her into retirement for a lapse of time," leaving open the question of whether Clifton had had a child out of wedlock or perhaps an abortion.[40] There was no redemption for the actress in Clarke's telling, which cut to the deep-seated anxieties of the very publics Clifton was cultivating. While Hamblin remained the clear villain, Clarke's characterization of his world affirmed the middle-class concerns, especially of moral reformers, that any exposure to sexual vice threatened the virtue of innocent young women and men.

The 1838 scandal rocked Clifton's career, though it did not destroy it. Though Clifton had allies in the press who defended her character and applauded her return to touring at the end of the summer, her bid for respectability had been shattered. The next decade was professionally uneven. In order to protect her hard-won stature, particularly in light of attacks on her virtue and deservedness as a public figure, Clifton allied with actors to reinforce her reputation as an American star. That fall, she toured with rising American tragedian J. R. Scott, who was also a product of Hamblin's Bowery culture and a rival of Edwin Forrest. This joint tour may have been the plan all along, but it probably also helped Clifton secure engagements from managers worried about her draw. She joined forces with Edwin Forrest in 1842 in a tour during which she was supposed to have committed adultery with him, or so witnesses testified in Forrest's 1851 divorce trial, four years after Clifton's death. Sketches published about Clifton during her tour with Forrest struggled to paint her as a tragic victim of salacious gossip. The memory of her brief and scandalous association with Hamblin clearly endured.

Clifton maintained a level of personal independence unusual for star actresses, though "universal prejudice" may have made it more difficult for her to secure engagements, hence her joint tours in this period. Clifton's periodic absences from the stage during the early 1840s were also a result of deteriorating health. She suffered from gout, as well as from uterine complaints that produced intervals of severe pain and heavy bleeding.[41] She remained unmarried until illness compromised her ability to endure the rigors of a touring schedule. In 1845 or 1846 she married a theater manager in New Orleans, entered semiretirement, and died of a "violent hemorrhage" in 1847 at the age of thirty-four.[42]

The shifts in Clifton's public reputation over her lifetime suggest that while she operated on the edge of respectability, her strategies mostly worked. While Mary Clarke cast Clifton as Hamblin's mistress, possibly the mother of an illegitimate child, and consequently as beyond redemption, Clifton pushed back using available moral reform frameworks of the virtuous laborer who followed a respectable path away from a life of infamy. This made it possible for Clifton to achieve unprecedented celebrity as an unmarried actress with an illicit past. Subsequent actresses used many of Clifton's same professional strategies, particularly Charlotte Cushman, who began her New York career in the context of Clifton's reemergence as a star. From very early stages in her own career, Cushman worked diligently to construct a reputation palatable to middle-class standards of respectability.

Charlotte Cushman's Maneuvers

In October 1844 Charlotte Cushman and her fourteen-year-old African American maid, Sallie Mercer, embarked for Liverpool. Cushman had an offer to join English tragedian William Charles Macready in Paris, letters of introduction to facilitate social and professional connections, and over a decade of experience with theaters in New York and Philadelphia. Acting with Macready during his most recent American tour brought Cushman new notice, but she was wary of allowing her professional advancement to be connected too closely with his celebrity—or any actor's. Cushman ultimately turned down Macready's offer to support him in Paris. She had also been warned by a friend that unseating Helen Faucit, one of the most popular actresses on the London stage, as Macready's costar would not bode well for Cushman's London debut.[43] Still, no other offer of a position in London was forthcoming. Cushman's limited funds were dwindling rapidly when she was approached by American actor Edwin Forrest about performing with him at the Princess's Theatre. She insisted on appearing for one night prior to Forrest's engagement to ensure that her debut was not overshadowed by his celebrity.

Cushman's London debut on February 13, 1845, as Bianca in *Fazio* was a "triumphant success," exceeding even her "most *sanguine expectations*." Charlotte understood her achievement in terms of both her nationality and her repertoire. When she reminded her mother, "I have done more than an *American* has ever done in London," Cushman referenced not only critical acclaim and public enthusiasm but also the roles she played in her first two weeks, "Bianca 3 times, Lady Macbeth 4 times, Emilia twice & Rosalind twice."[44] These were standouts from the legitimate English drama, associated with a lineage of leading dramatic actresses. Cushman's debut strategy proved providential. On February 17, when she played Desdemona to Forrest's Othello, Cushman was cheered but Forrest was hissed, the fruits of his emerging rivalry with Macready and negative responses to his acting.[45] Cushman's professional rise became the context for Edwin Forrest's failure, which still had the potential to jeopardize her uncertain position.

Both the London and the New York press situated Charlotte's success within the history of the transatlantic starring system, but the stakes looked different on either side of the Atlantic. The London press debated Cushman's merits and failings while celebrating her as "the best importation from the New World that we have yet had amongst us," an indirect jibe at Forrest. A critic imagined that Cushman's triumph "repaid" her country's "heavy dramatic debt for enticing away from us so many of our best actors."[46] In New York, surprise at Cushman's London success in the context of Forrest's failure folded into competing views of the polarizing American actor. The *Herald* was relieved to champion an alternative to Forrest, whom it considered a mere "second-rate or third-rate actor," while acknowledging that New York critics had failed to appreciate Cushman years earlier.[47] In a rare reversal of the transatlantic starring system, the comparatively underrated New York stock actress would spend the next four years starring in Great Britain. Cushman returned to the United States in 1849 a transatlantic stage celebrity with a fortune.

Cushman's strategies in the decade prior to her transformative London season suggest some of the real barriers facing American actresses who wished to compete with foreign stars in an economically struggling American market, especially women without family ties to the business.

Figure 18. *Charlotte Saunders Cushman "of the Walnut Street Theater"* by Thomas Sully, 1843. Library Company of Philadelphia.

Between 1835 and 1844, Cushman maneuvered mainly in the eastern market, cultivating alliances with men in the theater business and the press, looking to English stars as models and mentors, and seeking to develop a distinct persona onstage through her repertoire and offstage through the press. Unable to break out of stock work, Cushman pursued theater management, defying gender boundaries within the profession while framing her moves in the rhetoric of middle-class women's reform. Cushman understood the importance of theater's expanding middle-class publics and worked tirelessly to align herself with the values of genteel white womanhood. Cushman was remarkable for managing to simultaneously transgress gendered boundaries within the industry and achieve respectability as an actress. As Cushman maneuvered, she innovated on the available playbook for aspiring actresses not only in her pursuit of new roles and professional opportunities but also with her use of print culture, deploying middle-class gender ideals in order to appeal to this expanding theater public. Though these moves did not secure stardom for her in America, they provided the ground upon which she successfully broke into the English market.

Cushman pursued these strategies while remaining unmarried, which continued to be rare for women in the profession. Neither did she show any romantic or sexual interest in men, preferring women for intimate relationships and also as lovers. Cushman's life partnership with sculptor Emma Stebbins, whom Cushman met in Rome in 1857, followed a succession of intense romantic friendships with women, particularly while living in Philadelphia in the early 1840s. The few surviving portraits of Cushman from this period are testaments of these relationships. An unfinished portrait by Thomas Sully remained in the possession of Philadelphian Anne Hampton Brewster, whose diary indicates that she was the more besotted party (fig. 18). Meanwhile, Charlotte cultivated a romance with Rosalie Sully, who also painted Charlotte's portrait shortly before her departure for England. This world of female erotic desire, neither constrained nor named by the late nineteenth-century category of "homosexual" or "lesbian," was illegible to most of Cushman's male contemporaries, though her circles of female admirers later in her career suggest other forms of knowing.[48] In the twentieth century, biographers grappled with Cushman's woman-centered world and relationships, but during her lifetime and following her death in 1876, Cushman's lack of romantic ties with men were celebrated as evidence of her "purity" and "virtue."[49] Cushman's respectability was hard won, given her background and family, as well as the risks for a young, unmarried woman pursuing close professional alliances with male power brokers and attempting to compete with them.

Cushman was thirteen when she left grammar school to seek music instruction. She intended to become an opera singer. This was as much a matter of ambition as necessity. Years earlier, her father had declared bankruptcy and at some point deserted her mother, who was keeping a boardinghouse in Boston. Cushman's vocal career was cut short by a disappointing operatic debut, later attributed to vocal problems, so she focused on acting instead.[50] In 1836 the twenty-year-old novice obtained a position at the Bowery Theatre, where Thomas Hamblin offered a three-year contract at twenty-five dollars a week (worth almost $700 today) for Charlotte's first year with a ten-dollar raise each successive year, promising, as Cushman recalled, that "he would make as great a success for me as he had done for . . . Miss Vincent." Though Cushman later regretted her youthful ignorance at preferring Hamblin's tempting offer to the "advantage of . . . even an inferior place at the Park Theatre," the Bowery had indeed produced viable American talent who successfully competed with English stars.[51] But after her promising first week, the Bowery Theatre burned down on September 22, 1836. Cushman was left without a dramatic wardrobe, in debt to her seamstress, with her contract void, but she was desperate for the income she used to support her mother and siblings still living in Boston. She used new professional contacts to secure a position in Albany but remained focused on New York. In April 1837 she was hired by New York's Park Theatre as a walking lady, or utility actress, for twenty dollars a week, or about $550 today. Whereas in Albany she had been able to "get practice" in a range of leading characters, in New York she was at the bottom of the company hierarchy but hoped to earn the notice of New York critics and theatergoers to advance her stature.[52] Two years later, after Charlotte's sister Susan and her infant son were deserted by Susan's much older husband, their father's former business associate, Charlotte helped prepare her sister to join the company. The stage was a viable professional path for both Cushman women.

As a woman without family ties to the theater, Cushman deployed legible frameworks of economic necessary and family sacrifice to appeal to her publics. Across her long career, a narrative of "duty" in which Charlotte was the "'savior' of her family" helped "legitimate Charlotte's ambition" such that it "never overtly refuted 'appropriate' norms for women."[53] An early sketch from 1838 developed these themes, informing *Herald* readers that the new actress came from a "most respectable family" and was raised by her uncle, "one of our wealthiest merchants" (this merely hinted at the actual history of her father's ruin), but because she had "a soul above dependence, and talents of the highest order," Cushman "select[ed] the stage as a profession."[54] Later sketches described her Puritan ancestry, claiming (incorrectly) that she had relatives who arrived on the *Mayflower*. This transparent bid for respectability attempted to counter the shame of her father's ruin and the question of Susan's marital status. This became a serious problem during their British tours, when Susan joined Charlotte as support. In early 1846 a vengeful Edwin Forrest began spreading rumors about Susan's "immorality," implying that her seven-year-old son was illegitimate, which prompted Charlotte to "send for marriage certificates, bills, and papers to prove our respectability." The rumors could have jeopardized Charlotte's growing acceptance within elite English social circles, as well as her status in the profession.[55]

Unlike Clifton, Cushman recognized early in her career the potential of print to shape her reputation. During the 1830s, she followed Fanny Kemble's example, using print to expand her renown, align herself with literary culture, and supplement her income. She published poetry in newspapers in the cities where she was performing and in literary periodicals.[56] After a positive mention in the *New Yorker* in 1836, Cushman cultivated a relationship with its editor, E. Burke Fisher, and, through him, with other journalists, which helped her place her own compositions.[57]

She used print to create an explanatory framework for her career and align the theater with middle-class values of virtuous labor and respectable leisure.

An early story that Cushman placed in *Godey's Lady's Book* in 1837, "Extracts from My Journal: The Actress," took on persistent characterization of the stage as a demoralizing sphere by pitting the artistic promise of a young actress against the moral degradation of an abusive marriage. The tragic portrait of Leoline, who becomes an actress to support her family after her father's ruin and death, then enters a demoralizing marriage, was clearly designed to "win the sympathy of women readers who might hear of or see [Cushman] onstage."[58] The story played with themes of moral corrosion and dissemblance but contrasted woman's victimization in marriage, itself a prominent trope in drama and fiction, with the artistic value of a stage career. Leoline is a promising young talent until marriage takes her away from a respectable profession suited to her "intellectual accomplishments." When Leoline finally returns to the stage, the "tortures" of marriage to a profligate and indifferent husband have actually cost her her ability to act, and she dies shortly thereafter due to the strain of her marriage. Cushman thus took on the enduring critique of acting as dangerous dissemblance by pushing readers to consider the "mask" women wore in everyday life, especially due to private suffering. The story asks her readers to consider whether marriage and domesticity are always preferable or whether a woman might actually be able to live a virtuous life on the stage, one suited to her genius.[59]

Cushman also used her pen to connect herself with actor celebrities at key moments in her career. In Albany in December 1836, Cushman composed and delivered an address in honor of Edwin Forrest's first London success. It appeared two months later in the *Spirit of the Times*. By delivering the address, Cushman highlighted her authorship while connecting her rise with Forrest's career. The verses reference Forrest's former Albany appearances, when he "basked in your smiles, or wrung per chance a tear . . . And in his bearing Genius stood confest!" Cushman also mobilized nationalistic pride in the "Forrest of our native land," who had since humbled Britain, which now "bowed before this wonder of the stage":

> He sought to grasp the sceptre of his art
> That he deserv'd to win; all know full well
> That he *has* won it, England's praises tell![60]

Winning "England's praises" in 1836 was a vindication of Forrest's popularity with American audiences. Nearly a decade later, in 1845, Cushman earned "England's praises," while some of Forrest's former critics in America found vindication in Forrest's failure during his return. English approbation remained a dominant measure of artistic consequence.

Though Cushman had played leading business in Albany during the 1836–37 season, her eye remained trained on the New York market, which paid higher salaries and where critical notice could do more to advance her career. But when Cushman returned to take a position as a walking lady, or utility actress, at the Park Theatre in April 1837, she discovered that she had little room to maneuver within the existing stock hierarchy. Cushman developed a unique repertoire out of supporting parts foisted on the walking lady. She did what she could with the mixed bag of roles in which she was cast, "old women, young men, chambermaids, tragic queens, and comic ladies." She turned minor characters, such as the fortune-teller crone Meg Merriles, into prominent figures of interest and embodiments of "female power."[61] She also used benefit nights to try new roles, a strategy widely practiced by stock actresses who exercised little control over casting decisions. Ellen Tree and Josephine Clifton were clearly models for Cushman, as was Edwin Forrest. In May 1838, a mere month after Forrest had debuted the role of Claude Melnotte in the new drama *The Lady of Lyons*, Cushman chose to play Claude Melnotte for her benefit night rather than the ingenue lead, Pauline.[62] She revived the role to critical acclaim in London, inviting direct comparison with Forrest. In 1839 Charlotte selected Antonio Montaldo, a breeches part recently introduced by Josephine Clifton, for her benefit night, Susan playing the ingenue love interest. Charlotte used this strategy to great success in London years later, starring as Romeo opposite Susan's Juliet.[63] Cushman's artistic creativity made her reliable support for touring stars and popular with Park Theatre audiences, but this did not translate into a higher salary or a leading position.

Yet Charlotte did not choose to go on the road. A New Orleans editor, having heard about Cushman's unparalleled Claude Melnotte, advised, "Charlotte is big enough to do it well if she only knows how."[64] But Cushman may not have been ready to launch herself as a regional star or felt financially secure, given her status as family breadwinner. She also encountered contradictory messages about her viability. She was a clear favorite with Park Theatre audiences but was unable to satisfy critics like *Herald* editor James Bennett, who praised her potential while lamenting a "helter-skelter, random, devil-may-care kind of style" that he believed Cushman "mistakes . . . for ease and freedom." Cushman continued to work on her vocal control and dramatic finesse, yet the qualities criticized by Bennett were precisely those that excited

English audiences in 1845, making Cushman seem distinctly and excit-ingly *American*. In America, Cushman failed to conform to expectations of physical beauty and dramatic style in a potential lead actress. Her dis-tinctive dramatic style was often criticized as too forceful. In England, however, the "masculine" qualities in her acting affirmed British expec-tations of American national identity and helped elevate her, even over Forrest. His "'democratic,' explosive, unrestrained" form of manliness "appeared vulgar and uncouth" in the British context, while Cushman was read as both "chaste and respectable as well as powerfully mascu-line."[65] Her unique qualities as an actress carried different associations overseas, creating draw and affirming her national identity. British ce-lebrity changed the way Cushman would be received by critics in the United States and increased her draw with American audiences. As she predicted in a letter to her mother in early 1845, "The very idea of my being thought so much of here will make me so much more valuable at home."[66]

In New York back in 1840, as Cushman approached the end of her third season at the Park, she faced the dilemma of being employed at the most elite theater in the dominant entertainment market, serving the diverse casting needs of the manager with great success, yet her weekly salary did not change. The lingering depression that followed the finan-cial panic of 1837 made managers more tightfisted than usual. Manager Simpson clearly recognized that he had Charlotte at a disadvantage so long as she did not have a viable alternative to his theater. Seeing no op-portunity for advancement at the Park, Cushman looked to other theaters in need of a lead actress. The dismal economic climate created unusual opportunities as management of smaller theaters became a revolving door. After Simpson turned down Cushman's request for a raise for her-self and Susan, to twenty-five dollars and twelve dollars per week, re-spectively, the sisters left for positions at William Burton's newly built National Theatre in Philadelphia. Charlotte was hired to play leading business—at last. Unfortunately, Burton struggled financially. To save his fledgling venture, he poured everything into a new production, the *Naiad Queen*, a holiday production enhanced by a spectacle of over one hundred women onstage. The production featured tableaus of scantily clad sea nymphs and a parade of Amazons commanded by Cushman.[67] Unsurprisingly, Cushman's life partner, Emma Stebbins, made no allu-sions to the *Naiad Queen* in her biography, published in 1878 shortly after Cushman's death and carefully curated from Cushman's papers. This production did not fit with Cushman's celebrity as an avatar of the legitimate English drama, but it did reflect the realities of work as a stock actress in the early 1840s. After closing the Philadelphia theater, Burton brought the production to New York, determined to wring as much money from it as he could after his losses. Charlotte and Susan decided to return to the Park Theatre at their former positions and salaries.

In March 1842 Cushman made an unprecedented move to launch herself into theater management, announcing a subscription drive to build a more affordable but still respectable alternative to the Park Theatre. This was daring, not least because Cushman had witnessed Burton's failure, but also because women rarely entered theater management alone. Other women who had managed in New York, like Elizabeth Blanchard Hamblin and Annette Nelson, relied on male partners to help them maneuver in the male-dominated world of New York real estate. Still, their attempts were short-lived. They were established stars, and though Cushman had drawn critical acclaim in a number of productions, she hardly rivaled their stature. For these reasons, Cushman was a risky investment for a property owner. It is unclear how much money Cushman raised before New York scion John Jacob Astor, mortgagee of the property, had second thoughts and withdrew his support in June.[68] Fortunately, Cushman's scheme brought her to the attention of Philadelphia businessman E. A. Marshall, who was looking for a new manager for the Walnut Street Theatre.

While men had long used management to improve their stature and earning power, this strategy was less available to women, who were more likely to gain access to management during economic downturns. In fact, Marshall was probably drawn to the idea of hiring a "manageress" because the rival Chestnut Street Theatre was being managed by Mary Maywood in place of her father, pushed out by the stockholders, who attributed the theater's financial difficulties to his "mismanagement." Mary closed the theater before the season was over, unable to make up prior losses to pay the company or orchestra.[69] Cushman's equally brief tenure as manager underscored the real limits to women's professional mobility through management. Management required that women become not merely peers and competitors of men onstage but also authorities over them offstage. Before the end of the season, Cushman was pushed out of her position by stage manager William Rufus Blake, confirming for fellow Philadelphia actor-manager Francis Wemyss that women in management "were out of their proper sphere of action."[70] Actually, Cushman faced "belligerency" from Blake, who also mocked Charlotte's and her sister's aspirations for professional and social mobility.[71] In his memoir, Wemyss referred to this as an "era of petticoat government," mobilizing a metaphor long used to police women's involvement in politics through the specter of gendered inversion of authority.[72] Especially because actresses could and did command profits in the thousands, assuming public authority over men through management was deeply troubling to their peers, many of whom expected and clearly cheered to see Cushman (and Maywood) fail.

Cushman was unique in seeking to maneuver around some of the gender boundaries within the industry, but she did so with careful attention to intensifying respectability politics around the theater. Her established reputation as a poet aligned her with a form of genteel feminine accomplishment. This further suggested that Cushman would be an avatar for the elevation of theater both intellectually and morally. She made this appeal central to her bid to open a theater in New York and deployed it during her tenure as manager in Philadelphia. In March 1842 she announced that her New York theater would be affordable without compromising respectability, operating with reduced prices, no saloons, and no third tier. Eliminating the private boxes in the third tier was essential in a theater run by a woman and also appealed to middle-class reform. "We have begun a general movement of reform in every thing," *Herald* editor James Bennett joked, "and why not in theatricals!"[73] Cushman promised the same for the Walnut Street Theatre.

Cushman was at the vanguard of the theater reform efforts managers pursued more purposefully over the 1840s, especially when faced with competition from the museum theater, which emerged in Boston and New York in 1840 as a purveyor of "family amusement." Marketing entertainment as family amusement signaled the absence of prostitutes and alcohol. The "lecture room" theaters in museums promised no morally compromising content and gradually introduced didactic plays. With admission priced at twenty-five cents, equivalent to the cost of the theater pit, museums could draw upon a wider social demographic while addressing Christian scruples.[74] Cushman clearly had these publics in mind when she promised that the "smiling and happy faces of whole families" would look down from the boxes of the Walnut Street Theatre, while "order and quiet" reigned among the "artisan and man of leisure" in the pit. They would enjoy plays that nurtured a "healthy tone of feeling" with "morality and generous sentimentality." Under Cushman's management, theater would return to an imaginary past when it was enjoyed by a "respectable and cultivated audience."[75] Though Cushman tried to align herself with these publics, her efforts at cultivating genteel respectability intensified the ridicule from peers like Blake, who mocked the Cushman sisters' aspirations to the "upper ten sphere" and "female sacred button-hole society." Appeals to respectability were not embraced across the profession, yet they were vital for women who hoped to position themselves in highly visible entrepreneurial roles.

Cushman continued to work at the Walnut after being pushed out of her management role, but she shifted her focus to developing her credentials as a star. Her next professional opportunity was also secured by courting male power brokers within the industry. She assumed the appropriately gendered role of support for English tragedian William Charles Macready, but she did so by aggressively pursuing an uncertain opportunity that further violated gendered scripts within the industry. Her relationship with Macready reveals how Cushman defied tacit gendered double standards around ambition and self-promotion. In October 1843 she supported Macready during a starring engagement at the Walnut Street Theatre. Macready was so impressed with Cushman's acting that he invited her to perform with him in Boston for fifty dollars. She eagerly accepted, but the arrangement fell through when the Boston manager refused. Undaunted, Cushman followed Macready to Boston, delivering a letter with an enclosed poem. While Macready ultimately paid her the promised fifty dollars, he mistook her professional persistence and unstinting fandom for a romantic overture, writing in his diary, "I think it is only a duty to myself to be strictly circumspect," as he had "not the slightest purpose, dream, or intent of wrong or folly" in this "strange country."[76] Not sure how to interpret Cushman's overtures, Macready was careful to meet her in the common room of the hotel to avoid any appearance of impropriety. Cushman continued to patronize Macready's performances, sending notes, poetry, and even flowers, clearly hoping to ingratiate herself and remain in his sights as he continued his tour.[77] Cushman had been similarly persistent in cultivating a friendship with Fanny Kemble Butler back in Philadelphia. As Macready warmed to Cushman's advances, she shared gossip about Butler's personal and professional plans with him.[78]

Cushman's strategy worked. Macready hired Cushman as support for his New York engagement in December 1843 but bristled at her attempts to position herself as his professional peer. He was annoyed by the elaborate "puffs" for her in New York papers. When she asked him to play for her benefit, he determined to put her in her place by agreeing to play for another actor's benefit, which exacerbated his annoyance when after the performance he "was called for—and so was Miss Cushman! ! !"[79] Macready recognized Cushman's dramatic promise but was uncomfortable with her courtship, which he struggled to see in strictly professional terms. In addition to gender inversion, Cushman's Boston pursuit disrupted Macready's largesse as mentor. Two years later, while facing pressure from a

London manager to act with Cushman, Macready wrote angrily, "This woman is full of the idea of her own importance."[80] Macready was known for his temper, which he directed liberally at actors and actresses who failed to live up to his exacting standards. He abused his costar Helen Faucit in rehearsals and railed about her mediocrity in his diaries. Jealous of his own stature, overexacting in his dramatic standards, and expecting deference from his peers, Macready did not know what to make of the American novice actress who was determined to position herself as his equal. In 1844, prior to her transatlantic voyage, Cushman published a tribute to Macready in the *Anglo-American*, a literary periodical, recalling "the seasons when I in thy conquests shared." Cushman wrote nakedly of her "wild ambition," a daring confession, given the usual tenor of Cushman's writing about her career.[81] Having gained confidence and stature, Cushman continued to stretch the narrow gendered frameworks governing her career while strategizing her pivotal voyage overseas.

The Moral Dilemmas of Matilda Heron

Like Clifton and Cushman, Matilda Heron chose the theater as a profession. And though Heron was born in Ireland, her training and professional career occurred exclusively in US theaters. She moved rapidly from obscurity to national stardom by innovating on the playbook of ambitious American actresses. While Cushman struggled for close to a decade to maneuver within the stock system before her starring success, Heron's impatience for stardom led her to seek a distinctive role in which she could market herself. She also shared Clifton's understanding of the possibilities of itinerancy for reshaping her reputation, particularly as she faced attacks from men with whom she had worked. Heron ultimately became nationally renowned for her adaptation of Alexandre Dumas *fils*'s drama *La dame aux camélias*, popularized in America as *Camille*. While prior adaptations had transformed the protagonist from courtesan to "coquette," Heron reintroduced the problem of prostitution into the play but within a distinctly American moral framework. Heron's *Camille* was part of an expanding repertoire of female-driven melodramas adapted from French originals that focused on the "moral plight of women" and successfully appealed to a gentrified feminized audience in American theater.[82] But while dramas that featured women in moral dilemmas sold tickets, actresses still strained to shield from view personal lives that deviated from the respectability politics of their target publics.

Heron was from an upwardly mobile immigrant family. Her father was a lumber merchant from Ireland. Her elder brother entered the steamship business and became the president of the Heron Line. As a girl, Heron studied elocution in Beaugureau's French Academy in Philadelphia, which developed her interest in drama, a trajectory that helped legitimize her interest in the stage. The 1856 *Biographical Sketch* dealt frankly with her family's opposition to her chosen career: her father grudgingly gave "his blessing," while her brother offered "$2000 per annum, if she would quit the stage." Heron "respectfully declined," and they were estranged for two years. Struggles with her health precipitated her family's second attempt to "reclaim" Heron "from the profession," but their "efforts were futile."[83] Heron's biography presented a stage career as a legitimate avenue for a woman's intellect and artistic genius, much as Anna Ogden Mowatt argued in her 1854 *Autobiography of an Actress* (likely an influence on Heron): writing poetry and prose was merely a temporary "safety-valve to [Heron's] mind" compared with the stage.[84] When Heron's teacher, Walnut Street Theatre stage manager Peter Richings, told her that she had neither the "voice, conception or fire" required for success, Heron replied, "I cannot think of bidding adieu to all my

Figure 19. Mezzotint of Matilda Heron in 1851 as Bianca in Henry Hart Millman's tragedy *Fazio*, probably used to promote her debut that year in Philadelphia. Courtesy of the California History Room, California State Library, Sacramento, California.

cherished hopes and dreams, I WILL SUCCEED. By labor and long years of study, to which I joyfully doom myself, so long as the smallest spark of hope lights me to the prize, I will win it one day, Mr. Richings, be sure of that."[85] These disclosures in her biography enhanced Heron's claims to gentility while giving her publics reason to be invested in her success. Her success likewise vindicated her defiance of father and brother.

Actually, Heron's triumph as a star was far from assured at the time the *Biographical Sketch* appeared. Heron's acting career began in Philadelphia at the Walnut Street Theatre, where she debuted as Bianca in *Fazio* in early 1851, followed by periodic stints as a stock actress. A commercial mezzotint of Heron as Bianca survives and was possibly used to promote her debut (fig. 19). After a rocky few seasons in eastern theater during which she struggled with indifferent audiences and health problems, Heron traveled to San Francisco, California, where the growth of legitimate theater was part of colonizers' efforts to replicate eastern institutions in a rapidly gentrifying boomtown. Heron sought opportunities to star and develop her credentials as a viable headliner but was still clearly thinking about the transatlantic market. She probably was counting on financing a trip to Europe from the profits of her California tours—and did. In 1854 she traveled to London and secured a debut at Drury Lane but no successive engagement; she then went on to Paris. She returned in 1855, hoping to relaunch herself on the distant memory of her six months of popularity in California but with a new repertoire, her original translations of French melodramas. Heron deployed a range of strategies between 1851 and 1856 that followed a playbook similar to that of her predecessors. Her movements also mapped the shifting structure of American theater entertainment.

The very different venues where Heron acted in her early years, the Howard Athenæum in Boston and the Bowery Theatre in New York, epitomized the growing market segmentation of commercial entertainment. Large urban centers led by New York, then the most populous city in the United States by several hundred thousand, offered a growing array of entertainments venues that were increasingly segmented according to different demographics and types of entertainment. Throughout the country, as theaters competed with new venues like museums and music halls, as well as lyceum entertainments, managers faced the challenge of marketing theater as a broadly popular but genteel amusement. The third tier had all but disappeared from theaters by midcentury. New venues like Boston's Howard Athenæum were constructed in the 1840s to appeal to the values of middle-class consumers. These venues signaled alignment with respectable and family amusements through the term "athenaeum," associated with edification and literature and containing a more elite gloss than "museum." Neither athenaeum nor museum theaters sold alcohol or admitted prostitutes, which they attempted to ensure by refusing to admit unaccompanied women. The replacement of pit benches with a "parquet" of bucket seats discouraged rowdyism, while renaming the second- and third-tier boxes the "family circle" signaled family amusement. Family amusement, of course, was marked by the enhanced presence of women and children and required that all audiences regulate their behavior according to middle-class standards. Often, price structure was reversed, as in the renovated Walnut Street Theatre, so that more costly seats were closest to the stage, and the cheaper seats were relegated to the highest tiers.[86] In New York, the Park Theatre struggled to compete in this changing market, but it lacked the comforts of padded benches, bucket seats, and carpeting found in newer elite venues like the Astor Place Opera House. Manager Edmund Simpson repeatedly came under fire in the 1840s for continuing to allow prostitutes into his theater. When the theater burned down on December 16, 1848, just a few months after Simpson's retirement and death, its stockholders elected not to rebuild. In contrast, the Bowery Theatre cultivated its growing working-class public, alienated from the surrounding gentrification. The construction of venues explicitly marketed to middle-class and elite patronage exacerbated rising class tensions, culminating in New York in the Astor Place Riots on March 7, 1849, as fans of Edwin Forrest rallied in opposition to William Charles Macready's engagement at the Astor Place Opera House. The riot and its tragic aftermath catalyzed shifts well under way in the culture of theater spectatorship, which was propelled by market segmentation.[87]

For a novice like Heron, positioning herself within this shifting landscape could have lasting consequences for her career trajectory. After her Philadelphia debut, she took a position in the stock company of the National Theatre in Washington, DC, where she acted with Cushman, then secured entry to the New York market through an offer to join the Bowery Theatre company. This may have been too soon: Heron lacked the dramatic force to appeal to Bowery audiences, then quit before the season was over because of health problems, which compromised her next position at the Howard Athenæum. In 1853 American actor James Murdoch hired her to support him during his tours, much as Cushman had supported Macready. But Heron was impatient for solo stardom.[88]

Heron followed another strategy from the aspiring star's playbook and advertised for an original dramatic composition, offering $500, though reports of the amount varied considerably.[89] While some laughed, given

Heron's inexperience, this was no "fluctuating fancy" but a long-tested strategy of aspiring stars.[90] By midcentury, capital in original dramatic compositions had become important for both stars and managers. Long runs of new dramas were replacing the older practice of rotating plays nightly. Overall, repertoire also continued to decrease as resident stock companies featured fewer plays in a season but for longer runs. Stars, meanwhile, sought to link their reputations with two or three particular roles and control access to those plays. When she arrived in London in late 1844, Cushman paid close attention to new pieces that might be good vehicles for her sister, who was still employed in Philadelphia at the Walnut.[91] In Paris, Heron purchased and translated *La dame aux camélias* after seeing it performed by French star Eugénie Doche. Many of the plays that Heron introduced during the height of her professional career, between 1856 and the early 1870s, were her own translations and adaptations of French melodramas: Ernest Legouvé's *Medea* and *Adrienne Lecouvreur* by Legouvé and Eugéne Scribe, as well as the seventeenth-century tragedy *Phédre* by Racine.[92] Heron was also part of the first cohort to file copyright of dramas under a new American Dramatic Copyright Law, passed in February 1856, joining managers Dion Bourcicault, F. S. Chanfrau, Barney Williams, and Laura Keene. Heron's copyright history bespeaks her determination to protect her investments in these plays and secure the exclusive association of her celebrity with particular roles and productions, ensuring that she would continue to be able to debut new roles and productions or make money by selling production rights.[93]

Another of Heron's professional strategies, her use of professional middlemen, revealed the changing structure of the theater business. The eighteenth-century model of the artisan theater company composed of married couples and parents and children had opened up significantly over the intervening decade. It became more common for unattached young people like Heron to seek positions, functionally apprenticing themselves into the trade of actress or actor and learning new "lines of business" to increase their stature and earning potential, as Clifton and Cushman had. With the expansion of western markets and greater density of urban markets, stars looked to a professional class of middlemen to help them navigate professional bookings, similar to the role Henry Wikoff played for Fanny Elssler in 1840 and P. T. Barnum for Jenny Lind in 1850. Both Clifton and Cushman looked to family to fulfill this role. In 1845 Cushman was relieved to have her brother arrive after her London debut to arrange her British tour. Heron hired George Lewis, formerly prompter with a New York theater, to serve as agent for her California venture, making it possible for a woman with minimal professional connections and no family ties to obtain bookings in a new market. This was a speculative venture for both, a calculation against the prospects of the "actor's El Dorado."[94] But Lewis died of fever contracted during the arduous trip, and Heron arrived in San Francisco in late 1853 without her agent or any engagements.

Heron was not completely without professional connections, though reliance on male power brokers carried great risk for an unmarried woman, as Heron ultimately discovered. James Murdoch was playing at the American Theatre, and *Spirit of the Times* editor George Wilkes was another recent arrival in San Francisco.[95] Catherine Sinclair, who had launched an acting career on the back of her highly publicized divorce with Edwin Forrest and her sympathetic reputation as a wronged wife, joined a cohort of actresses who secured theater leases in the more open market. Heron starred opposite Murdoch the second evening that Sinclair's Metropolitan Theatre opened. She secured another agent, John Gihon, who probably arranged her California tour and then her return tour following her 1854 trip to Europe. The shift toward reliance on middlemen in what remained a male-dominated industry only intensified the gendered double bind governing starring women's relative professional autonomy. When Heron's business relationship with Gihon deteriorated, her reputation rapidly became collateral damage.

Heron arrived in St. Louis with Gihon in late 1855 following a string of lackluster appearances in "minor cities" that left her too broke to return "home." She managed to secure a final engagement in St. Louis through "the personal friendship" of Hezekiah Bateman, whom Heron had known in California, where he had been touring with his two daughters. Now manager in St. Louis, Bateman gave Heron "one week . . . to make a last trial." She opened on January 7, 1856, and played for a month to crowded houses and critical rapture. Reasons for the different reception in St. Louis are unclear; perhaps Bateman invested more in marketing. Extending the duration of her engagement increased Heron's exposure. On the strength of the St. Louis coverage, theaters in the region "open[ed]" to Heron again.[96]

Meanwhile, relations with her agent deteriorated rapidly, as Heron revealed in a letter that she published on August 20, 1856, during her return to St. Louis. She accused Gihon of spreading "slanders . . . stopp[ing] at nothing to blacken me with shame." Apparently, he was insulted by her public gratitude toward Bateman. In retaliation, Gihon "attempt[ed] to rob me of my reputation," Heron wrote. Heron's professional strategies had brought her to multiple crossroads, and, much like Josephine Clifton, she recognized how delicate but important an actress's reputation was. She used the press to reshape the narrative. In the letter, Heron invoked her gender to frame her public address, lamenting, "I cannot meet you with a pistol" nor "horsewhip you, for that would be unladylike," but she could "charge" Gihon with his "slanders and challenge" him to "proof." While Gihon exercised his male privilege to "drink with men in a public saloon" and gossip about her, Heron now addressed him on a public stage. "I come a woman, and I come *alone*," she declared.[97] Gihon also responded publicly, predicting that Heron would "repent" her "indiscretion."[98] Instead, houses were full for *Camille* and other new pieces Heron had prepared for her return to St. Louis. During the fall of 1856, she wrote repeatedly to managers in New York about an engagement. Her persistence and growing reputation secured a January debut at Wallack's Lyceum, one of the leading gentrified New York theaters. The trajectory of Heron's career shifted again.

Over 1856, as Heron toured in the trans-Appalachian West and South and then reentered the eastern market as a star in 1857, her shocking interpretation of *Camille* generated excitement and censure in the context of the gentrification and feminization of theater. Remarkably, Heron skirted personal scandal while popularizing a play about a prostitute. Heron's *Camille* lacked the historicism of some of her other pieces and the idealization of other versions of *Camille*. In Paris, the play had been controversial if wildly successful for its frank exploration of the social problem of the demimonde. The original drama examines the contradictions and consequences of the demimonde in French society through the romance between consumptive courtesan Marguerite Gautier and young Armand Duval. An adaptation was first performed in the United States by English actress Jean Margaret Davenport, a former child star, as part of her adult comeback. While the subject of the French original was known in the United States, adaptations by Davenport and later by Laura Keene transformed the framing of the piece to place *Camille* firmly within the bounds of middle-class respectability while keeping the basic story intact, a common strategy used for other French dramas. Davenport renamed the protagonist "Camille" and transformed her from courtesan to "coquette." Only Heron actually portrayed Camille as a prostitute, but unlike the French original, in which the protagonist chooses the life of the demimonde, in Heron's version Camille is driven to the sex trade by misfortune rather than choice. Like prior American versions, Heron's remained a redemption tale, tailored to the tastes of an expanding feminized middle-class public.

Camille and other French melodramas adapted for the American stage involved their protagonists in moral choices, usually a product of the woman's social circumstances, which culminated in some form of sacrifice that reinforced the protagonist's true womanly character. Though varied in their handling of illicit sex, American versions spoke to middle-class concerns about the specter of commoditized female sexuality. They followed contemporary moral reform discourses that connected a love of material wealth, artifice, and flattery with risks to sexual virtue. Generally, they offered a clear moral in which womanly virtue overwhelmed the dictates of passion.

It was Heron's interpretation of the character Camille rather than the script itself that generated controversy during her tours, for in addition to marking Camille as a prostitute, Heron rejected key conventions of dramatic acting, for example, by eschewing the grand entrance and incorporating vernacular gesture into her performance. All she had to do, according to the *New York Tribune*, was "cough and eat a lozenge, say a few saucy words . . . but there was about her a halo of individuality," though the critic disproved of Heron's "stride in walking . . . passing akimbo with the arms" and her practice of "picking up her ball-dresses, as if she was entering a coach."[99] She also turned her back on the audience, a startling break with convention. Decades later, bohemian writer Fitz-James O'Brien memorialized Heron in a work of short fiction for the "daring reality" of her performance, beginning with her "wonderfully unconventional" entrance. Rather than "wait for the mockery that is called 'a reception,'" Heron entered the stage "as if it really was the home apartment it was represented to be."[100] Heron's use of the stage, her gestures, and even her phrasing seemed to be drawn more from everyday life in defiance of English acting style, conveying an unexpected naturalism in which theatergoers were able to "forget [the actress] in the woman."[101] These choices created a successful illusion of voyeurism for theatergoers that enhanced the eroticism of the performance. To O'Brien, Heron seemed "unwitting of any outside eyes."[102] "There was no acting," the *Spirit of the Times* gushed. "It was all nature."[103] Clearly, craft had much to do with it, though critics were more likely to describe the effect and reduce Heron's mastery—and, as some argued, her dramatic genius—to gendered emanation rather than technique, such that Heron's acting became "all nature." This enhanced the affective qualities of Heron's performance, making it more shocking and more erotically charged. This also explains why Heron's *Camille* was her most controversial piece, for in subverting conventions of dramatic performance, Heron "subverted the innocence of the script," making "Camille seem common, even vulgar."[104]

Over the spring of 1857, as Heron introduced several other pieces, she faced more variegated criticism from journalists grappling with their expectations about the externalization of emotion in her tragic roles, whether they represented a coarse excess rather than the heights of tragic artistry. This criticism and Heron's defense of her pieces directly involved the question of her female publics. In early April, after a slew of attacks on the fidelity of her translation and her use of a press agent to control coverage of her debut, Heron published a letter in which she articulated her artistic vision and connected it to her female public. Heron countered that her version alone represented the play's "*truth—its terrible reality.*" She drew on long-standing defenses of the drama as a school of morals, explaining that her *Camille* offered a "solemn warning to the pure" and a "terrible example to the fallen" while featuring "the grandest type of lofty feminine nature that ever had a place upon the English stage." Heron then connected the appeal and significance of the play to her female public, thanking the "ladies—the mothers, wives, and daughters who have so frequently bestowed their presence, their sympathies and tears upon my representation."[105] She thus identified women and girls as interested parties *and* satisfied audiences.

However, Heron's entry into a wider debate over the acceptable realms of discourse about sexual vice rested upon her own appearance of virtue. In choosing to rebuild her career through her raw, daring *Camille*, Heron risked merging with the role's much vaunted "*truth—its terrible reality.*"[106] She simultaneously tried to identify her celebrity with her shockingly real portrayal of a prostitute while distancing herself as a known figure from the moral dilemmas Camille faced. This was no mean feat, particularly given some of Heron's own personal history, but it was also a calculation made in relation to a gentrified theater audience. Heron could perform the moral dilemma of a repentant prostitute because she performed in theaters from which the sex trade had been formally banished. During her engagement in Boston, debate about *Camille* exclusively considered its effect on a genteel female public. One writer worried that Heron's celebrity in the role "compel[led] the pure minds of our daughters, under penalty of not seeing [Heron] at all, to learn the ways of vice."[107] Readers who entered into a similar discussion in another paper hoped the play would inspire a more "Christian sentiment" for the "fallen," leading women to "[soften] . . . their hearts towards the abandoned" and thus be able to "help" women in "their fallen state."[108] Crucially, the graphic representation of sexual vice in *Camille* became possible through the absence of its reality, the debate turning on the implications of drama's representation of vice rather than theater as a world of vice. Yet for Heron, the reality may have been closer than her publics knew.

In 1854 in California, Heron had contracted a marriage to lawyer Harry Byrne. Byrne deserted Heron in the course of her return eastward, possibly over her reluctance to leave the stage, though after her death in 1877, it was reported that he deserted her over rumors that her sister, under the name Kate Ridgeley, was the madam of a house of prostitution in New York. The timing and reach of rumors connecting Ridgeley to Heron remain unclear and only first appeared in print in 1872. Barring a rumored connection between Heron and Ridgeley in 1856, reports about Heron's short-lived marriage could have done considerable damage to her reputation, shadowing her reemergence in 1856 and explaining why eastern theaters initially refused to engage her. Heron's public letter to Gihon suggested that she believed he was spreading rumors about her sexual virtue, including showing around a "paragraph from a newspaper" that Heron believed he wrote, "announcing" that she had "lately become a mother." Whether the "slime" of Gihon's "slanders" concerned her scandalously short marriage, a child out of wedlock, or worse, Heron took seriously the professional costs of Gihon's gossip.[109] Though she succeeded in publicly shaming Gihon into silence, naming those attacks was risky. Timing mattered. Heron disputed Gihon's rumors and framed herself as the victim of a vengeful former agent just as she was rebuilding her reputation as a compelling actress. Eastern theaters reopened to her when the buzz over her dramatic portrayal of a prostitute overwhelmed rumors about her sexual virtue—and possibly even about ties to the sex trade.

In a more bitter irony, struggles between men for control of Heron's wealth contributed to the poverty that preceded her death in 1877. In 1867, sometime after Heron's second marriage to musician Robert Stoepel, Henry Byrne resurfaced to lay claim to Heron's earnings, charging that she had not legally divorced him. This prompted Stoepel to sue for a "division of property," claiming half of Heron's fortune. In the course of the separation, Heron lost most of her property to Stoepel, perhaps to protect it from Byrne, though Heron and Stoepel ultimately divorced in 1872.[110] She attempted to recover some financial footing by appealing for money from Byrne's estate after his death in 1872. Destitute, she deployed a tested strategy of thespian parents and in 1874 arranged for the debut of her ten-year-old daughter, Bijou. Children continued to be valuable capital, even in the shifting business of midcentury theater.

For Josephine Clifton, Charlotte Cushman, and Matilda Heron, maneuvering for professional opportunities required that they pay attention to the terms of their public image, which often required an appearance of agency and virtue that belied the structural and personal realities of their lives. The strategies each pursued, of seeking out new roles, cultivating alliances with male power brokers, and touring regional markets, none-theless threatened to undermine elements of the public image starring women tried to cultivate. Lacking established family ties to the industry, these women were more vulnerable personally and professionally, espe-cially given the enduring importance of respectability politics to a suc-cessful starring career. Each attempted, with varying degrees of success, to mobilize gendered respectability politics while maneuvering within an industry that continued to be controlled by men. They correctly con-nected their ability to make a place for themselves in theater as relative outsiders to their successful identification with genteel white woman-hood, which also became more important as the industry oriented to an expanding middle-class market.

Each of these women managed to successfully use this playbook to achieve popular and critical notice, yet even then, controlling the terms of that notice proved difficult if essential to continued success. This involved presenting themselves as playing by one set of gendered rules when the realities of their lives and careers looked very different indeed. Josephine Clifton tried to distance herself from manager Thomas Ham-blin and align herself with Americanness through ties to literati like Nathaniel Parker Willis. As she pursued new repertoire she struggled against attacks on her sexual virtue and character, which led her to ally with actor Edwin Forrest, in spite of her prior attempts to carve out a more gentrified, Anglophilic model of American actress celebrity.

In her decade trying to maneuver within the stock system, Charlotte Cushman clearly emulated Clifton, but because she did not connect her-self with Clifton in constructing her celebrity, biographers have failed to consider how Cushman may have been adopting Clifton's strategies. Cushman was also aggressive in trying to link herself to established English celebrities. She successfully replicated Fanny Kemble's use of print, sought a relationship with Kemble and then English actor William Charles Macready, who was shocked by Cushman's persistence. Travel-ing overseas helped Cushman, like Clifton, remake her reputation to a historically unprecedented degree.

Matilda Heron practiced all of these strategies during her midcen-tury rise, demonstrating their efficacy as the structure and market of dramatic theater were rapidly changing. Heron's short-lived marriage to Byrne undermined much that she was able to accomplish professionally after 1856. She discovered that her professional wealth was not legally her own, a reality earlier generations of starring women had also lived.

Conclusion

Four years after her death, Josephine Clifton was named for adultery with Edwin Forrest in Catherine Sinclair Forrest's 1851 divorce suit. The trial became a battle of adultery accusations. Edwin charged that Catherine had engaged in adultery with members of her social circle, while Catherine's counsel brought witnesses who testified to her husband's patronage of houses of prostitution and alleged affair with Josephine Clifton years earlier. Catherine successfully played the wronged wife in the trial, overcoming adultery allegations.[1] While settlements from the divorce remained tied up for the next fifteen years, Catherine turned to the stage. She debuted in New York less than two weeks after the trial ended, commencing a seven-year career as an actress, including a three-year stint managing a theater in San Francisco.[2] Josephine Clifton would have been shocked to discover how much her own battles for respectability while living a relatively autonomous life as an itinerant star paved the way for Catherine Sinclair's move into the theater. This unprecedented leap from the notoriety of a sensational divorce trial to a theatrical career had little in common with Josephine Clifton's frustrated professional climb. Still, it demonstrated the expanded realms of opportunity that the starring system continued to hold out for women, even as the contradictory politics of respectability around female stage celebrity endured.

Edwin Forrest was found guilty of adultery, though whether this included the alleged affair with Clifton or merely his patronage of prostitutes remained unclear.[3] Enough doubt attached to the late actress's character and exercise of independence during her lifetime to produce the reasonable possibility that Clifton had carried on an extended extramarital affair with a married actor while touring with him.[4] As trial testimony underscored, starring women like Clifton defied many of the norms of white middle-class womanhood even as they tried to align themselves with its values. Testimony chronicled the degree to which Clifton's daily movements at the height of her starring career defied gendered expectations about mobility and sociability. In 1843, when the alleged affair was supposed to have taken place, Clifton was an unmarried wealthy professional woman in her late twenties who spurned a female chaperone.[5] Witnesses alleged that while traveling together, Clifton and Forrest slept in rooms with a shared parlor, had been seen coming and going from each other's quarters, and promenaded arm in arm on an overnight steamboat. There were also suspicions of an abortion, presented as a damning sign of adultery. A doctor and his wife testified that they had seen Forrest administer a draft to Clifton while traveling by train. Clifton was in severe physical distress, bleeding heavily from her menses, but Sinclair's lawyer asserted that their intimacy pointed to abortion and hence adultery. Clifton's physicians testified otherwise.[6] Edwin Forrest's counsel reminded the court that Clifton was not on trial and in closing remarks asked the jury to frame their "familiarity" in terms of the actors' "long friendly intercourse."[7] Still, assertions that Clifton had "maintained throughout her life a respectable character" did not stop the judge in the case from considering this "degree of intimacy . . . between a single lady and a married man" to be "extraordinary."[8]

So long as women were able to achieve levels of independence and personal license through stage careers and work closely with men to whom they were not tied by marriage or birth, they remained vulnerable to charges of sexual impropriety, which could damage a viable career and certainly worked against the pursuit of respectability within the profession. The allegations of the affair involved norms of heterosociability that Clifton and Forrest clearly violated, whether because of an affair or because of the "different" norms and conduct of stage people. If by midcentury the unmarried starring woman was less of an anomaly, women continued to grapple with the implications of their own mobility and independence for their social status and professional legitimacy. Women continued to stake out new ground for women's autonomy in entertainment and, like Catherine Sinclair, embrace the mobility, autonomy, and earning potential of the stage while playing strategically to the moral standards of white middle-class publics. Whatever their true attitudes toward marriage and sexuality, both Clifton and Sinclair understood the importance of middle-class sexual and domestic frameworks to their public roles.

Over the first half of the nineteenth century, as women and girls from England, continental Europe, and the United States developed English theater in America, these starring women mapped the boundaries of genteel white womanhood. The opportunities they pursued remained inseparable from the gendered parameters of their lives, but in ways that often deviate from how they appeared in popular media. While this deviation has contributed to their marginalization in work on entertainment capitalism and the gender politics of public life in the early nineteenth century, starring women's lives, careers, and celebrity revealed the gendered contradictions of new economic opportunities in early American entertainment. As starring girls and women from Europe and the United States pursued the economic potential of the American market, they ensured the economic viability and cultural purchase of English theater. For much of the period chronicled here, theaters struggled to stay open and remain profitable. Even while managers complained about the depredations of the American starring system, stars generated public patronage. Women in particular expanded the appeal of theater, introducing new entertainments that satisfied the omnivorous tastes of the theater's diverse publics, much to the dismay of some critics, and helped keep theater viable. They became among the most well known public figures in the young United States. Even as girls and women rarely encountered the economic opportunities of the emerging starring system as a straightforward path to professional autonomy, their careers offered exciting if contradictory images of womanhood during a period of narrowing domestic feminine ideals.

Starring girls and women introduced American audiences to new roles and repertoire that defied the standards mobilized by male tastemakers in the press. For this very reason, performers like Lydia Kelly drew enthusiastic female publics in the 1820s but little sustained critical interest, unlike male tragedians. The pantomime artistry of Celeste Elliott, who toured with racy sentimental adventure tales during the 1830s, existed uncomfortably with visions of "legitimate drama" or respectable theater. These tensions culminated in panic over the 1840–42 tour of Viennese ballerina Fanny Elssler, whose implications for American society were tied to readings of her publics. Even Fanny Kemble, tastefully marketed during her American tours from 1832 to 1834 as a model of literary womanhood and a reluctant celebrity figure, challenged expectations that ingenue debutants play ingenue roles. She also violated expectations around the gendered performance of celebrity itself. In the decades following Kemble, actresses from England and the United States continued to experiment with dramatic roles that offered more creative outlets, though most nineteenth-century entertainments reinforced sentimental lessons about female virtue and sacrifice. While starring women played swashbucklers, republican freedom fighters, distraught mothers, and noble courtesans onstage, earning exorbitant salaries, the terms of their celebrity narrowed to reinforce conformity to sentimental domestic ideals. Their celebrity personas were a distorted mirror of the patriarchal realities of family and industry governing their lives and careers.

Neither their marginalized social status nor their cultural power liberated starring women from the patriarchal expectations governing family and entertainment. As starring women and girls grew theater audiences, they negotiated competing patriarchal pressures and interests behind the scenes. Far more than men, women in the entertainment business pursued their careers relative to the pressures of the patriarchal family. Marriage was crucial in providing women with professional support, legitimacy, and companionship. However, while at the start of the century, women's access to professional opportunities were largely structured by their family ties, even though family continued to be important, by the 1830s, the eighteenth-century model of an artisan theater company composed of married couples and parents and children had opened up significantly, creating cracks through which ambitious girls entered the business and pursued stardom. Whether married or *femes sole*, starring women recognized that professional viability required a negotiation of the intensifying respectability politics around a gentrifying industry. Likewise, their careers depended upon male gatekeepers: theater managers, agents, and the growing press shaped celebrity. Starring women wrestled with these gatekeepers over the terms of their earning power and publicity. Meanwhile, the gendered frameworks governing celebrity presented these women very differently.

As the gendered terms of publicity narrowed around Christian domesticity, starring women played both sides to appeal to an emerging middle. That is, they neither repudiated theater's masculine sporting culture nor appealed exclusively to it; instead, they cultivated forms of "public intimacy" aligned with virtues of sentimental domestic femininity. From the 1820s on, the terms of female stage celebrity were caught up in battles over the social control and address of public amusements. Navigating the shifting publics and address of American theater required the appearance of conformity to gendered scripts, a disavowal of the very real cultural power and, in rare cases, personal autonomy that some starring women achieved. Starring women and girls navigated an industry in which they performed a level of conformity to a set of social ideals that rarely matched the realities of their lives. Between the 1790s and 1850s, starring women achieved unprecedented wealth, stature, and even personal autonomy and fulfillment that remained unprecedented in their day. As their labors grew American theater, starring women from Europe and America stretched though rarely shattered expectations about what theatergoers, especially women, should enjoy and about what public women should be.

NOTES

Introduction

1. Anna Mowatt, *Autobiography of an Actress; or, Eight Years on the Stage* (Boston: Ticknor, Reed & Fields, 1854), 38.

2. Ibid., 39.

3. The "cult of domesticity" is identified by Barbara Welter, "The Cult of True Womanhood, 1820–1860," *American Quarterly* 18 (1866): 151–74; and "redemptive womanhood" is from Barbara Cutter, *Domestic Devils, Battlefield Angels: The Radicalism of American Womanhood, 1830–1865* (DeKalb: Northern Illinois University Press, 2003), 7.

4. Mowatt, *Autobiography*, 39–40.

5. Theater entertainers in this period were overwhelmingly white, as theater in the early United States and stage celebrity operated within a strict color line, at least until midcentury. Theater managers neither trained nor employed black women as performers. In the early 1820s, New York's free black community attempted to establish their own pleasure garden and then theater, but rioting and police injunctions ultimately forced the African Theatre to disband by 1824. We know next to nothing about the women who acted at the African Theatre, though scholars have reconstructed the career of James Hewlett, who toured giving solo entertainments in northern manufacturing towns but never performed in a stage drama again. At midcentury, African American singer Elizabeth Greenfield successfully toured in the wake of Jenny Lind's celebrity, marketing herself as the "Black Swan"; however, theaters maintained a strict color line across the century. In the post–Civil War period, black women and men increasingly mounted their own entertainments and itinerant musical and dramatic companies. Shane White, *Stories of Freedom in Black New York* (Cambridge, MA: Harvard University Press, 2002); Sara Lampert, "Black Swan/White Raven: The Racial Politics of Elizabeth Greenfield's American Concert Career, 1851–1855," *American Nineteenth Century History* 17, no. 1 (2016): 75–102; Daphne Brooks, *Bodies in Dissent: Spectacular Performances of Race and Freedom, 1850–1910* (Durham, NC: Duke University Press, 2006).

6. Joseph Roach, "Public Intimacy: The Prior History of 'It,'" in *Theatre and Celebrity in Britain, 1660–2000*, ed. Mary Luckhurst and Jane Moody (London: Palgrave Macmillan, 2005), 25.

7. This project thus follows literary scholar and theater historian Tracy Davis's charge, delivered almost three decades ago, for scholars on women and theater not only to approach this terrain as recovery work but also to challenge the "terms, periodization, and categories" of theater history while bringing them into dialogue

with the themes and patterns of women's history. Tracy Davis, "Questions for a Feminist Methodology in Theatre History," in *Interpreting the Theatrical Past,* ed. Thomas Postlewaite and Bruce McConachie (Iowa City: University of Iowa Press, 1989), 63.

8. This argument about "feminization" appears in David Grimsted, *Melodrama Unveiled: American Theater and Culture, 1800–1850* (1968; Berkeley: University of California Press, 1987); Peter Buckley, "To the Opera House: Culture and Society in New York City, 1800–1850" (PhD diss., State University of New York at Stony Brook, 1984); Lawrence Levine, *Highbrow/Lowbrow: The Emergence of Cultural Hierarchy in America* (Cambridge, MA: Harvard University Press, 1988); Bruce McConachie, *Melodramatic Formations: American Theatre and Society 1820–1870* (Iowa City: University of Iowa Press, 1992); and Richard Butsch, *The Making of American Audiences: From Stage to Television, 1750–1990* (New York: Cambridge University Press, 2000). This work is connected with a wider literature on entertainment in nineteenth-century America that is concerned with the relationship between class formation and the beginnings of entertainment capitalism. Rosemarie Bank, *Theatre Culture in America, 1825–1860* (Cambridge: Cambridge University Press, 1997) complicates the rigid class analysis of some of the literature, while recent scholarship by David Monod, *The Soul of Pleasure: Sentiment and Sensation in Nineteenth-Century Mass Entertainment* (Ithaca, NY: Cornell University Press, 2016) and Gillian Rodger, *Champagne Charlie and Pretty Jemima: Variety Theater in the Nineteenth Century* (Urbana: University of Illinois Press, 2010) consider theater within a larger entertainment marketplace that saw expansion and diversification from the 1840s on.

9. Buckley, "To the Opera House"; Bluford Adams, *E Pluribus Barnum: The Greatest Showman and the Making of U.S. Popular Culture* (Minneapolis: University of Minnesota Press, 1997).

10. Rodger, *Champagne Charlie*; Alison Kibler, *Rank Ladies: Gender and Cultural Hierarchy in American Vaudeville* (Chapel Hill: University of North Carolina Press, 1991); Susan Glenn, *Female Spectacle: The Theatrical Roots of Modern Feminism* (Cambridge, MA: Harvard University Press, 2000); Renee Sentilles, *Performing Menken: Adah Issacs Menken and the Birth of American Celebrity* (New York: Cambridge University Press, 2003); Robert Allen, *Horrible Prettiness: Burlesque and American Culture* (Chapel Hill: University of North Carolina Press, 1991).

11. Heather Nathans, *Early American Theatre from the Revolution to Thomas Jefferson* (Cambridge: Cambridge University Press, 2003).

12. Faye Dudden, *Women in the American Theatre: Actress and Audiences, 1790–1870* (New Haven, CT: Yale University Press, 1994); Elizabeth Reitz Mullenix, *Wearing the Breeches: Gender on the Antebellum Stage* (New York: St. Martin's Press, 2000).

13. McConachie, *Melodramatic Formations*, 80. McConachie compares stars to the "shoemakers and carpenters who elevated themselves from craftworkers to capitalists." Stars "thrust themselves into the new business class by climbing up the backs of their peers," who in turn became mere "support." This comparison is also an apt way of characterizing managers, the majority of whom were themselves stock actors or erstwhile stars.

14. John Burge, *Lines of Business: Casting Practice and Policy in the American Theatre, 1752–1899* (New York: Peter Lang Publishing, 1986), 104–5.

15. McConachie, Melodramatic Formations, 80.

16. Ellen Hartigan-O'Connor, *The Ties That Buy: Women and Commerce in Revolutionary America* (Philadelphia: University of Pennsylvania Press, 2011), 6–7.

17. Jeanne Boydston, *Home and Work: Housework, Wages, and the Ideology of Labor in the Early Republic* (New York: Oxford University Press, 1990), 55, 158.

18. Cutter, *Domestic Devils*, 10.

19. J. S. Bratton, *New Readings in Theatre History* (Cambridge: Cambridge University Press, 2003), 178–80. Or as theater historian Tracy Davis has so eloquently explained, drawing upon Jürgen Habermas's conception of the "public sphere," actresses were "neither private citizens in the public sphere nor private women in the intimate sphere" and hence outside the framework for gendered respectability. Yet actresses were still able to "convey [a] normative ideology of the private/intimate sphere," even one to which they "clearly [did] not confine themselves" (Tracy Davis, "Private Women and the Public Realm," *Theatre Survey* 35, no. 1 [1994]: 68). However, the Habermasian public sphere has significant limits for my analysis because of a tendency for "theoretical slippages," as Judith Surkis has cautioned, "between spatialized notions of publicity and the public as a normative or political category" as conceptualized by Habermas. This distinction is useful for thinking about performers as public figures. In the early United States, as in republican France, analyzed by Surkis, women were "politically marginalized even when they were visibly present in *many* spheres of public life" (Judith Surkis, "Carnival Balls and Penal Codes: Body Politics in July Monarchy France," *History of the Present* 1, no. 1 [2011]: 59–83, emphasis added).

20. Anne Boylan, *The Origins of Women's Activism: New York and Boston, 1797–1840* (Chapel Hill: University of North Carolina Press, 2002); Mary Ryan, *Women in Public: Between Banners and Ballots, 1825–1880* (Baltimore, MD: Johns Hopkins University Press, 1990); Lori Ginzberg, *Women and the Work of Benevolence: Morality, Politics, and Class in the Nineteenth-Century United States* (New Haven, CT: Yale University Press, 1990); Christine Stansell, *City of Women: Sex and Class in New York, 1789–1860* (Chicago: University of Chicago Press, 1982).

21. The qualities associated with womanhood, therefore, were part of the process of middle-class formation, constructed in relation to the expansion of women's waged work. The "cult of domesticity," identified by Barbara Welter, remains useful for mapping hegemonic ideals mobilized in print culture, itself a major vehicle of female stage celebrity. However, scholarship in the intervening half century has added more nuance and complexity to this formulation, for example, by drawing a key distinction between ideas and behavior. Hence, April Haynes's intervention shows how "passionlessness" became a tool of white middle-class women's race and class hegemony. Barbara Welter, "The Cult of True Womanhood, 1820–1860," *American Quarterly* 18 (1966): 151–74; Nancy Cott, *The Bonds of Womanhood: "Woman's Sphere" in New England, 1780–1860* (New Haven, CT: Yale University Press, 1977); April Haynes, *Riotous Flesh: Women, Physiology, and the Solitary Vice in Nineteenth-Century America* (Chicago: University of Chicago Press, 2015), 18–19, 22.

22. Recent explorations of women's engagement with civil society in the early national period as writers, educators, and speakers include Mary Kelley, *Learning to Stand and Speak: Women, Education, and Public Life in America's Republic*

(Chapel Hill: University of North Carolina Press, 2006); Rosemarie Zagarri, *Women and Politics in the Early American Republic* (Philadelphia: University of Pennsylvania Press, 2007); Carolyn Eastman, *A Nation of Speechifiers: Making an American Public after the Revolution* (Chicago: University of Chicago Press, 2009), building upon a rich literature on the associationalism and reform activity of northern white women and women of color.

23. Cutter, *Redemptive Womanhood*, 7.

24. Mary Kelley, *Private Woman, Public Stage: Literary Domesticity in Nineteenth-Century America* (New York: Oxford University Press, 1984). Nan Mulleaneaux, *Staging Family: Domestic Deceptions of Mid-Nineteenth-Century American Actresses* (Lincoln: University of Nebraska Press, 2018) characterizes these as "domestic deceptions" that governed women's theatrical celebrity at the height of the century.

25. Helen Horowitz, *Rereading Sex: Battles over Sexual Knowledge and Suppression in Nineteenth-Century America* (New York: Vintage Books, 2002).

26. Most histories of celebrity emphasize the role of English theater, including circulation of early theater troupes between London and provincial cities, as in Fred Inglis, *A Short History of Celebrity* (Princeton, NJ: Princeton University Press, 2010).

27. Leo Braudy, *The Frenzy of Renown: Fame and Its History* (New York: Vintage Books, 1986), 14; Roach, "Public Intimacy," 25. In her study of Elizabeth Patterson Bonaparte, Charlene M. Boyer Lewis uses the distinction between fame and celebrity to map gendered terms of renown in the early republic, adding a layer of nuance to Braudy's distinction. Boyer Lewis argues that whereas fame was associated with "public-mindedness" and "virtue" and cultivated with an "eye on posterity[,] . . . celebrity was more temporary, the cultivation of renown during one's lifetime." And because celebrity was associated with "special talents" or attractiveness, usually through society and the arts, it was the avenue to public renown most associated with women (Charlene M. Boyer Lewis, *Elizabeth Bonaparte: An American Aristocrat in the Early Republic* [Philadelphia: University of Pennsylvania Press, 2012], 21). This distinction around attention to historical legacy is less useful for stage celebrity. Furthermore, while I recognize that there were clear gendered paths to renown, I choose not to adopt the fame and celebrity distinction, because for much of the eighteenth and nineteenth centuries, the terms "fame," "renown," and "celebrity" were used interchangeably. Actresses, incidentally, were most often described as having fame. Often, these terms were used to describe something an individual, object, or place *had* rather than *was*. The designation of an individual as a celebrity did not emerge until the middle of the nineteenth century. While I refer to starring women as celebrities, I also follow historical usage and use the terms "fame," "renown," and "celebrity" interchangeably.

28. Chris Rojek, *Celebrity* (London: Reaktion Books, 2001), 7. Roach notes that the stage in particular allowed for new realms of "visibility" that made it possible for "the intimate persons of its stars to become as familiar to the public" as the "trappings of monarchy" ("Public Intimacy," 24).

29. Claire Brock, *The Feminization of Fame* (Basingstoke: Palgrave Macmillan, 2006). Brock's arguments offer a key corrective to early studies of celebrity like Braudy's *Frenzy of Renown*, which reproduces rather than interrogates gendered constructions of celebrity.

30. Felicity Nussbaum, *Rival Queens: Actresses, Performance, and Eighteenth-Century British Theater* (Philadelphia: University of Pennsylvania Press, 2010), 26, 29–30.

31. Laura Engel, *Fashioning Celebrity: Eighteenth-Century British Actresses and Strategies for Image Making* (Athens: Ohio University Press, 2016), 8–11.

32. Sharon Marcus focuses on "continuities" rather than "change over time" in *The Drama of Celebrity* but without losing sight of developments from the eighteenth century on. Her characterization of celebrity as constituted through "triangular dramas" between celebrities, media, and publics that involves competition and cooperation is borne out by my analysis here. Sharon Marcus, *The Drama of Celebrity* (Princeton, NJ: Princeton University Press, 2019), 18, 4.

33. Laura Rosenthal argues that this self-fashioning of Siddons as a maternal figure in private life actually supported some of her more radical and unprecedented interpretations of characters like Lady Macbeth. Laura J. Rosenthal, "The Sublime, the Beautiful, 'the Siddons,'" in *The Clothes That Wear Us: Essays on Dressing and Transgressing in Eighteenth-Century Culture*, ed. Jessica Munns and Penny Richards (Newark: University of Delaware Press, 1999), 56–79.

34. Nussbaum explains that Siddons "withdrew her own person from the audience's scrutiny," which allowed her to "merge with the dramatic characters" in new ways. Nussbaum sees this shift as indicative of a lost possibility that "by repudiating the practice of incorporating a competing self-presence on stage as earlier actresses had done, [Siddons] may well have interrupted a certain line of thespian possibility" (*Rival Queens*, 281).

35. Early dramatic criticism developed in the context of these critiques, which drove the preference in theater criticism for the "legitimate drama" and the preference for acting deemed "chaste" and "natural," terms also used to police dramatic content. These terms reinforced the notion that theater should model social and moral ideals. Defenders of drama continued to grapple with the trade-off when moral lessons exposed theatergoers to unchaste possibilities. See Grimsted, *Melodrama Unveiled*, 11–14, 35–39; and on the rise of sentimentality in entertainment culture, see Monod, *The Soul of Pleasure*, 19–20, 32–41.

36. Boyer Lewis finds a similar tension in her examination of celebrity in the early republic, noting that "any woman or man who led a public life . . . faced the challenge of . . . presenting a public self that was a natural self." This "created many unhappy men and women" who grappled with the pressures involved in maintaining these "false" identities, as Kemble likewise discovered. Lewis, *Elizabeth Patterson Bonaparte*, 23.

37. Bratton, *New Readings*, 180.

Chapter 1. Between Stock and Star

1. This grew from the eighteenth-century practice in English theater of designating benefit nights at the end of a season for members of the company. This convention persisted into the next century and was adopted by stars for their engagements as well.

2. William Warren, Journal, April 1823. The journal covers the years 1796–1827 in three volumes and is available on microfilm at Indiana University, Bloomington. See also William Burke Wood, *Personal Recollections of the Stage* (Philadelphia:

Henry Baird Carey, 1855), 294. Relative worth was calculated using Measuringworth.com based on the historic consumer price index, reflecting the relative purchasing power of income or wealth in 2018. Samuel H. Williamson, "Seven Ways to Compute the Relative Value of a U.S. Dollar Amount, 1790 to Present," MeasuringWorth, 2020, https://www.measuringworth.com/uscompare/.

3. Warren, Journal, May 7, May 26, 1823.

4. *American and Commercial Daily Advertiser* (Baltimore, MD), May 26, 1823.

5. Warren, Journal, May 26, 1823; Williamson, "Seven Ways to Compute."

6. Bruce McConachie contrasts the "paternalistic admiration" of early female stars like Clara Fisher for her performance of fairy melodramas with the "hero worship" attending tragedians such as Edmund Kean in "American Theatre in Context, from the Beginnings to 1870" in *The Cambridge History of American Theatre*, vol. 1, *Beginnings to 1870*, ed. Don Wilmeth and Christopher Bigsby (Cambridge: Cambridge University Press, 1998), 148–50. In *Melodramatic Formations*, McConachie takes Clara Fisher's popularity seriously, whereas most scholarly accounts of the starring system privilege English tragic actors and introduce Fanny Kemble as the first major star actress. Simon Williams, "European Actors and the Star System, 1752–1870," in Wilmeth and Bigsby, *Cambridge History*, 1:310–18; Faye Dydden, *Women in the American Theatre: Actresses and Audiences, 1790–1870* (New Haven, CT: Yale University Press, 1994), chap. 2.

7. This was the case with Agnes Holman, who later married Charles Gilfert. She supported her husband's theater management career in Richmond, periodically making starring engagements, as discussed in chapter 2.

8. William Dunlap, *A History of the American Theatre from Its Origins to 1832*, ed. Tice L. Miller (Urbana: University of Illinois Press, 2005), 272; Williamson, "Seven Ways to Compute."

9. Gresdna A. Doty, *The Career of Mrs. Anne Brunton Merry in the American Theatre* (Baton Rouge: Louisiana State University Press, 1971), 87.

10. Jason Shaffer, *Performing Patriotism: National Identity in the Colonial and Revolutionary American Theater* (Philadelphia: University of Pennsylvania Press, 2007), 70.

11. Ibid., 70–71; Mary C. Henderson, "Scenography, Stagecraft, and Architecture," in Wilmeth and Bigsby, *Cambridge History*, 1:382–88.

12. Douglas McDermott, "Structure and Management in the American Theatre from the Beginning to 1870," in Wilmeth and Bigsby, *Cambridge History*, 1:194.

13. Doty, *The Career*, 46–48.

14. Theaters also went up in Richmond, VA (1785), Providence, RI (1795), Baltimore, MD (1794), Charleston, SC (1794), and Washington (1800). Don Wilmeth and Jonathan Curley, "Timeline: Beginnings to 1870," in Wilmeth and Bigsby, *The Cambridge History*, 1:48–55; Heather S. Nathans, *Early American Theatre from the Revolution to Thomas Jefferson: Into the Hands of the People* (Cambridge: Cambridge University Press, 2003); and George Bryan, *American Theatrical Regulation, 1607–1900* (Metuchen, NJ: Scarecrow Press, 1993).

15. Nathans, *Early American Theatre*, 8.

16. Dunlap, *A History*, 251–52.

17. John Burge, *Lines of Business: Casting Practice and Policy in the American Theatre, 1752–1899* (New York: Peter Lang Publishing, 1986), 97–105.

18. William Dunlap, *Diary of William Dunlap* (1930; New York: Benjamin Blom, 1969), 45.

19. David Grimsted, *Melodrama Unveiled: American Theater and Culture, 1800–1850* (1968; Berkeley: University of California Press, 1987), 8–9; George O'Dell, *Annals of the New York Stage*, 15 vols. (New York: Columbia University Press, 1927–49), 2:43, 52.

20. Burge, *Lines of Business*, 126.

21. Joseph Ireland, *Records of the New York Stage*, 2 vols. (1866–67; New York: Burt Franklin, 1968), 1:201, 206; O'Dell, *Annals*, 2:199, 137.

22. Doty, *The Career*, 109.

23. Ibid., 118, 119.

24. Dunlap, *A History*, 291.

25. Calvin Printer, "William Warren's Financial Arrangements with Traveling Stars, 1805–1829," *Theatre Survey*, November 1965, 86–87.

26. William Warland Clapp, *A Record of the Boston Stage* (Boston: James Monroe & Company, 1853), 47.

27. Don Wilmeth, *George Frederick Cooke, Machiavel of the Stage* (Westport, CT: Greenwood Press, 1980), 306.

28. Joseph Ireland, *Mrs. Duff* (Boston: James R. Osgood, 1882), 8.

29. Cooke had faced down crowds during the Old Price Riots and the full ire of the London press for uneven performances and periodic absences caused by alcoholism. Wilmeth, *George Frederick Cooke*, 250–55.

30. Ibid., 256–58.

31. William Dunlap, *Memoirs of the Life of George Frederick Cooke*, 2 vols. (New York: D. Longworth, 1813), 2:176.

32. Wilmeth, *George Frederick Cooke*, 260; Dunlap, *Memoirs*, 2:179.

33. Wilmeth, *George Frederick Cooke*, 275.

34. Dunlap, *Memoirs*, 2:199.

35. Wilmeth, *George Frederick Cooke*, 266, 256. In Philadelphia, according to William Warren's records, Cooke played on sharing terms ("Cook[e] gets 1/2 the profit—that is he divides with us after $390. pr night for 5 nights the 6th he gets all after 390 and the 13th a Clear Bent"), though there is some ambiguity over how exactly these profits were paid out. They may have been payable to Cooper, who in turn provided Cooke a salary. Warren, Journal, March 30, 1811; Printer, "William Warren's Financial Arrangements," 87; "Williamson, "Seven Ways to Compute."

36. Philip H. Highfill, Edward A. Langhans, and Kalman A. Burnim, eds., *A Biographical Dictionary of Actors, Actresses, Musicians, Dancers, Managers & Other Stage Personnel in London, 1660–1800, Volume 7: Habgood to Haubert* (Carbondale: Southern Illinois University Press, 1982), 385–90; T. Allston Brown, *History of the American Stage: Containing Biographical Sketches of Nearly Every Member of the Profession That Has Appeared on the American Stage, from 1733 to 1870* (New York: Dick and Fitzgerald, 1870), 145.

37. The trip was broken up by a brief stop in Halifax. War had been declared between the United States and Great Britain in June. A week short of arriving in New York harbor, their ship was boarded by the crew of a British frigate.

38. *Morning Post* (London), August 31, 1811, August 23, 1811.

39. Nan L. Stephenson, "Milestones in the American Career of Mrs. Amelia Holman Gilfert," *Theatre Symposium: A Journal of the Southeastern Theater Conference* 2 (1994): 100.

40. Wood, *Personal Recollections*, 172.

41. Warren, Journal, December 11, 1812.

42. Ireland, *Records*, 1:289; Williamson, "Seven Ways to Compute."

43. Sam Haynes, *Unfinished Revolution: The Early American Republic in a British World* (Charlottesville: University of Virginia Press, 2011), 78.

44. Quoted in Vincent Angotti, "American Dramatic Criticism, 1800–1830" (PhD diss., University of Kansas, 1967), 199.

45. Williams, "European Actors," 306.

46. This argument is developed in chapter 2, "(Dis)Obedient Daughters and Devoted Wives: The Family Politics of Stock and Star."

47. McDermott, "Structure and Management," 196; F. Arant Maginnes, *Thomas Abthorpe Cooper: Father of the American Stage, 1775–1849* (Jefferson, NC: McFarland, 2004), 140–41.

48. Philip H. Highfill, "Edmund Simpson's Talent Raid on England in 1818 (2)," *Theatre Notebook* 12 (Summer 1958): 130–32.

49. Ibid., 134–35.

50. Ibid., 133; Barnard Hewitt, "'King Stephen' of the Park and Drury Lane," in *The Theatrical Manager in Britain and America: Player of a Perilous Game*, ed. Joseph W. Donahue (Princeton, NJ: Princeton University Press, 1971), 98; Clapp, *A Record*, 157.

51. *National Advocate, for the Country* (New York), May 5, 1820.

52. Wood, *Personal Recollections*, 330. Relative value for 2018 was calculated based on the historic real price index. "Five Ways to Compute the Relative Value of a UK Pound Amount, 1270 to Present," MeasuringWorth, 2020, https://www.measuringworth.com/ukcompare/.

53. Williams, "European Actors," 315.

54. Edwin Booth, "Edmund Kean," in *Actors and Actresses of Great Britain and the United States: Kean and Booth and Their Contemporaries*, ed. Brander Matthews and Laurence Hutton (New York: Cassell & Company, 1886), 7.

55. Hewitt, "'King Stephen,'" 101–2.

56. Francis Courtney Wemyss, *Twenty-Six Years of the Life of an Actor and Manager* (New York: Burgess, Stringer & Co., 1846), 101.

57. Wood, *Personal Recollections*, 330.

58. This was Joseph Tinker Buckingham's reason for demurring when Kelly played in Boston in November 1824. *National Advocate*, November 16, 1824.

59. *Boston Patriot*, November 10, 1824.

60. *National Advocate*, March 28, 1825.

61. *New-York Statesman*, May 17, 1825.

62. *The Theatrical Contributions of Jacques to the "United States Gazette"* (Philadelphia: Ash & Mason, 1826), 62.

63. Ibid., 69.

64. Wemyss, *Twenty-Six Years*, 102.

65. Wood places this engagement in November 1825, but the dates match the February 1826 engagement covered in the "Jacques" columns. Wood, *Personal Recollections*, 310.

66. *Theatrical Contributions of Jacques*, 79.

67. Elizabeth Reitz-Mullenix, *Wearing the Breeches: Gender on the Antebellum Stage* (New York: Palgrave Macmillan, 2007), 39–40, 130.

68. *National Advocate*, December 29, 1820.

69. Marlis Schweitzer, "Casting Clara Fisher: Phrenology, Protean Farce, and the 'Astonishing' Career of a Child Actress," *Theatre Journal* 68, no. 2 (May 2016): 173–75.

70. Printer, "William Warren's Arrangements," 85–89.

71. Wemyss, *Twenty-Six Years*, 136–38.

72. Wood gives more precise numbers to the same effect: for ten nights over three weeks, including her benefit night, he recalls that Fisher earned $3,060, the equivalent of $83,600 today. Wemyss, *Twenty-Six Years*, 149; Wood, *Personal Recollections*, 287; Williamson, "Seven Ways to Compute." Fisher's February arrival in Philadelphia was also a function of Price's virtual New York monopoly on London debutants. Because Price often kept stars in New York for multiple engagements, Boston or Philadelphia theaters had to wait until the new year to see New York arrivals. Competition between American agents in London intensified in the late 1820s, with managers trying to outmaneuver Price, each hoping to arrange a performer's American debut at *their* venue rather than at the Park Theatre and to schedule the rest of a star's American tour for a cut of the profits, as Price clearly did with his stars. Actor-manager Francis Courtney Wemyss, who was sent to London as agent for a Philadelphia theater, described these maneuvers in his memoir, also noting the interest from English performers. Wemyss claimed that whereas he had been unusual in his willingness to sign a three-year contract for an American theater in 1822, when he arrived in London five years later, "applications from actors of minor repute flocked in upon me by dozens" (*Twenty-Six Years*, 128). Higher salaries at American theaters were a clear inducement.

73. Clara Fisher Maeder, *Autobiography of Clara Fisher Maeder*, ed. Douglas Taylor (New York: Dunlap Society, 1897), 26–28.

74. *New-York Spectator*, January 15, 1830.

75. Cooke had also been known for his performance of Richard III; thus, the medallion might also have called up Fisher's childhood performances of Richard III, serving as a reminder of her childhood genius. Fisher Maeder, *Autobiography*, 40.

76. *Baltimore Patriot & Mercantile Advertiser*, September 1, 1826.

77. Tom Mole shows this process of proliferation and the development of a recognizable visual iconography across diverse commercial images with Lord Byron's literary celebrity in *Byron's Romantic Celebrity: Industrial Culture and the Hermeneutic of Intimacy* (New York: Palgrave Macmillan, 2007), esp. chap. 5, 79.

78. Ireland, *Records*, 1:537–38.

79. Schweitzer, "Casting Clara Fisher," 188.

80. Theaters in this period restricted African American patrons either to a "colored gallery" or to the third tier. African Americans were also employed in theaters, for example, in Philadelphia, where "black women" tending bar apparently did quite "well" on the comparatively low weekly rents of forty-six dollars per week. James B. Johnson to Washington P. Gragg, January 27, 1831, Documents Concerning the Early Years of the Tremont Theatre 1827–41, Harvard Theatre Collection, Houghton Library, Cambridge, MA.

81. *Augusta (GA) Chronicle*, April 7, 1830; *Mechanics' Free Press* (Philadelphia, PA), April 24, 1830; *Newburyport (MA) Herald*, April 27, 1830.

82. Christine Stansell, *City of Women: Sex and Class in New York, 1789–1860* (New York: Knopf, 1986), 105, 111, 157; "How much is a dollar?"

83. Thomas Dublin, *Women at Work: The Transformation of Work and Community in Lowell, Massachusetts, 1826–1860,* 2nd ed. (New York: Columbia University Press, 1993), 66.

84. Claudia Johnson, *American Actress: Perspective on the Nineteenth Century* (Chicago: Nelson-Hall, 1984), 55.

85. Ireland, *Mrs. Duff,* 18–19.

86. Ibid., 30.

87. Ibid., 28–29.

88. Clapp, *A Record,* 116.

89. "Dramatic Communication," *Ladies' Port Folio,* March 11, 1820, 83.

90. Ireland, *Mrs. Duff,* 42.

91. Ibid., 74.

92. Ibid., 79, 84.

Chapter 2. (Dis)Obedient Daughters and Devoted Wives

1. Fisher Maeder, *Autobiography,* 19.

2. Ibid., 24.

3. Ibid., 27–28, 24, 95.

4. Most states followed English common law, retaining twenty-one as the age of majority for males and females. Nicholas Syrett, *American Child Bride: A History of Marriage and Minors in the United States* (Chapel Hill: University of North Carolina Press, 2016), 34.

5. Fisher Maeder, *Autobiography,* 93.

6. Bratton, *New Readings,* 79.

7. Fisher Maeder, *Autobiography,* 50.

8. Holly Brewer, *By Birth or Consent: Children, Law, and the Anglo-American Revolution in Authority* (Chapel Hill: University of North Carolina Press, 2005), 280–87, 329–31.

9. Claudia Johnson argues that theater was one of the forms of labor in which women had the potential to earn equal pay for equal work with men. Edna Hammer Cooley's analysis of several New York salary lists at midcentury demonstrates that a woman's salary was 80 percent of a man's average stock company salary; however, overall salaries show much more "economic equity" than in any other occupation, with starring making it possible for women to achieve parity. Claudia Johnson, *American Actress: Perspective on the Nineteenth Century* (Chicago: Nelson-Hall, 1984), 55–57; Edna Hammer Cooley, "Women in American Theatre, 1850–1870: A Study in Professional Equity" (PhD diss., University of Maryland College Park, 1986), 68–71, 87.

10. Faye Dudden, *Women in the American Theatre* (New Haven, CT: Yale University Press, 1997), 11–12.

11. Tracy Davis, *The Economics of the British Stage, 1800–1914* (Cambridge: Cambridge University Press, 2007), 274.

12. Bratton, *New Readings,* 180.

13. Ibid., 184.

14. Davis, *Economics*, 242.

15. Bratton, *New Readings*, 185.

16. Steven Mintz, *Huck's Raft: A History of American Childhood* (Cambridge, MA: Harvard University Press, 2004), 80.

17. Joseph Haslewood, *The Secret History of the Green-Room*, 2 vols. (London: J. Owen, 1795), 2:84–87.

18. Ireland, *Records*, 1:154.

19. John Bernard, *Retrospections of the Stage* (London: Henry Colburn and Richard Bentley, 1830), 2:67–68. This was published two years later in Boston.

20. Clapp, *A Record*, 91.

21. Modern biographer Gresdna Ann Doty surmises that whether or not John actually did train his daughter for the stage, Anne would have had "many opportunities to observe" the great Sarah Siddons act and tellingly chose to debut in Siddons's most celebrated role, as Euphrasia in *The Grecian Daughter*. Doty, *The Career*, 8.

22. Schweitzer, "Casting Clara Fisher," 173–74.

23. *Souvenir* (Philadelphia), February 27, 1828.

24. Brewer, *By Birth or Consent*, 260, 332–333.

25. Syrett, *American Child Bride*, 43–45, 88–89.

26. Nor was Holman liked by his fellow actors, who bristled at his "imperious disposition," aggressive efforts at self-promotion, and propensity for conflict. Wood had a poor opinion of Gilfert as well, considering him far beneath the "highly educated woman" and "delicate and finished actress" he married. Wood, *Personal Recollections*, 173–77.

27. Nan L. Stephenson, "Milestones in the American Career of Mrs. Amelia Holman Gilfert," *Theatre Symposium: A Journal of the Southeastern Theater Conference* 2 (1994): 104.

28. Philip H. Highfill, "Edmund Simpson's Talent Raid on England in 1818 (1)," *Theatre Notebook* 12 (Spring 1958): 89.

29. Philip H. Highfill, "Edmund Simpson's Talent Raid on England in 1818 (2)," *Theatre Notebook* 12 (Summer 1958): 139.

30. Highfill's account of these negotiations is a bit confused, perhaps because of his error in mistaking the original offer as being for the elder daughter alone when it clearly reads, "Wrote Leesugg offering his daughters—8 Guas a week." Diary of Edmund Shaw Simpson, Folger Shakespeare Library, Washington, DC.

31. Simpson Diary.

32. Highfill, "Edmund Simpson's Talent Raid (2)," 139.

33. Mary Wallack Hill did make it to America, first appearing in June 1827 at New York's Chatham Garden Theatre, probably invited by her brother and former manager Henry Wallack, who had only just let go of the theater's lease. In the preceding decade, both of her brothers maintained successful touring careers and attempted theater management, building on their stature and the connections they made while touring. Robert Maywood had similar success. By 1828 he had remarried and was manager in Philadelphia, Campbell, Maywood & Co. having replaced Warren & Wood at the helm of the city's theaters. Highfill, "Edmund Simpson's Talent Raid (2)," 135; Ireland, *Records*, 2:569.

34. Highfill, "Edmund Simpson's Talent Raid (1)," 88–89.

35. Highfill, "Edmund Simpson's Talent Raid (2)," 134.

36. Wood, *Personal Recollections*, 274.

37. Stephen Archer, *Junius Brutus Booth: Theatrical Prometheus* (Carbondale: Southern Illinois University Press, 1992).

38. *New York Spectator*, November 18, 1825.

39. *Federal Gazette* (Baltimore, MD), quoted in *New York Spectator*, November 22, 1825.

40. *Boston Commercial Advertiser*, September 11, 1827.

41. Franklin Graham, *Histrionic Montreal: Annals of the Montreal Stage* (Montreal: John Lovell, 1902), 89.

42. John Green, *Theatre in Dublin, 1745–1820: A History*, 6 vols. (Bethlehem, PA: Lehigh University, 2011), 5:4298.

43. *Boston Commercial Gazette*, February 4, 1828.

44. Boston Theatre Papers, Boston Public Library, Boston, MA; Relative worth calculated using Measuringworth.com based on the historic consumer price index, which reflects the relative purchasing power of income or wealth. Williamson, "Seven Ways to Compute."

45. *Boston Commercial Gazette*, February 4, 1828.

46. *American Traveller* (Boston), February 5, 1828.

47. *Evening Gazette* (Boston) February 9, 1828.

48. *American Traveller*, February 12, 1828.

49. Lori Ginzburg, "'The Hearts of Your Readers Will Shudder': Fanny Wright, Infidelity, and American Freethought," *American Quarterly* 46, no. 2 (June 1994): 196.

50. Elizabeth Clapp, *A Notorious Woman: Anne Royall in Jacksonian America* (Charlottesville: University of Virginia Press, 2016).

51. *American Traveller*, February 12, 1828, February 8, 1828; Williamson, "Seven Ways to Compute."

52. Ireland indicates that later in life, Mary Rock went by Mrs. Murray in her private life. Graham, *Histrionic Montreal*, 89; Ireland, *Records*, 1:563.

53. Dunlap, *A History*, 149; Williamson, "Seven Ways to Compute."

54. Dunlap, *Diary*, 259–60, 264.

55. O'Dell, *Annals*, 2:274, 468–69; "The Late Mrs. Hilson," *Ladies' Companion*, August 1837, 202.

56. Susan Klepp, *Revolutionary Conceptions: Women, Fertility, and Family Limitation in America, 1760–1820* (Chapel Hill: University of North Carolina Press, 2004), 114–17.

57. Citing an unpublished manuscript by Ireland, scholar Penny Landau notes that Duff "gave birth to thirteen children, ten of whom survived, seven reaching the age of majority," whereas in his published biography, Ireland writes that Duff was the "mother of ten children, seven of whom . . . reached maturity." Penny Landau, "The Career of Mary Ann Duff, the American Siddons 1810–1839" (PhD diss., Bowling Green State University, 1979), 17; Ireland, *Mrs. Duff*, 137.

58. Wood, *Personal Recollections*, 330.

59. Maria Hilson was adopted by Edmund Simpson, manager of the Park, but did not go on the stage, instead marrying a New York merchant. According to an 1837 profile of Simpson in the *Ladies' Companion*, ties between Thomas Hilson and Edmund Simpson reached back to their beginnings in English theater, Simpson "first introduced to theatricals" by Hilson. Philip H. Highfill, Edward A. Langhans, and Kalman A. Burnim, eds., *A Biographical Dictionary of Actors*,

Actresses, Musicians, Dancers, Managers & Other Stage Personnel in London,
1660–1800, Volume 8: Hough to Keyse (Carbondale: Southern Illinois University
Press, 1982), 177; "Edmund Simpson, Manager of the Park Theatre," *Ladies'*
Companion, July 1837.

60. The *Ladies' Companion* may have been in the pocket of Thomas Hamblin,
who became manager of the New York Bowery Theatre in 1829, who paid for
favorable reports on his theater as a strategy for appealing to genteel publics and
drawing theatergoers from the rival Park Theatre. Dudden, *Women*, 79; Highfill,
Langhans, and Burnim, *A Biographical Dictionary*, 177.

61. "The Late Mrs. Hilson," 203.

62. *Louisiana Advertiser*, January 24, 1827.

63. Noah Ludlow, *Dramatic Life as I Found It: A Record of Personal Experi-*
ence (St. Louis: G. I. Jones & Co., 1880), 451.

64. Wemyss, *Twenty-Six Years*, 84, 86.

65. Mary Fairlie (Cooper)'s sister Julia Fairlie married Samuel Ogden. Their
daughter, Anna Cora Ogden, married lawyer James Mowatt and in the context of
her husband's financial ruin commenced a career as a writer, elocutionist, and,
in 1846, a playwright and professional actress (see the introduction). F. Arant
Maginnes, *Thomas Abthorpe Cooper: Father of the American Stage, 1775–1849*
(Jefferson, NC: McFarland, 2004), 157.

66. T. Allston Brown, *History of the American Stage: Containing Biographical*
Sketches of Nearly Every Member of the Profession That Has Appeared on the
American Stage, from 1733 to 1870 (New York: Dick and Fitzgerald, 1870), 153.

67. Ireland, *Records*, 1:340.

68. "Famous Families of American Players No. 5: The Hacketts," *Theatre*,
January 1905, 13.

69. Leesugg's younger sister, now Mrs. Sharpe, debuted that season and also
commenced a starring turn before becoming an established actress in New York.

70. James W. Swain, "Mrs. Alexander Drake: A Biographical Study" (PhD diss.,
Tulane University), 38–39.

71. Ibid., 58.

72. *Cincinnati Daily Gazette*, March 13, 1828, quoted in ibid., 89.

73. Penny Landau provides the following dates and birth order: Mary (1810),
Eliza, James (1820), Thomas (1823), Mathilda, John, William. Landau, "The Career," 51.

74. *Cincinnati Daily Gazette*, February 24, 1830, quoted in Swain, "Mrs. Alexander Drake," 117.

75. *Philadelphia Inquirer*, September 13, 1831; H. P. Phelps, *Players of a Cen-*
tury: A Record of the Albany Stage, 2nd ed. (New York: Edgar S. Werner, 1880),
161.

76. *National Gazette and Literary Register* (Philadelphia), May 4, 1833.

77. Phelps, *Players*, 161.

78. *National Gazette and Literary Register*, May 15, 1833, in Swain, "Mrs.
Alexander Drake," 136; *Louisville Daily Focus*, January 9, 1832, in ibid., 127.

79. Joseph Jefferson, *Autobiography of Joseph Jefferson* (1889; New York: Century Co., 1890), 416.

80. An anecdote about the frustrated courtship of Richard Johnson, a legislative representative from Kentucky, sketches Denny Drake's well-known wit and
clear direction for her life and career. She had no intention to marry, but "if it so

happened he should need her assistance to govern the United States, she would, perhaps, sacrifice herself for her country's good." Swain, "Mrs. Alexander Drake," 182; Phelps, *Players*, 161–62.

81. Norma Basch, *Framing American Divorce: From the Revolutionary Generation to the Victorians* (Berkeley: University of California Press, 1999), 105–8.

82. Ibid., 117.

83. [Mary Clarke], *A Concise History of the Life and Amours of Thomas S. Hamblin, Late Manager of the Bowery Theatre* (Philadelphia, n.d.), 25.

84. Ibid., 25.

85. There is some discrepancy, perhaps deliberate on Thomas's part. He claims the terms were $600 alimony with $200 of child support, while in 1834 the *Evening Star* reported that Elizabeth would receive "$600 per annum, for herself and son." These were also the terms described by Mary Clarke. *Evening Star* (New York), reprinted in *Columbian Centinel* (Boston), August 12, 1835; *Evening Star*, December 4, 1834.

86. "Articles of Separation and Settlement, June 25, 1832," box 3, miscellaneous theatrical papers, Harvard Theatre Collection, Houghton Library, Cambridge, MA.

87. *Evening Star*, July 31, 1835.

88. [Clarke], *A Concise History*, 29.

89. Susan Branson, *Dangerous to Know: Women, Crime, and Notoriety in the Early Republic* (Philadelphia: University of Pennsylvania Press, 2008), 99; [Clarke], *A Concise History*, 25–26.

90. Thomas's publicity corroborates this. He reported, "Elizabeth's allowance was afterwards bartered by her for the sum of $2500, and paid by me at a time when my circumstances rendered it no easy manner." [Clarke], *A Concise History*, 31–32; *Evening Star* reprinted in *Columbian Centinel*, August 12, 1835; Williamson, "Seven Ways to Compute."

91. Blanchard Hamblin emerges as a patron of other star actresses attempting to parlay their renown into management. Though the terms are not available, it seems that she handed over management of Richmond Hill for periodic intervals first to Annette Nelson and then to Virginia Monier.

92. Mary Ann was also rebuffed by her sister, who refused to travel to London from Bath for a reunion.

93. Williamson, "Seven Ways to Compute."

94. *Philadelphia Inquirer*, May 3, 1831, May 5, 1831.

95. *Courier and Enquirer* (New York) quoted in Ireland, *Mrs. Duff*, 113; O'Dell, *Annals*, 3:581.

96. Landau, "The Career," 58.

97. Ireland, *Mr. Duff*, 121–22.

98. Nineteenth-century critic and theater chronicler William Winter quoted in Landau, "The Career," 79.

Chapter 3. The Promise and Limits of Female Stage Celebrity

1. *New-York Spectator*, January 5, 1835.

2. *Literary Journal* (Schenectady, NY), May 9, 1835.

3. *New York Mirror*, February 26, 1831, May 16, 1835.

4. *Boston Investigator*, September 7, 1832.

5. Frances Anne Kemble, *Records of a Girlhood* (New York: Henry Holt and Company, 1879), 534.

6. Ibid., 512; also see Catherine Clinton, *Fanny Kemble's Civil Wars: The Story of America's Most Unlikely Abolitionist* (New York: Simon & Schuster, 2000), 48.

7. Kemble, *Records*, 543, 536.

8. Frances Anne Butler, *Journal*, 2 vols. (Philadelphia: Carey, Lea & Blanchard, 1835), 1:93.

9. Kemble, *Records*, 544.

10. Ibid., 542.

11. Ireland, *Records*, 2:36, 52–53; Williamson, "Seven Ways to Compute."

12. Butler, *Journal*, 2:5.

13. Ibid., 2:10.

14. Rosemarie K. Bank, "Arbiters of National Culture: Newspapers, Thomas S. Hamblin, the Bowery Theatre, and the Miss Missouri Affair," *New England Theatre Journal* 24 (2013): 1–11.

15. *New York Mirror*, September 1, 1832.

16. *New York Mirror*, September 22, 1832.

17. *New-York Spectator*, November 19, 1832.

18. *New York Mirror*, September 29, 1832.

19. *Daily Chronicle* (Philadelphia, PA), October 23, 1832.

20. *Spirit of the Times*, September 15, 1832.

21. *New York Mirror*, February 26, 1831, September 22, 1832.

22. *Spirit of the Times*, September 15, 1832.

23. *Spirit of the Times*, September 8, 1832.

24. Carolyn Eastman, *A Nation of Speechifiers: Making an American Public after the Revolution* (Chicago: University of Chicago Press, 2009); Rosemarie Zagarri, *Revolutionary Backlash: Women and Politics in the Early American Republic* (Philadelphia: University of Pennsylvania Press, 2007); Mary Kelley, *Learning to Stand and Speak: Women, Education and Public Life in America's Republic* (Chapel Hill: University of North Carolina Press, 2006).

25. Anne Boylan, *The Origins of Women's Activism: New York and Boston, 1797–1840* (Chapel Hill: University of North Carolina Press, 2002); Lori Ginzberg, *Women and the Work of Benevolence: Morality, Politics, and Class in the Nineteenth-Century United States* (New Haven, CT: Yale University Press, 1990).

26. Joanne Dobson and Sandra A. Zagarell, "Women Writing in the Early Republic," in *A History of the Book in America, Volume 2: An Extensive Republic: Print, Culture, and Society in the New Nation, 1790–1840*, ed. Robert A. Gross and Mary Kelley (Chapel Hill: University of North Carolina Press, 2005), 376–77.

27. Paula Bernat Bennett, *Poets in the Public Sphere: The Emancipatory Project of American Women's Poetry, 1800–1900* (Princeton, NJ: Princeton University Press, 2003), especially chapter 1, see 28, 34–35, 38. Bennett is interested in how some women poets used sentimental poetics to address feminist issues and in some cases resist the dominance of this style. Kemble clearly grappled with the gendered aesthetic pressures that remained intertwined with the gender politics of her celebrity.

28. Tom Mole, *Byron's Romantic Celebrity: Industrial Culture and the Hermeneutic of Intimacy* (New York: Palgrave Macmillan, 2007), chapter 5.

29. Butler, *Journal*, 1:57.

30. *New-York Spectator*, November 19, 1832.

31. Butler, *Journal*, 1:110.

32. Ibid., 1:191.

33. Una Pope-Hennessey, *Three English Women in America* (London: Ernest Benn Limited, 1929), 163.

34. Ibid., 2:106.

35. Ibid., 2:103.

36. Sam W. Haynes, *Unfinished Revolution: The Early American Republic in a British World* (Charlottesville: University of Virginia Press, 2011), 32–34.

37. Frances Trollope, *Domestic Manners of the Americans* (London; repr., New York: Whittaker, Treacher & Co., 1832), 116.

38. Ibid., 271. These descriptions have been used by historians to characterize audience behaviors of the period; however, Rosemarie Bank cautions against generalizing too broadly from Trollope's particular observations and categories, including her characterizations of New York theaters. To say the Chatham Theatre was spurned by the class Trollope considered the "bon ton" or fashionables is not to say that it was the working-class theater. Likewise, as contemporaries noted, the behaviors Trollope described were commonplace in English theaters. English writer Lady Catherine Norton made this point in her critique of *Domestic Manners*. Rosemarie K. Bank, "Mrs. Trollope Visits the Theatre: Cultural Diplomacy and Historical," *Journal of American Drama and Theatre* 5, no. 3 (Fall 1993): 16–27; *Boston Evening Transcript*, September 5, 1832.

39. Haynes, *Unfinished Revolution*, 118–21.

40. Scholars have been quick to associate particular theaters, like the Bowery, with Jacksonian working-class politics. Hamblin's successful use of nationalist discourses as a marketing strategy, development of "native talent" as an alternative to foreign stars, and performance of original dramatic works by in-house dramatists certainly played right into Jacksonian nationalism and helped draw audiences away from the Park. However, it is an overstatement to cast the Bowery as a working-class theater, as some scholars have done, when both theaters continued to draw socially diverse patrons. Nor did the Bowery repudiate British cultural models or even the transatlantic starring system; instead, it continued to perform British repertoire and feature foreign stars throughout this period.

41. *New-York Spectator*, November 19, 1832.

42. Edward Thomas Coke, *A Subaltern's Furlough*, 2 vols. (New York: J. & J. Harper, 1833), 1:174.

43. Ibid., 1:174; *New York Evening Post*, September 19, 1832.

44. *New York American, for the Country*, September 21, 1832; *Daily Chronicle*, September 20, 1832.

45. Haynes, *Unfinished Revolution*, 83–85.

46. Philip Hone, *The Diary of Philip Hone, 1828–1851*, ed. Allan Nevins (New York: Dodd, Mead & Co., 1927; repr., New York: Kraus Reprint Co. 1969), 50–51.

47. *New York American*, October 18, 1831.

48. *New York Evening Post*, October 20, 1831.

49. Butler, *Journal*, 1:112.

50. Ibid., 2:102–3.

51. Ibid., 2:103.

52. Anna Cabot Lowell Quincy Waterston diary, April 16, 1833, Quincy family papers, Massachusetts Historical Society, Boston, MA.

53. Butler, *Journal*, 2:133.

54. Quincy Waterston diary, April 16, 1833.

55. Ibid.

56. Anna Quincy Waterston, *A Woman's Wit and Whimsy: The 1833 Diary of Anna Cabot Lowell Quincy*, ed. Beverly Palmer (Boston: Northeastern University Press, 2003), 54.

57. *Boston Evening Transcript*, May 18, 1833.

58. Kemble, *Records*, 323.

59. Henry Hart Milman, *Fazio, a Tragedy*, 3rd ed. (London: John Murray, 1818).

60. Butler, *Journal*, 1:120.

61. *New York Evening Post*, quoted in the *Albion*, September 22, 1832.

62. Reprinted in the *Daily Chronicle*, October 23, 1832.

63. Katherine Sedgwick to Charles Sedgwick, May 23, 1833, box 4, folder 27, Charles Sedgwick Papers, Massachusetts Historical Society, Boston, MA.

64. Joseph Sill diaries, December 15, 1832, Historical Society of Pennsylvania, Philadelphia, PA.

65. Dudden, *Women*, 32–33.

66. Sill diaries, December 14, 1832.

67. Quincy Waterston diary, April 16, 1833.

68. Quincy Waterston diary, May 10, 1833.

69. Rebecca Jenkins, *Fanny Kemble: A Reluctant Celebrity* (New York: Simon & Schuster, 2005), 350.

70. Butler, *Journal*, 1:154.

71. Ibid., 1:160–61; Jenkins, *Fanny Kemble*, 365–66.

72. Butler, *Journal*, 1:159.

73. Deidre David, *Fanny Kemble: A Performed Life* (Philadelphia: University of Pennsylvania Press, 2007), 104.

74. *Boston Courier*, reprinted in the *Pensacola (FL) Gazette*, June 12, 1833.

75. Catherine B. Burroughs, "'Be Good!': Acting, Reader's Theater, and Oratory in Frances Anne Kemble's Writing," in *Romanticism and Women Poets: Opening the Doors of Reception*, ed. Harriet Kramer Linkin and Stephen C. Behrendt (Lexington: University Press of Kentucky, 1999), 125–43.

76. *Southern Literary Messenger*, May 1835.

77. *Evening Post*, quoted in *Workingman's Advocate*, May 9, 1835.

78. *Literary Journal* (Schenectady, NY), May 9, 1835.

79. *Southern Literary Messenger*, May 1835.

80. *Fanny Kemble in America: or, The Journal of an Actress Reviewed* (Boston: Light & Horton, 1835), 13.

81. Sill diaries, May 3, 1835.

82. Philip Hone, *The Diary of Philip Hone*, ed. Bayard Tuckerman (Boston: Dodd, Mead & Company, 1889), 126.

83. Hone, *The Diary*, ed. Nevins, 340.

84. James Akin, *A Frontispiece for a Journal* (Philadelphia: James Akin Draughtsman & Lithographer, 1835), Library of Congress Prints and Photographs Division, Washington, DC, https://lccn.loc.gov/97508472.

85. *My Conscience: Fanny Thimble Cutler's Journal of a Residence in America* (Philadelphia: Alexander Turnbull, 1835), 10, 12, 5.

86. *Sketches Supposed to Have Been Intended for Fanny Kemble's Journal* ([New York]: Published by Endicott, 359, Broadway, [1835]; Philadelphia: Library Company of Philadelphia).

87. *My Conscience*, 16, 6, 32.

88. *Fanny Kemble in America*, 9.

89. *My Conscience*, 13.

90. *New-York Spectator*, January 5, 1835.

91. *New York Mirror*, May 16, 1833.

Chapter 4. Bringing Female Spectacle to the "Western Country," 1835–1840

1. Ludlow also sent Tree a pleading missive from Mobile, explaining that letting her off from the engagement "would so materially derange our business and compromise our faith to the public, that were you fully impressed with its extent . . . you would forgo your own convenience rather than disappoint" St. Louis (Smith to Ludlow, March 19, [1839], Solomon Franklin Smith Papers, Missouri Historical Society Archives, St. Louis; Ludlow & Smith to Ellen Tree, March 18, 1839, Letter Book, Smith Papers).

2. Sol Smith, *Theatrical Management in the West and South for Thirty Years* (New York: Harper & Brothers, 1868), 136.

3. Smith to Ludlow, March 13, 1839, Smith Papers.

4. Smith to Ludlow March 19, 1839, Smith Papers.

5. Smith to Ludlow, April 10, April 16, April 27, 1839, Smith Papers.

6. Smith, *Theatrical Management*, 138; Williamson, "Seven Ways to Compute."

7. *Spirit of the Times*, July 22, 1837.

8. Henry Elliott to Sol Smith, August 21, 1835, Smith Papers.

9. Smith to Henry Elliott, September 7, 1838, Letter Book, Smith Papers.

10. Ludlow and Smith to Augusta St. James, August 10, 1838, Letter Book, Smith Papers.

11. *Spirit of the Times*, July 22, April 22, 1837; Ludlow, *Dramatic Life*, 468. By way of context, the $60,000 price tag of the theater, which was completed without the "plastered . . . Portico," fell short of the total projected $80,000. The cathedral, built in 1833–34, which Pennsylvania native Henry Miller considered in 1837 "the most splendid Edifice in the City," was constructed for an estimated $80,000 as well. Henry Miller, "The Journal of Henry Miller," edited by Thomas Marshall Martland, *Missouri Historical Society Collections* 6 (1931): 255, 258.

12. Mary C. Henderson, "Scenography, Stagecraft, and Architecture in the American Theatre: Beginnings to 1870," in Wilmeth and Bigsby, *Cambridge History*, 404; Ludlow, *Dramatic Life*, 476–78.

13. Smith to Ludlow, March 24, 1838, Smith Papers.

14. Ludlow, *Dramatic Life*, 478; Miller, "The Journal," 254–55.

15. These reforms also eliminated private rooms in the third tier. See Minutes of Mayor and Aldermen, September 14, 1846, Boston City Archives, Boston, MA; Ludlow, *Dramatic Life*, 478.

16. Smith to Ludlow, August 11, 1837, Smith Papers.

17. H. Elliott to Ludlow & Smith, March 13, 1837, Smith Papers.

18. Ludlow and Smith to Thomas Davenport, March 1, 1839, Letter Book, Smith Papers.

19. Ludlow, *Dramatic Life*, 601, 74.

20. Smith to Ludlow, April 20, 1838, Smith Papers.

21. Conflicts over her commitment to her career in the context of her success and Elliott's poor health dogged their marriage, leading Elliott to sue unsuccessfully for divorce in 1841. He passed away in 1842. Elliott left most of the wealth from Celeste's career to their daughter and his sister-in-law, but had squandered most of it in bad investments. Mary Grace Swift, *Belles and Beaux on Their Toes: Dancing Stars in Young America* (Washington, DC: University Press of America, 1980), 195–200.

22. Ludlow and Smith to Alexander Gibbs, January 8, 1838, Letter Book, Smith Papers.

23. Refusing the $100 terms protected Smith and Ludlow from what amounted to a poor engagement. The highest receipts were $250 for the three nights and a $264 benefit, from which the house took a third ($88), while Mrs. Gibbs and Mr. St. Luke divided the remainder, their only earnings from the engagement. Ludlow and Smith to Alexander Gibbs, February 2, 1838, Letter Book, Smith Papers; Smith to Ludlow, May 13, 1838, Smith Papers.

24. Ludlow and Smith to Sophia Brown, April 17, 1836, Letter Book, Smith Papers.

25. Ludlow & Smith to Henry Elliott, April 23, 1836, Letter Book, Smith Papers.

26. Smith to Ludlow, March 13, 1838, Smith Papers.

27. Smith to Ludlow, March 10, 1838, Smith Papers.

28. Smith to Ludlow, April 13, 1838, Smith Papers.

29. Smith to Ludlow, March 31, 1838, Smith Papers.

30. *Daily Picayune* (New Orleans), April 20, 1838.

31. Smith to Ludlow, May 13, 1838, Smith Papers.

32. H. J. Finn to Ludlow and Smith, March 31, 1836, Smith Papers.

33. Summary of Ludlow and Smith to H. J. Finn, December 19, 1836, Letter Book, Smith Papers.

34. Ireland, *Records*, 2:182.

35. Smith to Ludlow, May 3, 1839, Smith Papers.

36. Smith to Ludlow, April 13, 1838, Smith Papers.

37. Playbill, Chestnut Street Theatre, Philadelphia, PA, January 2, 1837, Harry Ransom Center, University of Texas at Austin.

38. Smith to Ludlow, April 15, 1838, Smith Papers.

39. *Daily Picayune*, November 4, 1837.

40. *Commercial Bulletin* (St. Louis, MO), April 21, 1838.

41. William G. B. Carson, *Theatre on the Frontier: The Early Years of the St. Louis Stage* (Chicago: University of Chicago Press, 1932), 274.

42. Generally, critics read Tree's performance of the courageous foundling who gains the ear of the king as a model of ideal womanhood instead of manhood, thereby regendering the title character. Though Ion was very much an adult male character, established "actress-as-boy" conventions in Anglo-American theater made it possible for viewers to reimagine the role when Tree played it. Reitz-Mulleniz, *Wearing the Breeches*, 163–67.

43. Jona. Prescott Hall, *Reports of Cases Argued and Determined in the Superior Court of the City of New-York* (New York: Oliver Halsted, Law Bookseller, 1833), 2:212; Williamson, "Seven Ways to Compute."

44. Swift, *Belles and Beaux*, 88.

45. Playbill, Tremont Theatre, Boston, MA, November 28, [1827], Harvard Theatre Collection; Playbill, Tremont Theatre, Boston, MA, February 2, [1835], Harvard Theatre Collection.

46. Henry Elliott to Sol Smith, August 21, 1835, Smith Papers.

47. Swift, *Belles and Beaux*, 195.

48. Maureen Neeham Costonis, "Ballet Comes to America, 1792–1842: French Contributions to the Establishment of Theatrical Dance in New Orleans and Philadelphia" (PhD diss., New York University, 1989), 71, 99.

49. Playbills, Tremont Theatre, Boston, MA, February 2, 5, and 9, [1835], Harvard Theatre Collection.

50. Reitz-Mullenix, *Wearing the Breeches*, 155.

51. Jacky Bratton, *The Making of the West End Stage: Marriage, Management, and the Mapping of Gender in London, 1830–1870* (Cambridge: Cambridge University Press, 2011), 140.

52. "Editor's Table," *Godey's Lady's Book*, May 1836.

53. "Theatrical," *Ladies' Companion*, June 1837.

54. *Picayune*, March 7, 1837.

55. *Missouri Republican*, May 22, May 28, 1839.

56. Swift, *Belles and Beaux*, 91–92.

57. Costonis, "Ballet," 263; Williamson, "Seven Ways to Compute."

58. *Spirit of the Times*, March 26, December 17, 1836.

59. Henry Elliott to Sol Smith, August 21, 1835, Smith Papers; Williamson, "Seven Ways to Compute."

60. *Picayune*, March 9, 1837.

61. *The Celeste-al Cabinet* (New York: H. H. Robinson, 1836), Library of Congress Prints and Photographs Division, Washington, DC, https://www.loc.gov/pictures/item/2008661278/.

62. Charles A. Poulson, *Durang's History of the Philadelphia Stage Scrapbook, 1854–1863* (Philadelphia: Library Company of Philadelphia, n.d.).

63. Playbill, Tremont Theatre, May 13, 18[35], Harvard Theatre Collection.

64. *Picayune*, August 1, 1837.

65. *Picayune*, June 18, 1837.

66. *Public Ledger* (Philadelphia), June 12, 1840.

67. *New York Sun* quoted in the *Albany (NY) Argus*, June 16, 1840.

68. *Public Ledger*, June 8, 1840.

69. *Public Ledger*, June 12, 1840.

70. *New-York Weekly Whig*, June 11, 1840.

71. *Baltimore (MD) Sun*, January 30, 1841.

72. *Daily Picayune*, March 11, 1841.

73. Swift, *Belles and Beaux*, 200; Williamson, "Seven Ways to Compute."

74. Yet this fourth husband, Mr. Hosack, a businessman, was also connected financially to the St. Louis Theatre as one of its stockholders. Brown, *History*, 254; Ludlow, *Dramatic Life*, 488–89.

75. Smith to Noah Ludlow, August 7, 1837, Smith Papers.

76. *Missouri Republican*, August 18, 1837.

77. "The Wandering Cavite" was a satirical take on attempts at serious criticism, though it may have been written by the same author as "Asmodeus." The "faithful Cavite" inhabited the stance of an outsider, promising to "present things as they are . . . without prevarication." The "Cavite" columns that season featuring cutting send-ups rife with tortured classical references and puns. *Missouri Republican*, September 13, September 16, 1837.

78. For the 1836 engagement, Pritchard chose to play Rolla for her benefit, when it was customary for the recipient to choose the piece and casting, and probably used that tradition to override the managers' scruples. Ludlow, *Dramatic Life*, 460, 487.

79. Smith to Ludlow, March 18, 1838, Smith Papers; Ludlow, *Dramatic Life*, 463.

80. *Missouri Republican*, March 19, 1838.

81. *Missouri Republican*, March 26, 1838.

82. *Commercial Bulletin*, April 13, 1838; *Missouri Republican*, April 21, 1838.

83. *Commercial Bulletin*, April 27, 1838. This vociferous disagreement between critics over Lewis's Romeo contrasts with their studied silence about Tree's Ion, which reflected their unwillingness to criticize a star so celebrated and clearly aligned with the "legitimate" drama.

84. Jessica Litman, "The Invention of the Common Law Play Right," *Berkeley Tech Law Journal* 25, no. 3 (2010): 1381–1425; Oren Bracha, "Commentary on the U.S. Copyright Act Amendment 1856," in *Primary Sources on Copyright (1450–1900)*, ed. L. Bently and M. Kretschmer (2008), http://www.copyrighthistory.org.

85. The Barnes family also suffered John's failed attempt at theatrical management. Rebecca Jaroff, "Charlotte Barnes: A Life in the Theatre," in *Women's Contribution to Nineteenth-Century American Theatre*, edited by Miriam López Rodriguez and Maria Dolores Narbona Carrión (Universitat de València, 2004), 59.

86. Ludlow, *Dramatic Life*, 518.

87. Smith to Ludlow, March 26, 1837, Ludlow-Field-Maury Family Papers, Missouri Historical Society Archives, St. Louis.

88. Ludlow, *Dramatic Life*, 541–42.

89. John S. Kendall, *The Golden Age of the New Orleans Theatre* (Baton Rouge: Louisiana State University Press, 1952), 79, 81.

90. Smith to C. C. Hodges, March 3, 1836, Letter Book, Smith Papers.

91. Smith to Ludlow, July 20, 1836, Smith Papers.

92. Williamson, "Seven Ways to Compute."

93. In New Orleans, Hodges performed a rare gender reversal for his benefit night, using his tenor to sing Cinderella while Nelson performed as the Prince. The *Picayune* alluded to the greater demand for starring women, joking that "Hodges knows that they are wanting *prima donnas* at both the other theatres, and is evidently trying his hand for an engagement in that line" (April 18, 1837).

94. *New York Herald*, October 13, 1836.

95. *Missouri Republican*, October 14, 1837.

96. *Missouri Republican*, October 9, 1837.

97. Smith to Richard Corree, October 8, 1837, Smith Papers.

98. *Public Ledger*, September 28, 1842; *Picayune*, October 7, 1842.

Chapter 5. Danger, Desire, and Celebrity Mania

1. *Boston Courier*, September 28, 1840.

2. *Morning Post* quoted in *Boston Courier*, October 1, 1840.

3. Costonis, "Ballet," 297.

4. *Ladies' Companion*, July 1840.

5. Ivor Guest, *Fanny Elssler* (London: Adam and Charles Black, 1970), 185; Williamson, "Seven Ways to Compute."

6. Michael Schudson, *Discovering the News: A Social History of American Newspapers* (New York: Basic Books, 1978).

7. Chris Rojek, *Celebrity* (London: Reaktion Books, 2001), 7.

8. This argument is indebted to Robert Allen's analysis of how reception is shaped by readings of venue and publics. Allen tracks the shift in reception of Lydia Thompson's British Blondes burlesque troupe in 1868 once they moved to Niblo's Garden Theatre, "regarded . . . as the finest theater in America." Allen shows how "burlesque was 're-reviewed' as the 'leg-business' and 'nude drama'" and recast as a threat. In the earlier context of Elsslermania, which preceded the market segmentation of New York entertainment at midcentury, readings of Elssler remained tied to readings of her shifting publics, as venue alone could not ensure a particular social composition. Robert Allen, *Horrible Prettiness: Burlesque and American Culture* (Chapel Hill: University of North Carolina Press, 1991), 15–16.

9. *New York Herald*, May 4, 1840.

10. Hone, *The Diary*, ed. Nevins, 477.

11. All translations are my own. Katti Prinster, "Fanny Elsslers amerikanische Kunstreise im Jahre 1840," *Österreichische Rundschau* (Vienna), May–October 1905, 453–54.

12. Prinster, "Fanny Elsslers amerikanische Kunstreise," 453–54.

13. *New York Herald*, May 9, 1840.

14. Michael Schudson explains that the penny papers "sold a product to a general readership and sold a readership to advertisers" (*Discovering the News*, 17–18); see also James L. Crouthamel, *Bennett's "New York Herald" and the Rise of the Popular Press* (New York: Syracuse University Press, 1989), 43.

15. Crouthamel, *Bennett's "New York Herald,"* 24; Schudon, *Discovering the News*, 22–27.

16. Rojek, *Celebrity*, 19.

17. *New York Herald*, May 5, 1840.

18. Ibid. This scene reappeared in the 1845 volume *The Letters and Journal of Fanny Elssler*, allegedly written by Wikoff. Prinster also mentions the incident in her letters home—minus the embrace.

19. *Spirit of the Times* (New York), May 25, 1844.

20. *New York Herald*, May 18, 1840.

21. Competing accounts from *Spirit of the Times*, May 9, 1840, and *New York Herald*, May 3, 1840.

22. Hone, *The Diary*, ed. Nevins, 482.

23. *New York Herald*, May 29, 1840.

24. Guest, *Fanny Elssler*, 129.

25. Caldwell to Wycoff, n.d., Smith Papers.

26. *Evening Post* (New York), May 15, 1840; *Star* (New York), reprinted in the *Southern Patriot* (Charleston, SC), May 18, 1840.

27. *New York Herald,* June 15, 1840; Williamson, "Seven Ways to Compute."

28. *Spirit of the Times,* May 16, 1840.

29. *Daily Picayune* (New Orleans, LA), May 23, May 24, 1840.

30. *Daily Picayune,* August 26, 1838.

31. *Daily Picayune,* February 14, 1841.

32. This chronology is drawn from Guest's biography. Elssler took no engagements while traveling up the Mississippi and Ohio Rivers to New York, where she played a fourth engagement in June 1841. During her second year, she restricted herself to the North Atlantic coastal cities and returned to Cuba for an extended stay in early 1842, then performed a farewell engagement in New York in June 1842. She sailed for London in July 1842, ending her North American idyll.

33. *New York Herald,* May 24, 1841.

34. *New York Herald,* May 29, 1840. I have been unable to locate extant issues of the *Signal* from this period to verify how exactly Benjamin attacked Bennett.

35. Reprint in Fanny Elssler Clippings, NYPL Performing Arts Library, New York, NY; the original appeared in the *New York Herald,* August 5, 1840.

36. *New York Herald,* May 22, 1840, May 12, 1840.

37. *New York Herald,* May 29, 1840, May 12, 1840.

38. *Memoir of Fanny Elssler: With Anecdotes of Her Public and Private Life* (Boston: Turner & Fisher, 1840), 10.

39. Allison Delarue, ed., *Fanny Elssler in America* (New York: Dance Horizons, 1976), 5–6.

40. Helen Horowitz, *Rereading Sex: Battles over Sexual Knowledge and Suppression in Nineteenth-Century America* (New York: Alfred A. Knopf, 2002); Patricia Cline Cohen, Timothy Gilfoyle, and Helen Horowitz, eds., *Flash Press: Sporting Male Weeklies in 1840s New York* (Chicago: University of Chicago Press, 2008), 39–40.

41. *New York Herald,* May 5, 1840.

42. Mole, *Byron's Romantic Celebrity,* chap. 5.

43. *New York Mirror,* May 23, 1840.

44. L. N. Fowler, *The Phrenological Developments and Character of J. V. Stout, the Sculptor, and Fanny Elssler, the Actress* (New York: 135 Nassau Street, 1841), 17–18, 21.

45. Guest, *Fanny Elssler,* 133.

46. Prinster, "Fanny Elsslers amerikanische Kunstreise," 455.

47. *Daily Picayune,* September 27, 1840.

48. *Daily Picayune,* November 10, 1840.

49. Stuart Banner, *American Property: A History of How, Why, and What We Own* (Cambridge, MA: Harvard University Press, 2011), 130–31.

50. *Sun* (Baltimore, MD), September 16, 1840.

51. *Daily Picayune,* September 27, 1840.

52. Hone, *The Diary,* ed. Nevins, 481.

53. Guest, *Fanny Elssler,* 81.

54. *Sun,* August 4, 1840.

55. Ivor Guest, *The Romantic Ballet in England* (Middletown, CT: Wesleyan University Press, 1972), 63–64.

56. *New York Herald*, August 14, 1840.

57. Guest, *Fanny Elssler*, 135.

58. Swift, *Belles and Beaux*, 215.

59. Versions of the costume appear in portraits and as described by Theophile Gautier in Guest, *Fanny Elssler*, 101, and *Spirit of the Times*, May 16, 1840.

60. *Evening Post* reprinted in *Albany Argus*, May 22, 1840.

61. *Evening Post*, May 15, 1840; *Spirit of the Times*, May 16, 1840; the Willis original can be found in the *American Miscellany*, October 12, 1836.

62. *Evening Post*, May 15, 1840.

63. *New York Times* and *Evening Star* quoted in *Southern Patriot*, May 18, 1840.

64. It also irked the editor that Elssler generated so much "enthusiasm," whereas "more worthy . . . intellectual entertainments" had been met with "torpidity" ("Theatricals," *Ladies' Companion*, July 1840, 157).

65. Swift, *Belles and Beaux*, 212–13, 215.

66. *Memoir of Fanny Elssler*, 5–6.

67. Ibid., 10–11.

68. Wikoff's *Memoir* tried to put this scandal to rest, explaining that Elssler left Vienna rather than encourage Reichstadt and signaling Elssler's purity by praising her "adroit tact in evading—rather than repelling—the too pressing advances of her numerous admirers"—even kings. Delarue, *Fanny Elssler*, 19; *Memoir of Fanny Elssler*, 14.

69. Dance scholar Maureen Needham Costonis argues that Elssler came to personify desire in a variety of overlapping and often ambivalent ways, as a voluptuary who was "responsive to erotic desire" in her private life, an enchantress or goddess, and an exhibitionist. Elssler's audiences and critics responded to an "erotic overload of desire" through denial, displacement, and humor. Costonis rather cautiously suggests that Elssler may also have been an agent for change, a vehicle for more permissive eroticism in daily life. Maureen Neeham Costonis, "The Personification of Desire: Fanny Elssler and American Audiences," *Dance Chronicle* 13, no. 1 (1990): 47–67 esp. 49, 58.

70. Katherine Hijar, "The Pin-Up, the Piano, and the Parlor: American Sheet Music, 1840–1860," *Imprint* 30, no. 2 (2005): 14.

71. Caroline Healey Dall, *Selected Journals of Caroline Healey Dall*, ed. Helen Deese (Boston: Massachusetts Historical Society, 2006), 383.

72. *New York Herald*, August 1, 1840.

73. McConachie, *Melodramatic Formations*, 75–76.

74. Prinster, "Fanny Elsslers amerikanische Kunstreise," 454.

75. *New York Herald*, May 15, 1840.

76. Reprinted in the *Southern Patriot*, May 18, 1840.

77. *Sun*, July 29, 1840.

78. *Sunday Mercury* (New York), excerpted in the *Sun*, August 5, 1840; *Daily Picayune*, August 26, September 22, 1840.

79. J. Childs and Edward Williams Clay, *Fanny Elssler and the Baltimoreans* (New York: Published by J. Childs, 1840), Library of Congress Prints and Photographs Division, Washington, DC, https://www.loc.gov/item/2008661386/.

80. *Sun*, July 13, July 30, July 29, 1840.

81. *Sun*, August 1, 1840.

82. Childs and Clay, *Fanny Elssler*.

83. *The Baltimoreans Going the Whole Ass Tail and All* (author unknown, 1840), Library of Congress Prints and Photographs Division, Washington, DC, https://www.loc.gov/item/2008661780/.

84. Richard Bushman, *The Refinement of America: Persons, Houses, Cities* (New York: Vintage Books, 1993), 404–8, 411–15.

85. *Sun*, August 5, 1840.

86. Ronald J. Zboray and Mary Saracino Zboray, "Gendered Slurs in Boston's Partisan Press during the 1840s," *Journal of American Studies* 34, no. 3 (2000): 424–25.

87. *New York Herald*, August 17, 1840.

88. A Lady of This City, *The Life of the Beautiful and Accomplished Danseuse, Mademoiselle Fanny Elssler, of Vienna* (Philadelphia: Printed for the purchaser, and for sale, 65 Walnut St.; New York: 141 Fulton St. [1840?]), 31.

89. *Spirit of the Times*, May 30, 1840; O'Dell, *Annals*, 4:412–15.

90. *New York Herald*, September 10, 1840; Williamson, "Seven Ways to Compute."

91. *New York Herald*, May 24, 1841; Williamson, "Seven Ways to Compute."

92. *New-Yorker*, May 23, 1840.

93. *Sun*, July 13, 1840.

94. These narratives also played on the associations of fashion-conscious working woman with the prostitute. Wendy Gamber's examples come from midcentury novels, and I have found these tropes in both moral reform literature and the flash press of the 1840s. Wendy Gamber, *The Female Economy: The Millinery and Dressmaking Trades, 1860–1930* (Urbana: University of Illinois Press, 1997), 18.

95. George Warren, *History of the Bunker Hill Monument Association during the First Century of the United States of America* (Boston: J. R. Osgood, 1877), 311; Williamson, "Seven Ways to Compute."

96. From the *Sunday Morning News*, quoted in the *New England Review*, October 17, 1840.

97. *The Deipnosophists; or, Banquet of the Learned of Athenaeus*, trans. C. D. Yonge (London: Henry G. Bohn, 1854), 3:944.

98. *Public Ledger* (Philadelphia), October 1, 1840.

99. *Native American* (New York), quoted in the *New England Review*, October 17, 1840.

100. Hone, *The Diary*, ed. Nevin, 546.

101. Frank Luther Mott, *American Journalism: A History, 1690–1960* (New York: Macmillan, 1962), 270.

102. *New-York Daily Tribune*, June 9, 1841.

103. Ibid.

104. April Haynes, *Riotous Flesh: Women, Physiology, and the Solitary Vice in Nineteenth-Century America* (Chicago: University of Chicago Press, 2015), 9–10, 20–22.

105. Urban male sporting culture falls within the ideology of "libertine republicanism" identified by Haynes, according to which white men claimed unlimited right to various "sexual liberties" and in turn sought control of public space. Ibid., 7–10; Horowitz, *Rereading Sex*, esp. 155–58.

106. Minutes of the Mayor and Aldermen, 1840, 1846, Boston City Archives, West Roxbury, MA.

107. *New York Mirror*, May 30, 1840.

108. *New York Herald*, August 1, 1840.

109. Theatricals, *Ladies' Companion*, June 1837, 100.

110. Theatricals, *Ladies' Companion*, July 1840, 157.

111. Playbill, Chestnut Street Theatre, Philadelphia, January 7, 1840, Harry Ransom Center, University of Texas at Austin.

112. John Warren Williams Diary, Library of Congress, Washington, DC.

113. *Sun*, July 30, 1840. "Omega" singled out *La Sylphide* and *La tarentule* for censure, both ballets that foregrounded active female desire. The "indecent exposure of the figure" in her duet with Sylvain was also objectionable. He had no criticism of Elssler's solo character dances.

114. Horowitz, *Rereading Sex*, 216–17.

115. Duyckinck is scathing in his treatment of middle-class fashionables. He calls them the "mob who follow wherever they are led." Their "folly" for fashion and delight in self-display were a source of "entertaining mirth" for the sensible "democracy in the pit" ("The Ballet," *Arcturus*, July 1841, 122).

116. Reprinted in the *Public Ledger*, June 15, 1840.

117. Ralph Waldo Emerson, *The Journals and Miscellaneous Notebooks of Ralph Waldo Emerson*, ed. William H. Gilm and J. E. Parson (Cambridge, MA: Belknap Press, 1970), 8:109–11.

118. Reprinted in the *North American and Daily Advertiser* (Philadelphia), February 19, 1841.

119. *New-York Mirror*, October 24, 1840.

120. Timothy Shay Arthur, *The Maiden: A Story for My Young Countrywomen* (Philadelphia: Henry F. Anners, 1847), 53.

121. Ibid., 42, 140–42.

122. Celeste's career is again an instructive comparison. Her husband, Baltimore businessman Henry Elliott, died July 21, 1842, shortly before her return from London. While he left Celeste half of her fortune, which he controlled, he placed their daughter in his sister's custody. Elliott had already tried to divorce Celeste and secure her fortune in 1841, apparently because she refused to retire from the stage. The state of Maryland refused his divorce petition. In 1842, having lost legal rights to her child, Celeste returned to London, where she remained for the next decade. Swift, *Belles and Beaux*, 198–200, 202.

123. *New York Herald*, April 8, 16, 22, and 25, 1844; Guest, *Fanny Elssler*, 186–87, 192; Williamson, "Seven Ways to Compute."

124. This would not be his only attempt: in 1851 in Geneva, he was arrested, tried, and convicted for kidnapping an heiress whom he hoped to force into marriage. Wikoff later published his own account of the "courtship." Caleb Crain, "The Courtship of Henry Wikoff; or, A Spinster's Apprehensions," *American Literary History* 18, no. 4 (Winter 2006): 659–94.

Chapter 6. The American Actress's Starring Playbook, 1831–1857

1. *A Biographical Sketch of Miss Matilda Heron* (Cincinnati: James Bense, 1856), 3, 10.

2. Ibid., 16.

3. Hone, *The Diary*, ed. Nevins, 271.

4. Hone referred to the Bowery as the "cloven foot in relation to the riot at the Park Theatre" (ibid., 51).

5. Dudden, *Women*, 61.

6. Ibid., 67.

7. [Clarke], *A Concise History*, 23.

8. *Spirit of the Times*, July 7, 1838.

9. *Spirit of the Times*, June 23, 1838; Dudden, *Women*, 70.

10. One scholar speculates that this diagnosis may have resulted from combining alcohol with laudanum. Thomas A. Bogar, *Thomas Hamblin and the Bowery Theatre: The New York Reign of "Blood and Thunder" Melodramas* (New York: Palgrave Macmillan, 2018), 179.

11. Dudden, *Women*, 70.

12. *Observer* (London), October 5, September 29, 1834.

13. *Spirit of the Times*, February 20, 1836, quoted in Norman J. Myers, "Josephine Clifton: 'Manufactured' Star," *Theatre History Studies*, January 1, 1986.

14. Aldridge was part of a transatlantic circulation of black speakers, writers, activists, and performers who rose to celebrity through British antislavery circles, particularly over the 1840s and 1850s. See Bernth Lindfors, *Ira Aldridge: The Vagabond Years, 1833–1852* (Rochester, NY: University of Rochester Press, 2011).

15. *American and Commercial Daily Advertiser* (Baltimore, MD), November 7, 1836.

16. *Daily Sentinel* excerpted in the *Inquirer* (Philadelphia), November 22, 1836.

17. Excerpts in the *Inquirer*, November 22, 1836.

18. Butler, *Journal*, 1:121.

19. *Daily Picayune* (New Orleans), March 29, 1837.

20. *Saturday Morning Transcript* (Boston), June 25, 1836; Williamson, "Seven Ways to Compute."

21. Haynes, *Unfinished Revolution*, 70–72; Robert Gross, "Introduction: An Extensive Republic," in Gross and Kelley, *A History*, 46.

22. Haynes, *Unfinished Revolution*, 70; Andie Tuccher, "Newspapers and Periodicals," in Gross and Kelley, *A History*, 398.

23. "A Talk about Theatricals," *American Monthly Magazine*, August 1837, 344–48.

24. *Evening Star* (New York), November 21, 1837.

25. Thomas Baker, *Sentiment and Celebrity: Nathaniel Parker Willis and the Trials of Literary Fame* (New York: Oxford University Press, 1999), 86–89.

26. *Boston Transcript*, September 29, 1837, in the *Spirit of the Times*, October 7, 1837.

27. Epes Sargent to John Sargent, n.d., Anna Cora Ogden Mowatt Ritchie Papers, Schlesinger Library, Radcliffe Institute, Harvard University, Cambridge, MA.

28. *New York Herald*, August 26, 1837.

29. *Evening Post* (New York), August 26, 1837.

30. "The Bride of Genoa," *American Monthly Magazine*, May 1837, 448–57.

31. Edgar Allan Poe, "The Literati of New York Part IV," *Godey's Lady's Book*, August 1846.

32. *Spirit of the Times*, December 11, 1847.

33. *Spirit of the Times*, June 23, 1838; Bogar, *Thomas Hamblin*, 173–74.

34. *New York Spectator*, June 21, 1838.

35. *New York Whig,* quoted in the *Picayune,* June 6, 1838.

36. *Spirit of the Times,* July 7, 1838.

37. Ibid.

38. Bank, "Arbiters," 8.

39. She also claimed to have been a friend of Naomi Vincent but before she became Hamblin's mistress, a timeline that preserved Clarke's claims to respectability. Branson, *Dangerous to Know,* 98.

40. [Clarke], *A Concise History,* 16–18, 23.

41. *Report of the Forrest Divorce Case* (New York: Robert M. DeWitt), 128, 140.

42. Myers, "Josephine Clifton," 119.

43. Cushman to Mother (Mary Cushman), December 2, 1844, box 1, Charlotte Cushman Papers, Library of Congress, Washington, DC; Joseph Leach, *Bright Particular Star: The Life and Times of Charlotte Cushman* (New Haven, CT: Yale University Press, 1970), 140.

44. Cushman to Mother, March 2, 1845, Cushman Papers.

45. Leach, *Bright Particular Star,* 140–41, 149–50.

46. Ibid., 148.

47. *New York Herald,* March 21, 1845.

48. Lisa Merrill, *When Romeo Was a Woman: Charlotte Cushman and Her Circle of Female Spectators* (Ann Arbor: University of Michigan Press, 2000), 7–8.

49. Ibid., 244.

50. Merrill, *When Romeo,* 27–28.

51. Emma Stebbins, *Charlotte Cushman: Her Letters and Memories of Her Life* (Boston: Houghton, Osgood & Company, 1879), 26; Williamson, "Seven Ways to Compute."

52. Ibid., 28; Williamson, "Seven Ways to Compute."

53. Merrill, *When Romeo,* 21–23.

54. *New York Herald,* March 11, 1838.

55. Leach, *Bright Particular Star,* 174; Merrill, *When Romeo,* 113–14.

56. For example, see Charlotte Cushman, "Cromwell at the Coffin of Charles I," *Graham's Magazine,* November 1843; "Sonnet—Manhood," *Ladies' Companion,* February 1844; "Monody; on the Death of Henry Ware Jr.," *Ladies' Companion,* March 1844.

57. Merrill, *When Romeo,* 29–30.

58. Ibid., 37.

59. Charlotte Cushman, "Extracts from My Journal: The Actress," *Godey's Lady's Book,* February 1837.

60. Quoted in Leach, *Bright Particular Star,* 63–64.

61. Ibid., 68–70, 78; Dudden, *Women,* 86. Lisa Merrill argues that the story about the origins of the role of Meg Merriles, told much later during the height of Cushman's career, emphasized the "accidental" casting, which "helped mitigate criticism she might have received for creating this bold, unconventional woman" (*When Romeo,* 42).

62. *Evening Post,* June 28, 1838.

63. Leach, *Bright Particular Star,* 178.

64. *Picayune,* June 20, 1838.

65. Merrill, *When Romeo,* 93–94.

66. Cushman to Mother, March 28, 1845, Cushman Papers.

67. Merrill, *When Romeo*, 48–49.

68. *New York Herald*, March 18, June 13, 1842.

69. Wemyss, *Twenty-Six Years*, 378.

70. Ibid., 381.

71. Walter Moore Leman, *Memories of an Old Actor* (San Francisco: A. Roman Co. Publishers, 1886), 179–80.

72. Wemyss, *Twenty-Six Years*, 378, 381.

73. *New York Herald*, March 18, 1842.

74. Bluford Adams, *E. Pluribus Barnum: The Great Showman and the Making of U.S. Popular Culture* (Minneapolis: University of Minnesota Press, 1997); Jay Cook, *The Arts of Deception: Playing with Fraud in the Age of Barnum* (Cambridge, MA: Harvard University Press, 2001).

75. Charlotte Cushman, "Address I wrote and published on taking management of the Walnut Theater," box 1, Cushman Papers.

76. William Charles Macready, *The Diaries of William Charles Macready, 1833–1851*, ed. William Toynbee (New York: G. P. Putnam's Sons, 1912), 2:234–35.

77. Ibid., 2:235.

78. Ibid., 2:241; Merrill, *When Romeo*, 71.

79. Macready, *Diaries*, 2:242–43.

80. Ibid., 2:305.

81. Excerpted in Leach, *Bright Particular Star*, 123.

82. *Camille* was a distinctly American phenomenon, for unlike other French plays from the period, which usually appeared first on the London stage, *La dame aux camélias* would not be performed in England until 1875, state censorship keeping all versions except the opera *La traviata* from the English stage. Elaine Hadley, *Melodramatic Tactics: Theatricalized Dissent in the English Marketplace, 1800–1885* (Stanford, CA: Stanford University Press, 1995), 133; Sos Eltis, *Acts of Desire: Women and Sex on Stage, 1800–1930* (Oxford University Press, 2013).

83. *A Biographical Sketch*, 19.

84. Ibid., 7.

85. Ibid., 10.

86. Andrew Davis, *America's Longest Run: A History of the Walnut Street Theatre* (University Park: Pennsylvania State University Press, 2010), 105.

87. Buckley, "To the Opera House."

88. Alberta Lewis Humble, "Matilda Heron, American Actress" (PhD diss., University of Illinois, 1959), 14, 16–19.

89. Ibid., 24.

90. *Boston Daily Bee*, March 12, 1853.

91. Cushman to Mother, December 2, 1844, Cushman Papers.

92. These plays were associated with Rachel Felix, tragedian of the Comédie-Française in the 1840s. Felix achieved a transatlantic celebrity in America long before her sole American tour in 1855. See Rachel Brownstein, *Tragic Muse: Rachel of the Comédie-Française* (New York: A. A. Knopf, 1993). In September 1856 Heron presented her version of Ernest Legouvé's *Medea*, written for but never performed by Rachel. *Medea; A Tragedy, in Three Acts, Translated from the French of E. Legouve by Matilda Heron* (New York: Samuel French, 1857).

93. In my research into the New York copyright records of 1856 and 1857, I noted Heron's copyright of her translations of *Medea* in October 1856, *Phaedra* in June 1857, and *Fiammina* in August 1857. In 1856 Heron accused dramatic publisher Samuel French of publishing her translation of *Camille*. French professed his ignorance and apologized. Their exchange appears in the 1857 edition of Heron's *Camille*, published in Cincinnati, along with her notice of its copyright in Ohio 1856. *Camille: A Play in Five Acts, Translated from the French of Alexander Dumas Jr. by Matilda Heron* (Cincinnati: T. Wrightson, 1856).

94. Humble, "Matilda Heron," 23.

95. This included the editor of the *Spirit of the Times*, George Wilkes, who continued to champion Heron in his periodical over the years. See ibid., 25–26.

96. *Porter's Spirit of the Times*, September 6, 1856.

97. Ibid.

98. Quoted in Humble, "Matilda Heron," 80.

99. *New York Tribune*, January 23, 1857.

100. Fitz-James O'Brien, *The Diamond Lens with Other Stories*, ed. William Winter (New York: Charles Scribner's Sons, 1885), 126.

101. Bonnie Jean Eckard, "Camille in America" (PhD diss., University of Denver, 1982), 68; *Daily Missouri Herald*, January 12, 1856, quoted in Humble, "Matilda Heron," 70.

102. O'Brien, *The Diamond Lens*, 126.

103. *Spirit of the Times*, February 14, 1857.

104. Barbara Wallace Grossman, *A Spectacle of Suffering: Clara Morris on the American Stage* (Carbondale: Southern Illinois University Press, 2009), 116–17.

105. *New York Tribune*, April 2, 1857.

106. Ibid.

107. *Boston Daily Advertiser*, May 7, 1857, quoted in Humble, "Matilda Heron," 139.

108. *Boston Daily Courier*, May 14, 1857, quoted in Humble, "Matilda Heron," 142. This remarkable argument reflected shifting attitudes toward prostitution at midcentury. Moral reformers had long grappled with the question of whether prostitutes were truly innocent victims capable of redemption, though rescue had been central to their early work. By midcentury, their focus had shifted to guardianship and away from rescue, and they increasingly cast prostitutes as depraved predators. However, the image of prostitute as victim persisted in popular fiction and, as the popularity of *Camille* indicates, drama. Laura Keene's version of the play, *Camille: A Moral Life*, which was quickly overshadowed by Heron's, focused on the vulnerability of working-class women to the lures of the sex trade. It also incorporated a device from the French play *Victorine*, of presenting the drama of the play as the protagonist's dream. In Keene's *Camille*, as in *Victorine*, the heroine must choose between the virtuous path of marriage and domesticity and the pleasures of a life of dissipation. On shifting attitudes toward prostitutes, see Barbara Hobson, *Uneasy Virtue: The Politics of Prostitution and the American Reform Tradition* (1987; Chicago: University of Chicago Press, 1990), 70–72; Cutter, *Domestic Devils*, 53; and on different versions of *Camille*, see Humble, "Matilda Heron," 83–84; Eckard, "Camille in America," 49–50.

109. *Porter's Spirit of the Times*, September 6, 1856.

110. Humble, "Matilda Heron," 258–59.

Conclusion

1. Basch, *Framing American Divorce*, 176.

2. Jane Kathleen Curry, *Nineteenth-Century American Women Theatre Managers* (Westport, CT: Greenwood Press, 1994), 41–44.

3. In similar divorce cases, a hierarchy attached to men's adultery according to which "sex with prostitutes" was "tacitly accepted," whereas "sex with a woman of the middle or upper classes, or even worse, a family friend or relative . . . threatened marriage in ways prostitution did not" (Basch, *Framing American Divorce*, 165).

4. Conversely, her successful negotiation of respectability politics in her life may have helped jurors dismiss the "circumstantial" evidence of the affair, especially in relation to evidence that Forrest openly consorted with prostitutes. Though Forrest was ultimately found guilty of adultery, during deliberations the jury asked "whether frequent visits to a house of ill fame was to be taken as sufficient proof of adultery," referencing evidence that Forrest also frequented a boardinghouse known to be a brothel. *Report of the Forrest Divorce Case, Containing the Full and Unabridged Testimony of All the Witnesses* (New York: Robert M. DeWitt, [1852]), 186.

5. *The Forrest Divorce Case. Catherine N. Forrest against Edwin Forrest. Fully and Correctly Reported by the Reporter of the National Police Gazette* (New York: Stringer and Townsend, 1852), 100. Witnesses noted Clifton's "mulatto" servant, Susan Allen, though Allen was never called to the stand. She did, however, testify in an 1853 perjury trial related to the case. Clearly, Allen's racial and social status meant that she was not seen as a legitimate witness or guarantor of Clifton's virtuous behavior.

6. Sara Lampert, "'Immoderate Menses' or Abortion? Bodily Knowledge and Illicit Intimacy in an 1851 Divorce Trial," *Nursing Clio*, September 23, 2019, https://nursingclio.org/2019/09/23/immoderate-menses-or-abortion-bodily-knowledge-and-illicit-intimacy-in-an-1851-divorce-trial/.

7. *The Forrest Divorce Case*, 100.

8. *Report of the Forrest Divorce Case*, 87, 128, 13, 165.

INDEX

SARA E. LAMPERT is an associate professor of history at the University of South Dakota.

WOMEN, GENDER, AND SEXUALITY IN AMERICAN HISTORY

The University of Illinois Press
is a founding member of the
Association of University Presses.

———————————————————————

University of Illinois Press
1325 South Oak Street
Champaign, IL 61820-6903
www.press.uillinois.edu

Made in the USA
Coppell, TX
18 August 2021